Caroline Louisa Currie

Some Side-Lights on the Oxford Movement

Caroline Louisa Currie

Some Side-Lights on the Oxford Movement

ISBN/EAN: 9783337248901

Printed in Europe, USA, Canada, Australia, Japan

Cover: Foto ©ninafisch / pixelio.de

More available books at **www.hansebooks.com**

SOME SIDE-LIGHTS

ON THE

OXFORD MOVEMENT

BY

MINIMA PARSPARTIS

LONDON AND LEAMINGTON
ART AND BOOK COMPANY

1895

MUCH has been written during the last few years concerning the Oxford Movement. The present volume may perhaps not be without interest, inasmuch as it relates the influence of Tractarian principles on some of that comparatively insignificant, but not wholly unimportant, section of the community — the Young Ladies of England.

The story is intended for women. As, however, the foolish things of the world have sometimes confounded the wise, it may possibly contain a message for the men to whom they have been given as help-meets.

CONTENTS.

CHAPTER I. 1

Impressions on first entering a Catholic church. Woodchester and the Passionist Fathers. St. Paul's words about Purgatory. A controversial and disquieting discussion on the veneration of saints.

The Gorham case. My two friends and their parents. Sybella's views on Baptismal Regeneration. The sermons of Mr. Robbins. Perplexity as to how to behave in church so as not to displease any of my lawful superiors. Brother Martin and his penances. Dr. Pusey's teaching on the necessity of self-denial. The foreign devotional works translated and edited by Dr. Pusey and their effect. Observance of saints' days.

Oswald Middleton and his influence over us. Mr. Sewell's works. A country church some forty years ago. Mr. Dean. Bishop Samual Wilberforce and his Confirmation addresses. His mind an essentially Protestant one.

Life from ten to fourteen. Letters from friends. The freedom of the Church from State trammels predicted. Sybella's account of Mr. Magee's sermon on self-denial. Some letters from Milly.

CHAPTER II. 33

The Ancient British Church entirely independent of Rome. The opinions of a High Churchman on Roman corruptions and Anglican errors. A speedy union between Rome and England predicted. The Papal Aggression in connection with the validity of English Orders. Conduct of the English Bishops in Elizabeth's reign. Uncertainty as to the competency of Barlow to consecrate Parker, and as to the form actually used in Parker's consecration. Excitement at Bath caused by the Papal Aggression. Mr. Robbins' discourses on the subject. The regret they caused my mother.

Removal to Clifton. Preparation for Confirmation. Spiritual books. Mr. Herbert Graham. Archdeacon Manning's sermons. His secession.

Interview with Dr. Pusey. Milly. Her feelings about High Church views. Her account of the religious vagaries of her cousin. Her thoughts about the Church of St. Barnabas, Pimlico. Description of Dr. Christopher Wordsworth and an S.P.G. meeting.

CHAPTER III. 58

A Latitudinarian friend. His influence. Sir James Stephens' Essays in Ecclesiastical Biography. His estimate of St. Ignatius Loyola and of the Spiritual Exercises. The Catholic type of sanctity not understood outside the Roman Catholic Church.

Visits to Convents in and near Clifton. Converts to Catholicism. Mr. Aubrey de Vere urges the duty of inquiry into the claims of the Roman Catholic Church. The testimony of those who have submitted to her guidance. The English Church powerless to witness to the truth. It allows contradictory doctrines to be taught. Oswald's views on the duty of inquiry. His sister Ethel a resolute defender of the Anglican Church. She undertakes to read Milner's *End of Controversy* and other Catholic works. Several letters from her. The Councils of Nice and Chalcedon. Extracts from Anglican writers to show that the Papal Supremacy was not recognized by these Councils. Answer.

Moehler's Symbolism. The unity of the Church, the proof of her Divine Mission. Oswald's views of the impossibility of arriving at certainty. Evil of such views.

CHAPTER IV. 99

Misgivings excited by Protestant calumnies. Their effect on the imagination. Mr. de Vere's advice on the importance of attending only to the one question: Is there a Divine Teacher in the world? The question can never be a subordinate one. Difficulties to be surmounted. Necessity for perfect sincerity.

Visits in Ireland. Newman's book on Anglican difficulties. The effect it produced. Why the principles of the Oxford movement made it impossible for those who would retain them, to remain in the English Church. Lessons learnt from the first seven lectures. The difficulties dealt with in the second part of the work. The superiority of Protestant States in material prosperity. The world and the Church have different standards of right and wrong. Protestants cannot understand that faith may exist without works. That there is perfect unity of doctrine throughout the Roman Catholic Church, an undeniable fact. A parallel to the position of the Greek Church to be found in that of the Nestorians. It is no argument in favour of Anglicanism. Consoling reflections with regard to those who have been brought up in heresy and schism. Arguments derived from ecclesiastical history in favour of the Church of Rome.

Return to Clifton. Depression of spirits. Mr. Manning's Lectures giving the reason for his secession. Oswald's remarks about them. Reflections about Faith. Two letters from Mr. Aubrey de Vere. Our Lady of La Salette. Analogy between the manifestations of God recorded in the Old Testament and those which take place in the Catholic Church.

CHAPTER V. 139

Letters from Mr. de Vere. God's action through secondary agencies. The intercession of God's Saints and the one Mediator. Holy Scripture and the honour due to the Saints. A question for the Church, rather than for private judgment. The functions of the Church. Our duties towards the Church.

Doctrines not defined by the Church until definition is necessary. Many examples of the cultus of the Saints in the first centuries. Their intercession referred to in the ancient Liturgies. The Roman Liturgy. Explanation of certain prayers *for* Saints. The Notes of the Church in their plainness.

The old Cathedrals of England, and some thoughts which they suggest.

Protest of the High Church party at the time of the Gorham judgment. If the Church of England did not proclaim her faith in Baptism because she had no power of making her voice heard, she found power of voice to pronounce judgment against the Papal Supremacy. On that doctrine her members were agreed.

Authority found only in the Catholic Church. Her "Notes" easily perceived even by the unlearned.

The point really at issue. Are the difficulties greater now than they were at Pentecost?

CHAPTER VI. 167

High Church friends. Mr. Allies' book on *St. Peter, his Name and his Office*. Ethel's opinion on the danger of a hurried inquiry. A Colonial Bishop points out the danger of any inquiry at all. *Margaret Percival*. Her uncle's advice.

A long letter from Milly. Her views. Her fears. Her desire for the restoration of the godly discipline of penance. Her appreciation of suffering, mental and physical. Description of the death she wished to die. How her wish was realized.

Archdeacon Wilberforce's Sermons *On the New Birth of Man's Nature*. Dr. Arnold's opinion of the English divines. Wrong ideas about the Sacramental system.

Charles Kingsley's novels. First visit to Oxford. Ethel's letters from Scotland. Her description of the Presbyterian service.

Extracts from Diary on religious difficulties. Letters from Mr. Aubrey de Vere. The "Church of our Baptism." Mr. Manning comes to Clifton. Interviews with him, and the effect of them.

CHAPTER VII. 217

Visits to Protestant friends. Vexation. Oswald's collection of books.

Archdeacon Wilberforce's *Treatise on the Holy Eucharist*. Its definite teaching. This doctrine the key to Christianity. The Sacred Humanity the appointed channel of grace. St. Augustine's testimony.

Lessons learnt from study of Archdeacon Wilberforce's book. Practical difficulties that it suggested. Milly's letters on the subject. Her doubts and perplexities.

The Holy Communion, by Father Dalgairns. How Christianity satisfies the yearning of the human soul for union with God. Jewish saints contrasted with Christian saints. The sixth chapter of St. John's Gospel.

CHAPTER VIII. 241

Difficulties in the way of conversion. Reasons why it was delayed. The Crimean War. A first great sorrow. The state of the soul after death. Tennyson's *In Memoriam*. Letters from sympathizing friends. Prayers for the dead. Notes of a High Church sermon on the Communion of Saints. The necessity for penance taught in Scripture. The consolations of Purgatory.

Bournemouth. St. Peter's Church. Spiritual helps in the English Church. The Definition of the doctrine of the Immaculate Conception. Mr. Dean's secession. Extracts from Diary. Thoughts suggested by Mr. Woodford. Extracts from Mr. Woodford's published sermons. The punishment that rejection of any article of faith entails. The mystery of the Gospel. Lectures on the latter part of the Creed. The Holy Catholic Church. The Alliance of Church and State.

Courbon on *Mental Prayer*. Spiritual consolation. A foreign tour projected.

CHAPTER IX. 284

A foreign tour. Morning at Bruges. High Mass in the Cathedral. Rubens' pictures at Antwerp and Malines. Church of St. Appolinaris at Remagen. Arrival in Switzerland. Thun. An earthquake.

Mr. Barker. His ideas and conduct. My brother's letters from Kandersteg and Weggis. Grindelwald. The churchyard at Weggis.

Arrival in Italy. Journey from Cività Vecchia. First impressions of Rome.

CHAPTER X. 312

The varied attractions of Rome. Its highest interests appreciable only by the children of the Church. Aggravating Protestants. Mr. Barker's remarks on St. Peter's. Visits to various churches. Benediction at the Trinità dei Monti. Evening parties. The Sistine chapel. Impressions in Santa Maria Maggiore. Olivia's lines on the grave of Keats.

Visits to the Catacombs. Description of the chapels and their paintings. Altercation with Mr. Barker. Christmas Eve. Midnight Mass at the Trinità. Matins and Lauds, and the Aurora Mass at St. Peter's. The Pope's Mass. Pius IX.

Mr. William Palmer. His early partiality for the Russian Church. His visit to Russia. Conversation with him about his submission to Rome. His method of controversy. His devotion to his friends. Mr. Palmer's discussion with the Archimandrite Philaret on the Invocation of Saints.

Mr. Robert Isaac Wilberforce. Visits to the Mamertine Prison and to the Palace of the Cæsars. The Convent of the Trinità dei Monti. Church of St. Cecilia. Crypt of St. Peter's. The Christian Museum in the Lateran. A letter from my mother.

Uneasiness of Mr. Barker. His behaviour. A general upset. An episcopal warning. My reflections. Some remarks from Olivia. Mr. Barker's pupil. The last days of the Carnival. Studios. Di Rossi, Tenerani, Overbeck. Dome of St. Peter's. Holy Week. Easter Sunday. Illumination of St. Peter's. Depression at the thought of leaving Italy. Audience of His Holiness Pius IX.

CHAPTER XI. 379

Regret at leaving Rome. Assisi. Dante's description of St. Francis and his Bride. Florence in 1856. Thoughts suggested by the old painters.

The Baths of Lucca. A summer in Tuscany. Extracts from books. The *Divina Commedia*.

A second winter in Rome. Drive in the Campagna. Children's First Communion in a convent. Monsignor George Talbot. The Aurora Mass in St. Peter's on Christmas morning. Miss Congleton. New Year's Eve at the Gesù.

San Lorenzo. Queen Christina. Lady Lothian. Dr. Manning.

Candlemas day. Illness and death of Robert Isaac Wilberforce. Consecration of the Bishop of Clifton in the Sistine chapel. Dr. Manning's sermons. The different impressions which these sermons produced. Devotion to the Blessed Virgin. Sermon on poverty of spirit. Reflections. Holy Week services. Easter Sunday.

Visits to sites connected with the holy Apostles. St. Philip Neri's delight in making the pilgrimage to the Seven Churches.

CHAPTER XII. 438

Painful impressions that some Protestants receive from foreign churches. They do not understand the Catholic idea of worship. Advantages of familiarity with foreign lands in youth. The choice of a state of life. Necessity of coming to a decision about religion. Motives which conduced to the decision. The Sacrament of Penance.

Dr. Pusey's satisfaction in the Church of England. Dean Church's views. Mr. Keble's views. The *Christian Year*. Ash Wednesday. The Commination Service.

Father Faber's books and sermons. Difficulties and their solutions. Interview with Father Faber. Reception into Church.

CHAPTER I.

Impressions on first entering a Catholic church. Woodchester and the Passionist Fathers. St. Paul's words about Purgatory. A controversial and disquieting discussion on the veneration of saints.

The Gorham case. My two friends and their parents. Sybella's views on Baptismal Regeneration. The sermons of Mr. Robbins. Perplexity as to how to behave in church so as not to displease any of my lawful superiors. Brother Martin and his penances. Dr. Pusey's teaching on the necessity of self-denial. The foreign devotional works translated and edited by Dr. Pusey and their effect. Observance of saints' days.

Oswald Middleton and his influence over us. Mr. Sewell's works. A country church some forty years ago. Mr. Dean. Bishop Samuel Wilberforce and his Confirmation addresses. His mind an essentially Protestant one.

Life from ten to fourteen. Letters from friends. The freedom of the Church from State trammels predicted. Sybella's account of Mr. Magee's sermon on self-denial. Some letters from Milly.

IT was an epoch in my life when I first entered a Catholic church (I was but twelve years old). There was a sense of a longing satisfied—something I had been craving for that I had at last found. Here was something that was supernatural —did it come from God or the devil? Certainly it was unlike anything in the world.

The church at Woodchester, in Gloucestershire, to which I refer, had lately been built and was then served by Passionists. It is now the Dominican Novitiate, and a large Priory is attached to it. In those days the church stood alone, and the Passionist Fathers lived in an ordinary little house close by. They were Italians mostly, and we made friends with one of them, Father Honorius. He gave us each a little crucifix, which much delighted me, and which I have worn ever since. He told us about Father Ignatius Spencer, who, he said, had been at Woodchester. Then he explained to us the Rule of St. Paul of the Cross, which is one of the most severe of modern times, and when one of our party rather carped at asceticism and the necessity for so much self-denial and mortification, Father Honorius pointed to an inscription in the church: "When Christ, Who is our Life, shall appear, then shall we also appear with Him in glory. Mortify, *therefore*, your members." Often afterwards did I think of those words, and contrast the lives of the Passionist Fathers with the standard of Christian life set before us in the so-called Church of our Baptism.

We had a discussion with the Father about Purgatory, and he quoted St. Paul's words in his first Epistle to the Corinthians (c. iii. 12—15), and asked us how we explained them. We undertook to send an explanation. Mant and d'Oyley were consulted, but we were somewhat dismayed at the feebleness of those commentators when treating of the passage in question. However, we had to forward the explanation, such as it was, to the good Padre, and in return came a very long answer with cogent arguments from Holy Scripture in proof of Purgatory. This letter we looked on as a great treasure, and read and re-read many a time. Father Honorius also lent us some of Dr. Wiseman's essays.

One of our visits to Woodchester was rather disturbing. We were a large party, and amongst the number was the incumbent of a London church, a gentleman of an argumentative turn of mind, very sure of the superiority of his position, and very anxious to improve the occasion. So in the sacristy, where we were being shown some vestments, he made some insulting observations about idolatry as practised in the Roman Church. The Italian Father, who did not possess much English, was kindly trying to put him right, when in came a recent convert, who grasped the situation at once and immediately joined in the discussion.

"I beg your pardon, sir," he said to the parson, "but are you married?"

"Yes, I am," was the expected answer.

"Then, why did you say to your wife in the marriage ceremony, 'With my body I thee worship'? Was not that idolatry?"

The question was aggravating, but very much to the point. The discussion was pursued, and I appreciated the logic displayed by the Catholic controversialist, but our friend was not so well pleased at being handed over to one of his own nationality, thoroughly well up in the question, very different to a benighted Italian. He became somewhat irritated, and his wife looked as if she wished she were anywhere else. As long as she stood there, witnessing to the fact that her husband had said he worshipped her, that husband could not have it all his own way in condemning Catholics because they worshipped saints. The result was loss of temper.

It was comic, but also vexatious. I did not like my peaceful associations with Woodchester to be disturbed; it seemed a sort of profanation. However, I had the comfort of knowing that the Anglican parson was completely worsted—that he should be ashamed of himself was too much to expect.

My mother said, "What a pity it was that *our* clergy could not keep their tempers." I was young and I believed it to be a fact that not many of the English clergy *could* keep their tempers when arguing with Roman Catholics!

This was the time of the celebrated Gorham case, which brought the doctrine of Holy Baptism into prominence. I had been taught the orthodox doctrine and believed it firmly. Some of my friends were "not sure" about it, and we used to have great discussions. Sybella was a very stolid young person, the exact opposite to Milly, her elder sister, so far at least that whereas the latter possessed the sense of the ludicrous to an inordinate degree, Sybella was made quite unhappy by any want of gravity. She looked on fun as inconsistent with the seriousness of life. These young ladies were very well educated. Their father was somewhat eccentric and lived very much alone with his books and his family. He read every book that was worth reading. His wife shared his literary tastes, but not his anti-social disposition. She possessed a great power of sympathy with others and was more ready to make friends than her husband was the reverse. She and my mother became much attached to each other, and frequent meetings took place. And so it came to pass that Sybella was much thrown with me.

Sybella was three or four years older than I was and very tall, so I had to look up to her, but this did not prevent me from being anxious about her views on Baptism. She did not see that Baptismal Regeneration could be proved from the Bible, or indeed that the Bible warranted the Baptism of infants. I looked up all the passages that spoke of Baptism. Sybella gave due consideration to them, but declared herself unconvinced. I found out thus early in life by practical experience how hopeless it is to prove any doctrine however plain it may appear to oneself from the Bible. I myself was just as firmly convinced of the truth of Baptismal Regeneration as I was before we began the discussions, but it was evident that people might read their Bibles with a good-will and an earnest spirit and not find it taught there. But the Church had always taught it—was that the reason why I believed it so firmly?

"*Our* Church," Sybella said, "did not require any doctrine to be believed unless it could be proved that it was contained in Holy Scripture. The Regeneration of infants could not be so proved." And yet our Church was very explicit on the subject of Baptism, quite wonderfully explicit, compared to the vagueness of her teaching on many points. I used to wonder how Mr. Robbins, the clergyman of our parish, could read the baptismal service with such unction and emphasis, and give thanks to Almighty God that He had been pleased to regenerate this infant, and then get up into the pulpit and tell the congregation that it was a Popish superstition to believe that any inward grace had been conferred on the child by the ceremony that it had just gone through. His remarks on these occasions were made especially for the benefit of my mother and of us her unfortunate children whom she was misleading, as no other members of his congregation were inclined to these "Popish delusions." He used to denounce very strongly "the bowing of the head" and "the turning of the body," which "some amongst us trusted in for salvation." Mother used to insist on our turning to the east when the Creed was said. This embarrassed us greatly, as our governess did not approve of it, and if the curate was reading the service, Mr. Robbins was in the adjoining pew to ours, and we had to confront his Protestant countenance as he stood there with his back resolutely turned to the altar and feel as though we were defying him. It did seem hard that our pew should be almost the only one in the church which called for this manifestation of principle. The others mostly faced the east.

Father Honorius had given us a little book containing the history of Brother Martin—a very holy youth—and this was our first introduction to the ascetical life. The quaintness and ingenuity of Brother Martin's penances delighted us much. Milly especially was desirous of emulating them. His proceedings, I need not say, were not at all in accordance with Sybella's ideas. That was another point of dispute between Sybella and me—the necessity of doing penance and practising self-denial.

I remember a sermon of Dr. Pusey's (it must have been in his volume of the *Plain Sermons*, the third, I think) which was very strong on this point. He said our Lord taught plainly that unless we took up the cross and denied ourselves, we could not be His true disciples, and that what He said then was just as true now; there were no other terms on which we could be His followers; He had not died again to open the Kingdom of Heaven to those whom He had declared unworthy of Him. Dr. Pusey reminded us that St. Paul dealt hardly with his body to bring it into subjection and *had* suffered the loss of all things. The *Tract for the Times*, too, on "Fasting" made an impression on me. My mother always taught us the excellence, or rather necessity, of mortification and self-denial in food. It was owing to her example and teaching that I had no Protestant ideas on the subject, and it is a matter for great gratitude to have been taught the doctrine of the Cross from Thomas à Kempis early in life. Mother used to value *The Imitation of Christ*. She had also, though she did not use them so much, those Catholic books adapted by Dr. Pusey for the use of members of the English Church, *The Spiritual Combat* and *The Paradise of the Christian Soul*, and from these I imbibed the spirit of Catholic devotion. I shall always feel that I owe a great deal to Dr. Pusey for *The Paradise*. I do not understand how any one can use that book and remain long contented in the Church of England. Dr. Pusey, it is true, cut out the special devotions to the Blessed Virgin Mary and the Saints, which however form but a small portion of the book. What taught me so much, were the devotions to the Holy Trinity, the Contemplations on the Divine Perfections, the Acts of Faith, Hope, and Charity, the Acts of Contrition, of Gratitude, of Resignation, &c., the devotions to the Blessed Sacrament and to the Sacred Humanity. It was by using *The Paradise* that I got acclimatized (if I may so speak) to the atmosphere of Catholic doctrine and devotion, so that when I really found myself within the Church nothing seemed difficult or strange. It was from the same source no doubt that the aversion arose which I soon began to feel to English forms and ceremonies. The reciting of the Psalms was what I liked best in the Anglican service, but it was no sacrifice to me, as I believe it is to some, to give up our reformed Liturgy, and I heard "Dearly beloved Brethren" for the last time without a pang of regret.

Certainly what we were taught at home was not the same religion as that which was preached by Mr. Robbins and the majority of the clergy at that time, and we were week after week much diverted by the anti-Puseyite discourses we had to listen to. As a sort of protest we used to be taken on Saints' days to a church some three miles distant where "good Church doctrines" were preached. These festivals occur about once a month in the Anglican calendar, and we used to like them very much. My mother's observance of them was considered a very bad sign by Mr. Robbins and his curate.

Our cousin Oswald Middleton was a considerable personage in our lives for two or three years about this time. He was at Oxford and much bent on distinguishing himself there preparatory to taking Orders, but his hopes received a severe blow from the failure of his eyesight for all practical purposes of reading. He was melancholy in consequence and took the gloomiest view of men and things. He never could say anything in a plain way, but had a habit of making use of the best language he could find, so that simple folk were apt to be rather perplexed as to his meaning. We used to read to him a great deal and to write an analysis of what we read—a habit he taught me which has been of great service to me ever since. He was a great admirer of the writings of Robert Isaac Wilberforce, and used to speak of *The Five Empires* by that author as one of the books that had given him his taste for reading. Schlegel's *Philosophy of History*, I think, was the other.

Oswald was at Exeter College and had there come under the influence of the Rev. William Sewell, the author of a romance—and very much of a romance—bearing on the Roman controversy. I have a dim remembrance of the fearful ends that the Roman Catholic personages—Jesuits, I think—who figured in the tale came to. One was consumed in melted lead. Another was devoured alive by rats. The third met with a fate not less deplorable, but it has escaped my memory.

Another of Mr. Sewell's publications was a pamphlet which professed to examine *The Plea of Conscience for seceding from the Catholic Church to the Romish Schism in England*. One of the maxims he laid down for the guidance of the English Churchman was that he might always trust his conscience when it was prohibitory and told him *not* to do a thing. The Ten Commandments were mostly so framed: "Thou shalt *not* covet, thou shalt *not* steal, thou shalt *not* kill," &c., therefore the dictate of conscience might be trusted when it said, "Thou shalt not leave the Church of England," but not when it said, "Thou shalt join the Church of Rome," seemingly overlooking the obvious rejoinder that conscience might put the matter thus: "Thou shalt not remain in the Church of England," or that this rule would authorize a Dissenter to say, "Thou shalt not join that Apostolical Church." Although we whom he addressed had not yielded to the fascinations of the Romish schism, yet we could not be exonerated altogether from the guilt of those who had. There was an eloquent passage describing our shortcomings to which perchance the error of those misguided men was partly due, ending with, "And had we prayed for them as we might have prayed, God's mercy might have spared them all." It suggested that these unfortunate men had somehow through our fault met with the boiling lead and the hungry rats described in *Hawkestone*, but this we knew was not the case.

Christian Morals was the title of a work of Mr. Sewell's which Oswald was fond of recommending to his young lady friends. We read this when staying with our aunt, Mrs. Wrangham, at Lystone, as also Coleridge's *Aids to Reflection*

—another favourite book of Oswald's. We used to spend some weeks at Lystone every year. It was in the diocese of Oxford, and Bishop Samuel Wilberforce, who then occupied that see, was greatly revered by my mother and my aunt. They were much impressed by his confirmation charges. When the time came for my sister Olivia to receive that rite we went to Lystone that she might have the benefit of his administration of it. I wanted to be confirmed at the same time, and considered myself quite old enough, but Bishop Wilberforce objected to any one much under sixteen being confirmed. He looked on Confirmation as the great turning-point for good in life, and certainly did his best in the exhortations he was accustomed to give on these occasions to make it so, and to stamp the remembrance of it indelibly on the minds of the assembled congregations. These congregations indeed were unused to being so addressed. He spoke simply and earnestly. They could understand, and he took pains that they should understand what he said. Perhaps the instructions of their ordinary pastors had hardly prepared them to view what they were about to do in so very solemn a light.

Lystone Church was an old-fashioned edifice, with the pulpit, reading-desk, and clerk's desk of those days, and the Squire's large square pew immediately under these erections. The pew was so situated that conversations used sometimes to take place between the clergyman and Mr. Wrangham or Mrs. Wrangham. Much went on that was a trial to our gravity, beginning with the half-tremulous, half-threatening intonation of the clerk when he gave out the first verse of a hymn and called on his soul to awake and run its daily stage of duty with the sun. In this exhortation he was vigorously joined by Mrs. Wrangham, though in her case the admonition to "shake off dull sloth" was not often obeyed. She usually managed to drop asleep during the discourse, sometimes much to the embarrassment of the other members of the pew, as when on one occasion she dreamed that she was being pursued by a mad bull and woke with a loud shriek.

When old Mr. Baker went away for a time and left his parish for an indefinite period to the care of an elderly curate—one Mr. Sherwyn—the change was considered satisfactory. Mr. Sherwyn was more active than was his predecessor, and he tried to do his best. He used to enliven us too with very curious notices interspersed up and down the service about blankets which were to be had of Mrs. Sherwyn on advantageous terms, or about a sack of potato seed which he had acquired and which he was willing to share with those who might wish to purchase a few pecks, or about a bit of ground for which he required labourers. On one occasion I remember his having an altercation with Mrs. Wrangham as to the Lesson which was to be read. He had given out a wrong one according to Mrs. Wrangham's calendar, whereupon she immediately jumped up and put him right and quite a long conversation ensued in consequence. Once he announced in his sermon that it had long been his custom on Sunday to partake of a cold dinner and "in the evening," he said, " Mrs. Sherwyn and I take tea, and I could wish our example were more generally followed in the parish." Eventually he took to preaching a farewell sermon every Sunday, informing us with emotion that this would be his last appearance amongst us. I was rather touched the first time I heard this announcement, believing it to be true, till I heard my uncle mutter to himself, " No such luck!"

Mr. Dean, then a Fellow of All Souls and vicar of Lewknor, a village a few miles from Lystone and not very far from Oxford, was a great friend of my aunt's. He was very much in the movement, and possessed an unusual amount of wit and cleverness, and his statements were rather startling to those who take everything quite literally. If my aunt had some ultra-Protestant friend staying with her, she would beg of Mr. Dean to be careful of what he said, but nevertheless, would perhaps hear him shortly afterwards announce to his indignant listener that the principal things taught in his parish school were dancing and the Catechism of Trent. In these early days we were rather afraid of him. Later on he became one of my greatest friends.

I remember that he gave my sister a little book on self-examination when she was going to be confirmed. It was Mr. Sherwyn, however, whom she interviewed in order to obtain the certificate for the Bishop that she was duly qualified. Mr. Dean declared that Mr. Sherwyn's idea of the communion of saints was a few neighbours coming to tea with him and Mrs. Sherwyn, and reading a chapter in the Bible afterwards.

Confirmation is not regarded as a sacrament in the Church of England, there being two sacraments only, the Catechism says, "as generally necessary to salvation," whilst the 25th Article expressly repudiates its sacramental character. But as young people are not admitted to "the Lord's Supper" as a rule in the Church of England till they have been confirmed, the importance which in the Catholic Church is attached to First Communion seems to have been transferred to Confirmation. Bishop Wilberforce, as I have said, made the rite very impressive. He was accustomed to watch the conduct and countenances of all the candidates. If he saw any who appeared distracted or less serious than they should be, he would mention it and address the culprits publicly in his charge—and when the turn came for them to approach the altar-rails he would speak separately to each one and advise him or her to stay away unless duly prepared, and sorry for the smile or the wandering looks which had given rise to the admonition.

Much confusion and even tears ensued. "Confirmation," he said, "is not a charm. The laying on of my hands will not do you a bit of good unless your dispositions are right." Dear old Mr. Sherwyn was so pleased with the Bishop's address that at one part he began to rub his hands vigorously as though he were about to clap. This occasioned the Bishop to stop and look at him with great sternness. It did not tend to restore that prelate to good-humour with him when, after we were all assembled in the Parsonage, Mr. Dean chose to allude to Mr. Sherwyn's having spoken on a recent occasion of Cranmer, Ridley, and Latimer as the founders of our holy religion!

Bishop Wilberforce has been accused of treating his clergy with great imperiousness, as though they were quite an inferior race of beings. He had very exalted ideas of the office of an English Bishop, but he had no reverence apparently for the English priesthood. Indeed his was an essentially Protestant mind, wholly destitute of Catholic instincts. Unlike many who were not considered more High Church than he was —he never grasped the doctrine of the Eucharistic Sacrifice. It is not therefore to be wondered at that he did not consider his clergy entitled to honour in virtue of their calling. Mr. Allies' view of him in *A Life's Decision* may seem perhaps too severe. Mr. Dean used to say that he forgave Bishop Wilberforce much on discovering that he had a great deal more heart than head, and it was this no doubt that endeared him so much to his family. I remember with what affection his brother spoke of him and what excuses he made for his anti-Catholic spirit on the ground that the Bishop's life was one of such excitement and rush that he never gave himself time for thought. "He will not face his position," Mr. Henry Wilberforce said. "If he could but have an illness and be *forced* to think, or if all his occupations were taken from him and he could be alone with himself for half an hour, I should have hopes of his conversion." The words surprised me not a little; anyhow, the half-hour did not come; the illness which was to effect such a change was never sent. On a summer afternoon, on a sunny, pleasant down, suddenly and without a moment's warning that life of ceaseless activity came to an end. Men of the world said, "Let my last end be like his," and of the more religious not a few echoed the words, for "surely," said they, "no one was better prepared to die."

But in the days of which I am writing many years of work and enjoyment were before Samuel Wilberforce. Mr. Allies was still at Launton, giving trouble to him whom he called the modern Vigilantius, and the bust of Henry Edward Manning at Cuddesdon was not yet covered with a veil!

The four years from ten to fourteen seem equal to three or four times as many in after life. How very long a time it was one seemed to be in growing up and coming to what is called years of discretion. And how much one resented being treated as a small child and being supposed not to understand things. One attraction in my aunt Wrangham was that as a rule she gave very young people credit for being just as capable as their elders. This habit of hers and the line of conduct it induced was a trial to the governesses and instructors of youth with whom she came in contact. She would say when she saw us studying languages and history, we should not know nearly as much when we were forty. She was a great enemy to over-education and any pursuit that interfered with taking plenty of bodily exercise and being much in the open air.

The monotony of our life was varied by visits to Lystone and to the houses of other relatives, and by the friends my eldest brother used to bring home. These were usually older than himself, and were particularly nice quiet youths. I call them youths, but in those days we looked on any one of twenty-one or twenty-two years of age as quite old. They generally began or ended by falling in love with Olivia. She being still in the school-room was not supposed to think of such things, although by the time she was seventeen she had lived through more than one little romance.

I find a good many letters which bring back those days, and it may be as well to insert two or three belonging to the last year of our life in Gloucestershire, which bear more or less on religion.

The first is from a cousin.

"August 9th, 1850.

". . . Mrs. N—— thinks the vicinity of the Fathers very dangerous and does not at all like hearing of your going to Woodchester. She seems to think it tampering with Romanism in a most unnecessary manner, but *I* have not many fears of your conversion, attractive as the Fathers doubtless are; and I confess I should like as a matter of curiosity once to pay them a visit.

"I *did* read the opinions of the press in *The Guardian* last week, and was rather amused at the differences in opinion on the same subject. Our friend takes a very hopeful view of the case, and as you wish to know his opinion I will kindly transcribe what he says: 'I was very much interested with the notices of the meeting from the different newspapers. Altogether, I think the gathering most encouraging and begin to have real hopes for the vitality of the Church *in* England—not however as *joined to the State*. I don't think anything can save it from virtual extinction if that bond is kept up; but everything seems to me to point the other way; and a few years hence we shall I think see the Church *free* and *effective*. Now she is neither. It is a very mockery to appeal to the results or rather the fruits (to use Scripture language) as our test of the system in proof of its adaptation to the end which it professes. It has not come near to purifying a peculiar people zealous of good works.'

"And again, 'The times are past for a building standing by its own weight; it may do so when the air is calm and still. The storms and gusts that are now rising about every institution will overthrow all that have not a foundation: the Church has one, but it is not Downing Street or even Windsor.'"

Our dear friends the Burtons had moved to Bath, and Sybella in the following letter refers to the discussion at Woodchester before alluded to, and details her views about self-denial as expressed by Mr. Magee (afterwards Bishop of Peterborough and Archbishop of York), who was then a popular preacher at Bath.

"Thanks for your letter which I was delighted to receive. Jem told us of your expedition to Woodchester and also the substance of the argument, with which I suppose you were very much edified. I wonder which had the greatest weight —the Father's opinions or those of our clergymen?

How very sorry you will be when these Passionist Fathers leave! I only hope the friars 'of orders black' will not be so attractive. . . .

"I must now give you a slight account of Mr. Magee's sermon yesterday, more especially as it was on a subject on which we have so often talked together, viz., self-denial and bearing the cross, from the text 'He that beareth not his cross and cometh after Me cannot be My disciple,' but the view he took of it more coincided with what I vainly attempted to express, than with your favourite sermon of Dr. Pusey's.

"He began by saying that the Christian religion might be comprised in two sentences. Looking to Christ on the Cross on Calvary as our strength and our Redeemer, and looking to Jesus bearing His Cross thither as our example; that most of the errors which have arisen amongst Christians have come from their attempts to separate these two which God has eternally joined together. While some have looked entirely to the first and have imagined they can be saved by faith alone, others have lost sight of the Cross of Christ which justifies, by fixing their hopes on *bearing* the Cross, but that we ought no more to hide from the living sinner the Cross which is to be the rule of his life, than we should from the dying one that which is his hope in death. He then went on to say in what the bearing of the Cross consisted, that there was necessarily connected with it the idea of pain and shame; the pain of the Cross was self-denial, the difficulty of which we may feel from the effort which it costs us to deny ourselves from prudential motives any present gratification even for a future good: that the Christian's self-denial consisted in bringing his rebellious will into full harmony with the almighty will of God, by mortifying our corrupt affections and desires, substituting humility for pride, forbearance and love for revenge, malice, &c., that as the Cross might be avoided in affliction by a repining or self-satisfied spirit, so might it be found in prosperity by making it an occasion of exercising the virtues of humility, charity, &c. The shame of the Cross arose from the hatred of the world to those who professed it, who shone forth before men who hated light and reproved their ways both by word and example. Before concluding he called the attention of his hearers to some other crosses which people bear in the world which were not the sanctifying Cross of Christ. There is a cross which great sinners sometimes have to carry even in this world, when in the righteous judgment of God, he who is going to the place of his eternal execution is made to bear even in the sight of man the cross of his punishment, his sins going beforehand to Judgment. Secondly, there is a cross of self-imposition, consisting of fastings, laceratings of the flesh and such-like tortures by which men supposed they were bearing the Cross of Christ, when in reality they were going their own way to salvation, having their reward in the praise of men for their imagined sanctity, but what will such men answer to the Judge's question at the last great day: 'Who hath required this at your hand to follow Me?' saith the Lord. Finally, there is a cross of punishment which the Almighty sometimes lays upon His people who through carelessness or weakness have fallen from the faith and are wandering in sin and error—but such crosses are like the thorns which are planted round the path of the believer to keep him in the way, rather than the crown of thorns on earth which shall be his diadem of glory in Heaven.

"He then concluded by an address to those who had not begun to bear the Cross and to those who do bear it. To the latter he spoke of the comfort which they should have under it, for as when on earth a mortal was allowed to bear with our Saviour the burden of His Cross, so from the throne of glory in Heaven shall He now stretch forth His almighty hand to lighten the burden of this Cross which is now laid on Christians that it press not too heavily on them.

"I must not write more. I only hope you will feel the truth of the self-denial which the sermon recommends—the *real* mortification of self: only do not think I am going to preach as though you did not feel it; but it seems such self-denial is the only one really necessary for the Christian, and oh! what a constant labour and toil for the longest life *thus* to keep under the body and bring it into subjection to the law of Christ."

Thus wrote my good Sybella in her zeal for my improvement and wish that I should be enlightened as to what was faulty in the ascetic doctrines that were inculcated by Dr. Pusey.

Milly writes in a different style:

"I confess I *am* rather astonished to hear that you like my serious letters best: perhaps this may be from their variety and novelty, and consequently their pleasing effect may be greatly diminished when you become better acquainted with my sermonish style of composition. . . . I have been reading a very beautiful sermon by Dr. Pusey on the 'Bliss of Heaven.' I do so like him and reverence his pure unworldly spirit. I believe I am getting more and more of what is called by the various names of miss-ishy, fanatical, Romanistic, &c., by my many wise friends. *How* came you to hear that I argued with Miss Lyndon, and asserted my own views so strongly. Sometimes I assure you I can hardly help it, for I feel myself constrained to defend what I think right against accusations or insinuations, and also I confess with shame I *am* too fond of argument for its own sake. I have come to the conclusion founded on self-experience, that it is a bad thing for me to live much with people of very Low Church views and ways: it 'tends' too much to puff one up with an idea of superiority and to induce a contemptuous or bitter feeling against them, which is far from being really High Church (if so we must call it) or Christian. I don't know that I am yet fully established in the belief of that doctrine[1] to which you helped to convert me —not that I am gone back in my faith in it— don't be afraid of that, but I hardly *dare* to believe it certainly. I read a *very* good sermon on the subject, by Dodsworth, the other day, with excellent arguments in it which Sybella and I liked much.

"I think I should agree with you in not liking quite everything in Mr. Magee's sermon which Sybella sent you. I did not *hear* it, so I can hardly judge, but from what I have heard of it I think it would not altogether have pleased me.

"We had a treat last week, which was going with Dr. Reid to the Roman Catholic chapel here to hear him play the organ. While he was playing we, including Walter, sat in the chapel and I looked eagerly around in the hope of seeing a priest, but I saw nobody but a woman who came in for her devotions, and who rebuked us all most severely for our irreverence in being in the chapel for any other purpose than that of devotion. I was very meek and told her how sorry I was to have done wrong, though indeed we were very quiet, reading little Romish books, and then she became more calm and said she

[1] Baptismal Regeneration.

knew we didn't mean any harm, but that it was a very shocking thing to come lightly into that chapel, as it was peculiarly sacred. Whereupon I entered into a slight argument with her, in which she testified great compassion at our miserable state, and then she left poor heretical me and went to pray. I envied her being able to go into the quiet church to escape a while from the discord and hurry of the world, but we need not go to Rome to find open churches for this purpose, though alas! they are as yet but few. We must be patient and trustful, and all will be well.

"Do tell me about your visit to Woodchester. I hear the Passionists are going away and will be replaced by some Dominican Fathers, who will be very different and we shall not like them so well. This report will I know fill you with grief and dismay, but it may break one of your strongest ties to the neighbourhood. Alas! that this should be said of daughters of the Church of England.

"How sorry you must be that Mr. Middleton is going away so soon, and how sorry I am for your sakes. What will become of your minds when he is gone with the restraining influence of his wisdom and true churchism!

"Your affectionate
"MILLY."

"January 30th, 1857.
"On a wild and stormy day—fit celebration of the martyrdom of the blessed King Charles I.

after having duly been to church I willingly and gladly retire from the scenes and thoughts of Bath to spend a short time with you. . . . First I must just make a small observation or two on the subject of Mr. Bennett, but I won't give you much of my opinion on this head. . . . You will think me I fear very wicked when I say, I cannot help thinking Mr. Bennett very much in the wrong in not submitting at once to his Bishop: and though it seems wrong to condemn so good a man for acting according to his conscience, yet one can hardly help doing so when we remember that it is quite possible to follow our conscience and yet to do *wrong*, and this seems to me to be what Mr. Bennett has done—however unwillingly. All this is strictly in accordance with the opinion of Mr. Wood, to whom I talked a great deal about him, one evening when Jem and I went to dine with him and his sister. However, I do pity Mr. Bennett very much, for he must feel all this, I am sure, most deeply: it is grievous to think of losing all the good he did at St. Barnabas, and I hate and detest to have people talking as they do in those wretched newspapers about him.

"I hope you liked the Bishop of Fredericton's Charge as much as I did. I thought the part about Baptism excellent, and all he said about the office and duties of the clergy.

"I find you tell me in your letter not to let myself be corrupted here by Mr. Magee, &c., so you fear for me? If you knew the array against me on all sides you would be better able to appreciate my firmness of character and principle. Mama thinks me wild and romantic, Sybella and Jim are of the same opinion. Miss Lyndon says I am unstable and imitative. John pronounces me an ignorant bigot, and Walter, how can I express the feelings of grief and horror with which that excellent Protestant regards me. Not only does he think me of dangerous Romanizing tendencies, but he looks upon my whole character as that of one little if at all better than a pagan. This is by no means an exaggerated representation of his sentiments, though he would not be pleased at my revealing these dark thoughts concerning his unhappy cousin. But now the dear youth has departed for Oxford and I am not sorry for his departure, though how he will fare in that place of error and superstition, and thrown, as he is, into the power of 'a regular Puseyite,' I cannot imagine.

"I have heard a good many evil things of Dr. Pusey lately, and even Mr. Wood, to whom I talked about him a good deal, does not think him quite *sound*. *Why*, I never can find out, and I don't intend to think about it at all, but to go on admiring and loving what I *do* know is perfectly right and excellent in him, without troubling myself to discover what the 'something' is which frightens and shocks the rest of the world in such a strange manner.

"A week or so ago Father Faber came to Bath

and was staying with Mrs. Gordon, a great friend of Mr. Macpherson. The latter heard him preach and was enchanted, being affected almost to tears according to his account. Mr. Macpherson also saw Father Faber at Mrs. Gordon's, and had an argument with him, and says that his power of argument was wonderful.

". . . What you said in your letter to-day about feeling disheartened, weary of the daily struggle of our life, is just what I have been feeling so sadly lately. I have felt, as it were, quite tired of the strife against evil, against *self*, almost hopeless, and looking forward to perhaps a long life of such struggles, such hard fights to gain even a very little victory, and this to go on year after year, the same falls, the same petty trials and base yielding to them; I have felt a longing, a wrong, cowardly, selfish longing, I fear it is, to escape and be at rest from it all and feel *safe*. These feelings are very wrong—I am not so brave as you. I have not a heart for any fate I fear, but a very muffish and soft one. Fancy my being called on to be a Martyr, or to spend such a life as St. Francis Xavier! It all seems so great and noble and beautiful when one thinks and reads of it, yet when such principles (and surely they are or ought to be the very same principles) have to be carried out in daily life, its little trials, momentary vexations, &c., how poor and weak one is! I could go on far more about this, but Mary tells me I am too fond of talking of myself, my *faults* even, and this I am afraid is true. I am not sure whether it *is* good to talk of these things, and yet a talk with *you* about them always does me good, and at any rate it is an immense comfort, for sometimes I get really desponding, in which case to speak cheers and strengthens me, and then too, I know that you think as much as I do on such matters. I have longed for Dr. Pusey to talk to lately: he would help me. I believe the best thing is, not to sit down and despond. *That* is not the way to gain strength, but to go and *do* something, to put in *practice* in some way one's good resolves, and not to shrink from so doing, because the occasion which next offers itself may be trifling or unexpected, and therefore one's mighty resolutions are often nearly forgotten.

"Thus far had I got yesterday evening when tea and the reading aloud of *Jane Eyre* came to stop my further writing, but now a wet afternoon prevents me from thinking of going out, while Geraldine is solacing himself by industriously practising the bars of a polka assisted by mama, and Sybella is on her knees before the range of cupboards, which she is 'putting tidy,' whence occasionally issues a clattering sound of palettes and paint-boxes, &c. In this general scene of virtuous activity I endeavour to compose my mind, withdrawing it from polka and palettes with some difficulty to finish this letter. . . . Hobart Seymour is going this day to deliver a lecture to gentlemen only, on various enormities committed in nunneries, in answer to Cardinal Wiseman's sermon, which, by-the-bye, I have never yet seen. . . . Yesterday we three went to the Octagon and heard a very excellent discourse from Mr. Magee, more pleasing to *me* than almost any I have heard from him, because it was free from all uncharitableness, and because it gave me great satisfaction on points of which I had lately been made to feel almost doubtful. It was on the Holy Trinity, and gave very clear proofs of the *necessity* of our having a *right* belief of this great doctrine, and why creeds are needful, and such a strongly expressed creed as the Athanasian to fence the truth and guard it from the attacks of heretics, and to keep it undefiled.

"I thought of you on Whit Sunday when I went alone to early service, and remembered the last time when we went together on that dear happy Easter Day. When is my little book to come?[1] I anxiously expect it, as my soul is beginning to get dry and thirsts for a little rivulet from Paradise!

"I have just been reading four lectures on Church History by Mr. Woodford—very excellent—intended to strengthen me against Romish tendencies. They don't do that *especially*, because I have them not, but they do give a very good view of the general history of the Church, and

[1] Of extracts from Dr. Pusey's edition of *The Paradise of the Christian Soul.*

of the way in which our Church threw off the errors of Rome, without severing herself from the unity of the Church Catholic, so that we are still one with Rome and the Eastern Churches, and may hope for the day when we may yet be one outwardly, as we still have the four requisites, Unity, Holiness, Apostolicity, and Catholicity... Aunt Richard having just arrived, to spend a long wet afternoon here, the which afternoon I meant to have employed in a good long talk with you, I must close this, and go and entertain my respected relative, and hear little tales of Bill and Walter and of their various cracky doings! I should like to go on with you, but, because I do like it, it is more 'Brother Martinish' to say good-bye.

"Your ever devoted,

"MILLY."

CHAPTER II.

The Ancient British Church entirely independent of Rome. The opinions of a High Churchman on Roman corruptions and Anglican errors. A speedy union between Rome and England predicted. The Papal Aggression in connection with the validity of English Orders. Conduct of the English Bishops in Elizabeth's reign. Uncertainty as to the competency of Barlow to consecrate Parker, and as to the form actually used in Parker's consecration. Excitement at Bath caused by the Papal Aggression. Mr. Robbins' discourses on the subject. The regret they caused my mother.

Removal to Clifton. Preparation for Confirmation. Spiritual books. Mr. Herbert Graham. Archdeacon Manning's sermons. His secession.

Interview with Dr. Pusey. Milly. Her feelings about High Church views. Her account of the religious vagaries of her cousin. Her thoughts about the Church of St. Barnabas, Pimlico. Description of Dr. Christopher Wordsworth and an S.P.G. meeting.

WE were taught in our youth that the British Church originally had nothing to do with Rome. Christianity had been planted here long before the days of St. Gregory. It was indeed Gregory who sent St. Augustine, but Augustine was ordained by French Bishops, and his Creed, it was assumed, was very different from that of modern Rome. Some friends of my mother who were staying with us in the Woodchester days, encouraged us in our admiration for the

Passionists, and our love for visiting their church. We were greatly devoted to Mr. and Mrs. Cleveland. They were very High Church, and Mr. Cleveland used to maintain that certain doctrines which we had been told were Roman corruptions were on the contrary true Catholic teaching and to be received and held by a good churchman. As regards the Holy Eucharist, I believe he said the Church of Rome held the right doctrine in a wrong way! Praying for the dead, invoking saints, honouring the Blessed Virgin, were all primitive practices which had been very much lost sight of since the Reformation. These practices would now be gradually restored. They might have been carried too far in the Roman Church, but we on the contrary had completely given them up, and our error was probably the worst. Each Church had something to learn from the other. We had all our Protestantism to unlearn, and till we had done that, it was hardly to be anticipated that Rome would come far to meet us. Now, however, our Church architecture was being more cared for, a stir was being made about ritual, Catholic doctrines were preached, everything soon would be very different. Rome had never denied our Orders, but the English Bishops hitherto had not cared to claim spiritual kinship with their episcopal brethren on the Continent. Soon things would come right. We must have patience and pray for unity, and in theory and practice go as near as we could to our Roman brethren.

All this sounded hopeful and was very welcome to us, though I privately wished that it was not considered so very necessary that English churchmen should remain in the Church in which they were born, if it were really the same as the Church of Rome. That the Head of the Church of Rome did not so regard it was, however, distinctly proved in 1850, the year of the famous Papal Aggression. How were we to interpret this act of Pius IX.'s? Surely it proved that he had no belief in the validity of English Orders,. or at any rate in the Divine mission of the Church of England.

We had learnt little of the Church history of the early years of Elizabeth's reign. I did not know that all the Bishops who were in occupation of sees at Mary's death—fifteen in number—refused to perjure themselves by renouncing their allegiance to the See of Rome and recognizing Elizabeth as Head of the Church of Christ in England, and as supreme in all matters *spiritual* as well as temporal. The Bishops who boldly declined to take the oath of supremacy—for which oath no warrant could be found in Holy Scripture—were ejected from their sees and for the most part imprisoned. Who consecrated Parker Archbishop of Canterbury? I think I had a vague idea that Parker had behaved in the same way that Cranmer did. I do not know why

I thought such evil of him. He had not sworn obedience to the Vicar of Christ, and, on being nominated to the see of Canterbury, he was quite ready to promise submission in things spiritual as well as temporal to Elizabeth. But then the lawful Bishops would not consecrate him. To perform this ceremony an accommodating man of the name of Barlow was found. He does not seem to have been consecrated, being styled Bishop-elect of Chichester, and having previously been Bishop-elect of St. Asaph, St. David, and Bath and Wells. While no record of Barlow's own consecration is to be found, we read that Elizabeth as Supreme Head undertook to make good by her authority anything that might be wanting to the validity of Parker's consecration. Thus began the line of Bishops who have reigned in the Established Church ever since. Of course there is a possibility that Barlow may have been consecrated and that he used the proper form in the ceremony which placed the Protestant Parker in the see of St. Augustine. For either fact, however, no testimony is forthcoming. It must be taken on trust. The elimination of Orders from the class of sacraments would indicate that no great importance was attached by the Reformers to the rite.

When Brother John, a Passionist, tried to explain this to us at Woodchester, Mr. Cleveland assured us there was no doubt that the

Church of England possessed the Apostolic Succession, and that it was therefore a true branch of the One Church Catholic. How inconvenient it seemed to us that Pius IX. should take such a different view and inaugurate a new Hierarchy in England, as if no real Bishop already existed there!

The Burtons had taken a house in Bath, and we were staying with them when the nation was suffering from the panic caused by the Papal Aggression. Great Protestant demonstrations were made in Bath. There were public meetings, and special sermons in the churches on week-days as well as Sundays. Bath possessed a clergy that preached great variety of doctrine. In one church which had belonged to an old Mr. Mount there were two ministers—Mr. Wood, who was regarded as a sound churchman, and Mr. Way, who was decidedly Evangelical. Some lines occur to me which thus describe the situation:

> The traveller on his way to aid
> How much has here been done!
> The path is smooth and easy made,
> The wearying Mount is gone.
> The Wood remains 'tis true, but light
> Shines through with steady ray,
> And those who object to wooded height
> May choose the lower Way.

A choice which we did not make! The wooded heights were indeed very moderate, and not such as could be found fault with even by Sybella. Mr. Wood preached a sound Church of England sermon against the errors of Rome on the occasion of the aggression. Mr. Way's sermon was much more vehement. It was in another place of worship in Bath that I heard a very ultra-Protestant discourse, in which the Church of Rome was spoken of as the Temple of Satan, and High Church doctrines were described as the steps which led up to it. Tractarianism was the door at the top by which you went in. These denunciations used to amuse us young people, and I fear that we liked the diversion they afforded and were glad of a change from the ordinary unexciting sermon.

When we returned home we found that Mr. Robbins had not finished his remarks on the subject. Perhaps he thoughtfully postponed them that we might have the advantage of profiting. The texts for these instructions were selected from St. Paul's Epistle to the Galatians, c. ii. It remains in my mind that Mr. Robbins impressed upon us that the Church of Rome taught in contradiction to St. Paul, that a man *is* justified by the works of the law. All St. Paul's arguments against the necessity of observing Jewish rites he applied to those who believe that if they would enter into life they must perform a certain amount of good works and at least keep the Ten Commandments. "Works," he would say, "are nothing; it is faith that justifies us." Not the theological virtue of faith such as Catholics understand it, *i.e.*, belief in whatever God has revealed, because He has revealed it; but a vague sort of *feeling* (in no way an act of the understanding) that Christ has done everything for us, that we have nothing to do but to believe that He has taken away not only the guilt of our sins, but also any punishment that may be due to them. We had but to sit down and rejoice in our justification, and above all to be very careful not to think that any good works which we might perform could have any merit in them or be entitled to any reward. Mr. Robbins must have spoken a good deal against the worship of the Virgin, the sacraments, and other Catholic doctrines, but what he said about the mode of justification dwells most in my memory. "How any one with the Bible in his hand could fall into the errors of Romanism was what he (Mr. Robbins) had never been able to comprehend"!

Mother said that it was a great mistake, she thought, to tell the poor people who attended the church about these errors of which they need never hear, and that as there was but little danger of their trusting overmuch in their good works, it was a pity they should be in any way discouraged from performing them by being told such works were worth nothing. Mr. Robbins could not really have meant that it did not signify what sins you committed, provided you believed that Christ had died in order to procure forgiveness for those sins, but what he *said* amounted nearly to this, and the uneducated might so interpret it. Our works never could have any merit, mother said, but it was necessary that we should perform good works and especially the works of mercy. She would point out how in the twenty-fifth chapter of St. Matthew, our Lord makes eternal salvation to depend on whether we have fed the hungry, visited the sick, &c. She always considered caring for the poor one of the main duties of life, one which could not be neglected without great peril to the soul, and she would cite the authority of St. James, that faith without works is dead, and would tell us that Luther had a great objection to St. James's Epistle, and wondered if Mr. Robbins had also.

Sunday services, as conducted by Mr. Robbins and his curates, were, however, coming to an end for us. When I was fourteen we left the country, and said good-bye to our governess because, as we were going to reside for a time at Clifton, it was thought that our education might be carried on by means of masters. The change was agreeable and profitable. The Burtons having left the neighbourhood for three years, our chief attraction to our former residence was gone. French, German, music, and drawing-masters, gave a fresh stimulus to exertion and made work more interesting. We were abundantly supplied with books too, of which there had been rather a scarcity before, and very much did we enjoy this new phase of existence. Clifton, which was chosen on account of my mother's health, seemed a lively enough place to us at that time, accustomed as we were to the extreme quietness of the country.

Karslake's book-shop at the bottom of Park Street, which we passed as we walked to Bristol Cathedral, had a peculiar fascination for us. Still more fascination did the Catholic shop a little higher up possess, then kept by Mr. Reader. We used to get our stationery there as an excuse for looking at the images and books. All the newest Catholic publications were to be seen in the windows. Dr. Newman's *Lectures on University Education*, which I have always considered the finest of his works, I remember coming out in numbers. An acquaintance gave us the first five numbers. These I read over and over again, especially the splendid passage in the third lecture, "On the Divine Attributes." I was glad to be free from the dull routine of school-room life, to be able to arrange my studies as I liked, and to have plenty of books to interest me. We used often to attend the week-day services at Bristol Cathedral in the afternoon, and also on Sundays. The two churches at Clifton were very Low Church, so those we did not frequent. At first we went to Redlands, but afterwards to St. John the Baptist's, in Bristol, a beautiful old church with ancient associations, where the service was reverently performed, and where there was a weekly "celebration," a thing not so common in those days in the English Church as I understand it is now. We should have attended St. James', had not its incumbent, Mr. Woodward, been received into the Catholic Church just before we arrived. This event interested me greatly.

Very shortly after we were established at Clifton it was announced that a Confirmation would be held at the parish church. Here was a chance for me, and this I determined not to miss. Mother did not much like my receiving this rite with such very Low Church surroundings. She consulted the Rev. Herbert Graham, a connection of hers, who had a living some five miles from Clifton. It was arranged that he should give me the preparatory instruction that was required, and should furnish me with a certificate, which would obviate the necessity of my attending the classes of the parish clergyman. The latter's doctrine would not be the same as Mr. Graham's and mother's, but more in accordance with that of Mr. Robbins from whom we had suffered so much.

A little prayer-book I made use of for my preparation introduced me to a good translation of the *Veni, Sancte Spiritus*, a hymn that became very dear to me. *Steps to the Altar* was recommended in those days as the best devotional book for Holy Communion. I liked it, but the work that had most influence on my spiritual life at that time was one containing some six or seven instructions *On the Blessed Sacrament from the Writings of the Saints*, which had been published by Father Faber whilst he was yet in the English Church. Mrs. Cleveland had given it to mother, who was not quite sure that she liked it. It was very Roman, and rather exaggerated in its style. From it I learned to say the Psalm *Quam dilecta*, as a preparation for Communion, a Psalm which Faber told us was so used by hundreds of thousands throughout Christendom. I liked this. It gave me the feeling of being united in a new and real way with those numberless pious souls. The tone of this book and of its companion, *On the Examination of Conscience, from the Writings of the Saints*, was very unlike the tone of Anglican books. The writer seemed thoroughly to know what he was about, to have a definite purpose in view, and to be resolved that those whom he was instructing should be in earnest. It was this definiteness that was such a rest to me: I was always craving for something definite, to know exactly what to believe and how to carry out that belief in daily life.

The spirit of Faber's book on the Blessed Sacrament, as of his *Life of St. Wilfrid*, was so essentially Catholic and Roman that it was difficult to believe that these little books were written by an English clergyman. Faber belonged to that school of the Oxford movement, of which Mr. Ward was the exponent in his *Ideal of a Christian Church*. The members of this school did not shrink from teaching Catholic doctrines in all their fulness. If the Church of England would accept these doctrines and reform herself, well and good! If not, if these doctrines were declared incompatible with the Thirty-nine Articles and the religion as by law established, they must give up those Articles and that religion, and betake themselves to Rome. This they did without hesitation when an authoritative pronouncement had been made. No half and half measure, no compromise recommended itself to them.

The sweet spirit of Catholic devotion taught by Faber was most attractive to me. "Like as the hart desireth the water-brooks, so longeth my soul after Thee, O God," was the text of the first of these instructions. "My soul is athirst for God; oh, when shall I come to appear before the presence of God!" We were to aim at having that longing for God's presence, we were not to think such language wild and exaggerated and unfit for us. Like St. Paul, we were to desire to be with Christ, but we were never *so* to desire His glorious presence in Heaven as to make light of His hidden presence on earth. We ought so to realize our Lord's Presence in His Sacrament as to feel the aspect of the whole world around us changed, from the knowledge that He is present on it still, in His Manhood as well as in His Godhead. We were to contemplate our Lord's Life as divided into five deep mysteries:

His Hidden Life, His Public Life, His Suffering Life, His Glorified Life, and, lastly, His Mystical Life—His blessed Presence both as God and Man vouchsafed upon the altars of the Church. It was plain that our future happiness must very much depend on the way in which we realized this Presence, and therefore it was most necessary we should learn how to prepare for Communion, how to behave when in the presence of the Blessed Sacrament, how to make a good thanksgiving, what a blessing frequent Communion was, and how we might make at any time a spiritual communion.

On all these points the instructions were clear and definite. I can never be too thankful for having such beautiful Catholic practices suggested to me at that time. Holy Communion was the most important action of our life. Faber did not hesitate to say that it was more important than dying, for, he argued, "to go to God is surely not so important as to receive God into ourselves."

One thought which he suggested I will mention here, as a helpful thought in temptations against faith. This form was first celebrated in a private room in Jerusalem by One Who was supposed to be a carpenter's Son. A few poor unlearned men were the only witnesses, yet now this form was to be found all over the world and in every country thousands of churches have been built in honour of it and to provide for its more beautiful celebration. All who received this Blessed Sacrament, kings and priests, learned and unlearned, old and young, received it on their knees. How could this be if it were not from God? The very sight of an altar ought to satisfy us that the Catholic faith is true. The fact that this very doctrine has been most spoken against and denied by the world and perverted by misbelievers and been the cause of such enmity and strife, proved what a great thing it must really be.

I think at this time I implicitly believed the Catholic doctrine of the Real Presence, but it was not till I read Archdeacon Robert Wilberforce's treatise, which was published in 1853, that my ideas about it became very definite.

Mr. Herbert Graham was not a person with whom I could discourse about any difficulties with regard to faith. He gave me a set of questions to answer in writing. This exercise interested me. I asked him what the word "oblations" in the Communion Service referred to, "We offer Thee our alms and oblations." He said it was uncertain, it might mean an offering that was not money, such as a ring or some other ornament which might be put into the plate, or it might mean our prayers, *or* the bread and wine. In reading my answers to his questions, he asked whether I meant what I had written in reference to the Sacrament of the Eucharist, for if I did it was a very *high* view to take. He did not say it was a wrong view. There was nothing very definite to be got out of him, and I did not carry out some half-formed intentions of asking advice on practical subjects.

· · · · ·

Archdeacon Manning's four volumes of sermons were great favourites with my mother, and we used to read them to her very often. She was especially fond of those on suffering and trials, in the first volume. *The hidden power of Christ's Passion* is one in particular that remains in my memory. When the fourth volume appeared its Popish tendency was much animadverted on, greatly to mother's annoyance, who felt certain that everything that Archdeacon Manning wrote must be thoroughly sound. It was his language on the Holy Eucharist and also on the Communion of Saints which was objected to by moderate Anglicans. They discerned very unmistakeable signs in this last volume of the step he was so soon to take. Mother would not believe it. She would have considered it wrong to doubt his loyalty to the English Church. It was to her a great and unexpected blow when the news came that he had actually been received into the Church of Rome. I remember that morning. It was at Passiontide, and there wanted little more than two weeks to my Confirmation, which was to be on St. Mark's day, a feast falling that year on the Friday in Easter week. At first I had a wild hope that this step of Archdeacon Manning's might induce my mother to take the same step. What a relief it would be to feel quite free, nay more, to feel that authority (and apart from the Church parental authority was to me the only recognizable authority) guided me away from Protestantism. Mother had always, as she expressed it, "pinned her faith to Archdeacon Manning." Now that he had proclaimed his belief in the Church of Rome, surely it would have a great effect on her. That was my first idea. Great was my disappointment on finding that it did not really lessen her prejudices in any degree, these prejudices being far more deeply rooted than I could understand. I did not participate in her grief. It was truly to her a day of lamentation and woe, that day when she learnt, as she expressed it, that

> The grey-haired Saint may fail at last,
> The surest guide a wanderer prove.

For consolation she betook herself to Herbert Graham and Lady Millicent his wife, her great friends and counsellors in all her difficulties at Clifton. Mr. Graham, who was a comfortable and hopeful person, took a cheerful view. He thought that a way might be opened for the reunion of the Churches, through our best men going to Rome, and he was sure there was something providential in it. This idea had, I think, been promulgated by Dr. Pusey when Mr. Newman left the Church of England.

We had read a little volume by Mr. Gresley on the ordinance of confession, and it was one much advocated also by Dr. Pusey. Vague ideas about the desirableness of confessing my sins floated before me while preparing for Confirmation, but I perceived that however expedient and profitable in theory, the practice was entirely out of the question under existing circumstances. We had indeed once seen Dr. Pusey at Clifton. Mother got him to talk to Olivia and me, and after this she had a long private conversation with him herself. He told us that in our studies of foreign languages, music, drawing, &c., we must remember, if ever tempted to think such studies useless, that over and above the immediate object of them we were, if we were in earnest, really acquiring virtues far more valuable than learning or accomplishments—such as patience, perseverance, obedience, humility, &c. I liked this. The thought brightened many a weary hour and helped me through drudgery and exercises which without it I might have given up. I can imagine that Dr. Pusey was a great help to many. We had a great reverence for him, but this was the only occasion on which we met him.

Milly wrote: "I do so dreadfully envy you having seen Dr. Pusey, and I must say you were very good to tell me about him and to give such a capital description of him, though it was tantalizing and provoking not to hear what he said. . . . I have often longed to be able to talk to him. I think he might help me so much, for his sermons do more than any I know, and one does so want some good advice at times. I don't fancy he is like most clergymen, who seem too much like one's ordinary polite acquaintances, for one to be able to talk to them of one's thoughts and doubts and troubles, and this want I have often felt, but I think it would be supplied in such a man as Dr. Pusey."

How shall I describe my dearly-beloved Milly? In the first place, she was very different from any one else I ever knew, and strangely different from any other members of her family. She was a very decided individuality. Hers was a joyous nature. She always saw the comic element in everything, and that must have been one reason why I derived such immense gratification from her society. Her sense of the humorous was just as keen at the age of forty-six as it had been at sixteen, but in some points—so it appeared to me—she was very different in later life. In her youth she seemed—it may have been only seeming—to be too much influenced by those she loved, and these were many, for Milly had a large heart and a power of sympathy, a capacity for entering into the feelings and ideas of others which ensured for her a very great number of friends. She had an intense admiration for them and a disappreciation of herself. Had I been given to jealousy, I might have been jealous of her friends; as it was, they bored me rather. I thought Milly ought to know better than to go into raptures over some such common-place mortals. It was not, however, silliness and young ladyishness, but rather her great gift of sympathy that made her see souls in some sort as the angels do. Their beauty struck her and not their tiresomeness. She *seemed* unduly influenced by her friends, and too ready to adopt their opinions and peculiarities; in fact, those who did not know her well were inclined to think her weak and rather foolish. In reality hers was a very strong character. She possessed unusual powers of thought and reasoning, although to the end she was a little wanting in judgment. Numerous as were her friends, her immense devotion to her mother overpowered every other feeling. It made her sometimes doubt whether she really cared for any one else.

I have a predilection for people who are very frank, and unreserved, and trusting, though these qualities are apt to get their possessors into difficulties. Milly was abundantly endowed with them. We used to lecture her on her want of discretion, and yet it was impossible not to confide all one's secrets to her. I said before that we used to talk a great deal to each other about the religious questions of the day, and when we were separated these formed the chief subject of our correspondence. Our inner lives moved on side by side, and perhaps a few extracts from her letters will give the best idea of our views at that time.

"October 25, 1851.

". . . As I feel in a very steady mood, I will talk a little good sense about your letter. It was almost a comfort for me (forgive me) to think you are a partaker sometimes in *my* 'wicked' thoughts and can sympathize with me in them, which I think few people can do. I think I am becoming more and more warmly *attached* to High Church principles than ever. I feel I should give up such great privileges and happiness in relinquishing them, and though, as I used to tell you, I often have little doubts and misgivings about some things (now you will call me a heretic, I don't doubt, and apply to me that favourite little text), yet these things perplex me much less than they did. I think the less one dwells on doubtful and disputed points, and the more one tries to feel the solemn practical *reality* of what one professes, the better. Not that I do this, alas! You can't imagine how utterly bad I feel at times, . . . and my especially wicked feelings still go on, particularly when I attend St. Stephen's Church, where all goes so against my taste and disgusts me almost. This must be very bad, for at least one has the Church prayers even there, and I know what shocks *my* feelings is *really* the way of expressing *good* feelings, though it is a way which gives me the horrors. Sometimes I feel charitable and make such good resolutions never to abuse my spiritual pastors, but when next I go to church they say something irritating and all my strength fails. . . . How I long for a good talk with you. There are several things on which I can talk to you better than almost any one else, as you understand me, which few do here. Sybella is very good, and at times charming to talk to, but there are things which I dare not say, as I know they would sadly shock her, and I am in fact *la femme incomprise* on many points at home.

"I was going to tell you about Newman's correspondence with the Bishop of Norwich, but I dare say you have seen it, as it is in the papers. I like the spirit of them both so much, and it is a comfort to think that two men, who think even widely differently, *can* discuss a disputed matter with kind feeling and without mutual abuse. Newman is vindicating his opinions and expressions about miracles, and our R.C. friend here, Mr. Macpherson, says that *modern* miracles are not obligatory, but of merely voluntary belief in their Church, which people don't seem to understand. I am always glad when I can find anything which clears the Romanists from any misunderstanding or unjust charges; for I never can think that it is needful to see their Church painted in the blackest colours (a little *got up* too by clever artists) in order to be aware of her real errors. To me these are far too serious to need *painting* of any kind to increase their importance, consequently I am accused of dangerous leniency, of 'tampering with destruction,' or such like; but I hope I am not so doing.

"I read on Sunday such a beautiful sermon of Dr. Pusey's, *The Rule of Faith of the Fathers and the Church of England*. I was delighted with it, and think you would like it, and the end is so beautifully meek and so like him. Jim brought it from Wells for Sybella's edification, and even Sybella likes it, though she says it does not quite satisfy her with regard to Apostolic Succession; its subject being Apostolic Tradition, which I never understood before reading it.

"Now, to come down to Walter; he is, I believe, or thinks himself to be, safe, as Mr. Macpherson expresses it, from 'the fisherman's net,' to wit, the snares of 'Babylon.' He really was very near to it at one time though, and used to go to Prior Park to consult one of the Fathers there. The beginning of his 'dangerous tendencies' was the reading of Father Newman's Lectures, which he thought unanswerable until he fell in with Butler's refutation of them and found that that was unanswerable too. So he was obliged to give up Newman and with him all hopes of Fra Martinism, and after writing a penitent letter to his old tutor has returned to Oxford, determined to give no heed to seducing whispers again, but equally undecided as to *what* he will be, disliking the Church of England for good reasons of his own, I suppose, not to be fathomed by me, and not yet determined into the arms of what sect or party he shall throw himself, only of one thing I am pretty sure, it will be a fanatical sort of one, as he is given to vehement rhapsodies and can't be content with sober truth, poor creature! We had a grand quarrel while he was at home, but it ended in his giving me a beautiful engraving as a peace-offering. . . .

"How happy you will be at dear Mrs. Cleveland's! Miss Arkwright saw them both for a minute the other day at Wells, where they went to attend a meeting, *not* a Protestant one. The 5th of November will soon be here. Do you remember last 5th, when you were with us, and what fun we had? . . .

"Your devoted,
"Milly."

". . . I do envy you your delightful sight of St. Barnabas (Pimlico). I wonder if the meek verger was the same who fascinated Geraldine the day we were there! He had such a good, nice face. I very often long to see St. Barnabas again, and sometimes when I am feeling melancholy and dissatisfied (which unfortunately occurs at church at times) the thought of that beautiful church with its soft, dim, unworldly light and the deep reverent tones of its choral services comes over my mind with such a sense of beauty and repose, as makes me feel (as I think all these beautiful things were meant to make us feel) what comfort and peace the Church is made to bring in the midst of this world's turmoil and restlessness, and how we should try more and more to have our souls and lives, as well as our tastes and sentiments, penetrated and swayed by her influences.

"I am reading now a very interesting book, Ruskin's *Modern Painters*. He speaks of the *beauty* of outward things, both animate and inanimate, as having their great power and excellence in so far as they are types of the Divine attributes. It seems to me that we might make this outward world so much fuller of beauty and gladness than it is, if we looked more, both in lower creatures and in man, for that inward beauty of which their outward glories are types, but then, alas! *I* feel so empty of beauty and entertain so strong a disgust against my unfortunate self, that it is a great quencher to all my high and soaring ideas of 'typical beauty,' &c. You see I have fallen into a very moral strain. I think this letter will be quite as edifying, if not quite as Protestant, as the long effusion which Geraldine concocted last night for you, and read to me, expressing herself sure all the time that you would hate it. I suppose from the conviction that it contained some spicy little Protestant sentiments. . . .

". . . On Tuesday, from half-past ten till five o'clock, our whole time was occupied in an S.P.G. sermon and meeting, of which I must try to give you some small account. Dr. Christopher

Wordsworth preached the sermon. Have you ever seen him? Lest you have *not*, I proceed to describe him. He has a very interesting picturesque face and look: dark and sallow in complexion, with very black hair, somewhat wildly tossed about. Thin hollow cheeks, a fine forehead, and eyes deep sunken and full of expression, and a very sweet smile. He is rather tall, and looked very well in his ample black gown, and his manner is most solemn and earnest, not a sweet voice, but most expressive in tone. His sermon Geraldine and I thought beautiful, but Sybella considered it too political. It was on the Jubilee—comparing our celebration with that of the Jubilee of the Jews, and then he spoke much of the sin of England in having left America so long without a Church, which was justly punished by its revolting from us. He said much more, which I can't tell you now, being so hurried. We then went to the meeting and heard some goodish speeches—one very nice one from the deputation, Mr. Penrose, and many little compliments, &c., ensued—but these I may leave you to imagine, there being somewhat of a sameness in the flattering terms in which one speaker praises another and the importance attached by all alike to 'the meeting of this day.'"

CHAPTER III.

A Latitudinarian friend. His influence. Sir James Stephens' Essays in Ecclesiastical Biography. His estimate of St. Ignatius Loyola and of the Spiritual Exercises. The Catholic type of sanctity not understood outside the Roman Catholic Church.

Visits to Convents in and near Clifton. Converts to Catholicism. Mr. Aubrey de Vere urges the duty of inquiry into the claims of the Roman Catholic Church. The testimony of those who have submitted to her guidance. The English Church powerless to witness to the truth. It allows contradictory doctrines to be taught. Oswald's views on the duty of inquiry. His sister Ethel a resolute defender of the Anglican Church. She undertakes to read Milner's *End of Controversy* and other Catholic works. Several letters from her. The Councils of Nice and Chalcedon. Extracts from Anglican writers to show that the Papal Supremacy was not recognized by these Councils. Answer.

Moehler's Symbolism. The unity of the Church, the proof of her Divine Mission. Oswald's views of the impossibility of arriving at certainty. Evil of such views.

BEFORE we came to Clifton we had not known any one who belonged to the Broad or Latitudinarian school. At Clifton we saw a great deal of a very clever man whose opinions were anything but orthodox. He had a great deal of influence over us, if not in unsettling our minds, at least in showing us that there are many sides to a question, in making us think, in teaching us to appreciate poetry, and in helping us to form a taste for literature. He had a good library, and was most kind in lending us books and telling us what we ought to read and admire. In many ways it was a great advantage to see so much of Mr. Somers. He kept us alive to all that was going on in the literary world. He opened our minds, as it is called, instilling into us a great contempt for narrow-mindedness and intolerance. On the other hand, he was imbuing us with a respect for Latitudinarian theories to which they are not entitled. It was new and startling to hear the genuineness of certain passages of Scripture called in question, the necessity for creeds ridiculed, doubts cast upon inspiration, so much regard paid to mere intellect. What was the good of a creed? Mr. Somers asked. It made no difference when people came to die. He had seen many people on their death-beds, and whatever form of religion or non-religion they might have professed, they mostly died happily, and what more could be desired than peace at the last?

Mr. Somers had a fondness for quoting the lines:

> I sit as God holding no form of creed
> But contemplating all,

and,

> Behold we *know* not anything,
> I can but trust that good will fall
> At last, far off, at last to all,
> And every winter change to spring.

Besides Macaulay's Essays—so attractive to the young mind—we were greatly interested in those of Rogers and Stephens with which he furnished us, and in Charles Kingsley's *Yeast*, which had lately appeared.

It is curious and interesting late in life to take up books that have had a great influence on us in our youth. The Essays in Ecclesiastical Biography, which Sir James Stephens had contributed from time to time to the *Edinburgh Review*, were revised and enlarged by him, and republished in two volumes in the year 1849. It was two or three years later that I read them. The first of these volumes is occupied mainly with some saints of the Catholic Church or with characters connected with her history. Martin Luther and the Port Royalists figure towards the close. The first Essays deal with St. Gregory VII., St. Francis of Assisi, St. Ignatius and his first companions. It was in the dress provided for them by that brilliant but essentially Protestant writer that I first became acquainted with these great Saints. It was a grace to know them even under this disguise. Do what you will, the Lives of the Seraph of Assisi and of the Founder of the Society of Jesus and of the world-famous Apostle of the Indies, contain lessons and awaken an enthusiasm which all the worthies of the Church of England fail to inspire.

A man of the world trying to understand the interior of a saint of God! What a curious sight it is! What a pitiful failure is his endeavour to explain the supernatural in their lives on natural principles! It is like the attempt to account for the existence of the Church on the hypothesis of its being a merely human institution. The tone of superiority assumed by the average Protestant would irritate me if it had not its comic aspect. The kindly commendation of heroic acts of self-sacrifice if they should result in some tangible benefit on a fellow-creature, the commiseration for such acts should they have only the greater glory of the Creator for their end, the pity for a superstition which can believe that that Creator ever requires his creatures to leave houses and lands and father and mother and wife and children, for His sake; or that He can literally expect them to deny themselves and to take up their cross daily with no other motive than to follow Him—how should men with such sentiments, comprehend the story of Mount Alvernia? They seem to think it an irreverence to imagine the great Creator of all things really caring about such atoms as we His creatures are, and exerting Himself about every one of us, individually. They almost despise those who believe that Almighty God has knowledge of the number of hairs on the head of every one of us, that He notices how many sparrows fall to the ground every day, and that he takes account of every cup of water that one of His children gives to another in His Name. They do not see that these saints whom they look down on as ignorant enthusiasts are simply products of the Sermon on the Mount, and that theirs is the character that would be developed by obeying literally the counsels as well as the precepts of the Gospel. Father Faber indeed goes farther and says that, "If Christianity were not true, the conduct of a wise man, who acted consistently as a creature who had a Creator, would strangely resemble the behaviour of a Catholic saint. The lineaments of the Catholic type would be discernible upon him, though his gifts would not be the same." Sir James Stephens is not without a considerable amount of admiration for the saints with whom he deals, but he does not know how to unravel their eccentricities. He cannot understand the folly of the Cross. It is the old difficulty, "to the Greeks foolishness." St. Ignatius is especially puzzling, because the book which he wrote is, says our author, "invariably dry and didactic, even when it delineates and enjoins the highest rapture of devotion." Sir James Stephens gives us an analysis of the Spiritual Exercises. I observe that he passes over what St. Ignatius calls the "Foundation," and begins at once with the Exercises on Sin. If he could have made one or two prolonged meditations on the End of Man and on the Use of Creatures, perhaps his view of the lives of saints might have undergone some alteration. As it is he cannot grasp the idea that men like St. Gregory VII. and St. Ignatius, had no other motive than the greater glory of God in all things that they did. There must have been self-seeking, spiritual ambition, some earthly motive at work, some human reward on which they were bent. Thus, when Ignatius is elected General of the Society, it is assumed that his reluctance to accept the office was feigned. Not until he had received the solemn injunction of his confessor, would Ignatius of Loyola " ascend the throne of which he had been so long laying the foundations. It will be credible," continues Sir James Stephens, " that he seriously contemplated the renunciation of that high reward, when it shall be ascertained that Julius became Dictator, Cromwell Protector, and Napoleon First Consul, in their own despite; but not till then."

What I thought of such remarks in those days, I may not altogether remember. They could not have made much impression as I know I was filled with an intense admiration for these heroes of sanctity, and with no admiration at all for their rival, Martin Luther. A yearning to be encouraged or at least to be allowed to love God as they loved Him, took possession of my soul. I particularly disliked the lines in the *Christian Year*:

> We need not bid for cloister'd cell,
> Our neighbour and our work farewell,
> Nor strive to wind ourselves too high
> For sinful man beneath the sky.

" Be ye therefore perfect as your Father in Heaven is perfect." That is the perfection recommended to sinful man in the Gospel. "Christ suffered for us leaving us an example that we should follow His steps," said St. Peter. "Be ye followers of me as I also am of Christ," said St. Paul. No lower pattern is put before Christians. They are enjoined to love God with their whole heart, with their whole soul, to do His will after the example of Him Who came on earth to show them what that will required of them.

The idea of sin and the idea of sanctity have been lost outside the Roman Church. The very notion of sanctity is not understood, it is looked upon as superstitious and mean-spirited. Perhaps some might admire it if they were not afraid of being called on to imitate it, or to make an act of humility by acknowledging themselves the inferiors of those who do. It is so pleasant to lead a self-indulgent life, never giving up one's own will, to make reflections on the easiness of practising the virtue of obedience, and to sneer at subjection as a renunciation of the gift of freewill, the greatest natural gift which God has seen good to bestow upon men. I don't mean that *Mr. Keble* did not appreciate holiness or that he intended to imply that we need not aim at it. But it was not to be the holiness of "the counsels," or of the *state* of perfection. The desire for such a state would imply that we were not content with that "trivial round" and "daily task" which was sure to bring us nearer to God by the constant little acts of self-denial which it imposed, and that we wanted something very heroic, which would gratify our self-love, and gain us the esteem of others.

Nevertheless, such as they were, these studies on the lives of saints by a Latitudinarian writer interested me greatly at the time when I first read them. I was depressed, however, by the remarks that their type of sanctity must be displeasing to God and unfitting the dignity of man. This was a view which Mr. Somers was very strong in upholding, in conjunction with the great apostle of muscular Christianity, Charles Kingsley.

. . . . .

There was a Catholic atmosphere at Clifton which could not be without its effect. I am a great believer in the influence of "atmosphere," physical, moral, and spiritual. Clifton had been chosen to give its name to one of the new Catholic sees. The Pro-Cathedral, a very unfinished looking building, was an object of great interest to us. Adjoining it was the lately erected Convent of St. Catherine of Sienna. There the Sisters of Penance of the Third Order of St. Dominic were established with their Superior, Mother Margaret Hallahan. Greatly have I regretted that we missed the opportunity of knowing this holy and remarkable servant of God, whose life has been so beautifully told by one of those who had the privilege of being her spiritual children. I like to think, however, that we had a share in the fervent prayers which she offered for the conversion of the souls around her, and in the Rosaries so constantly said in that little chapel which it was our delight to pass. Once we were taken to see the convent and made the acquaintance of the Rev. Frederick Neve, Mother Margaret's faithful friend and adviser, after the departure of Dr. Ullathorne for Birmingham. We thought Mr. Neve rather severe and formidable on that occasion. Later we met him in Ireland and made great friends with him. We also visited the Convent of the Good Shepherd, Arno's Court, Bristol, and that of the Visitation at Westbury. These religious houses made a great impression on us. There was an element of mystery about them which added to the interest which they inspired.

Clifton attracted many converts, and amongst the number were a few who influenced us greatly: Mr. Spencer Northcote, Sir Vere and Lady de Vere, and Mr. Aubrey de Vere. Mr. Aubrey de Vere had not long been a Catholic when we first made his acquaintance. We saw a good deal of him during that summer, and he was always ready to speak of the peace and joy which were to be found in the Church. Indeed the happiness and thorough satisfaction in their religion of the converts to Catholicism whom we knew, seemed a great argument in favour of that religion. We were warned by friends like Oswald, that it was a dangerous peace, a delusive happiness, that the certainty which they professed to have in the truths of Revelation, was not a certainty that God meant us to have, that it would do away with a large part of that which He intended should be our probation here on earth. How were we to know? Ought we not to inquire? This, Mr. de Vere was ever pressing on us—the duty of inquiry and of praying for light. Oswald said such a prayer implied that we had not sufficient light and sufficient knowledge of the truth where we were. I was ready to admit that it implied this. Was it not a fact of which we were too painfully conscious? We had the Holy Scriptures, true, but as Mr. de Vere wrote in a little essay he composed for us, "Is it not a simple duty to inquire what is the Rule of Interpretation by means of which we shall be enabled, in studying the Scriptures, to distinguish between the *Mind of the Spirit* by Whom the Prophets spoke, and the fancies of individuals or the traditional gloss of recent and separated bodies at variance with each other? God has constituted a Visible Church in His Son, Who died to redeem it, Who feeds it ever with His own Body (the Mystic Body sacramentally sustained by the Natural Body), Who ever sends it His Spirit to lead it into all Truth, Who raised it upon earth to be the Pillar and Witness of the Truth, appointing it thereby to be as the Apostolic College remaining amongst us, occupying for ever thrones 'in the Kingdom of the Regeneration,' reiterating for ever the same Divine message, and 'telling us plainly' what that message is. Is it then or is it not a duty to know surely which among the claimants on our respect is indeed the Prophet of God, in listening to whom we listen to the voice of God, and in obeying whom we obey not man but God? How can we have *Divine Faith* if we do not *know* with the spiritual certainty of Faith, that it is God to Whom we are listening, through His appointed organ, and not any other authority, however respectable which yet is not that one which God has commissioned? . . . The question at issue is the gravest of questions, for what do we come into the world for except that we may serve God; and how can we serve Him except according to the way He has revealed? The question is one in which *all* are concerned, the rich and the poor, the wise and the simple. The solution of it therefore cannot be beyond the strivings of the unlearned."

One solution which has commended itself even to some thoughtful people outside the Roman Church, is that each individual should live and die in the sect or church in which he was born, that being the manifest will of God in his regard. This view would justify Unitarians, Quakers, Baptists, Jews, &c., and to speak of its being the *will* of God that any one should believe that which is in direct contradiction to His truth, seemed to me little short of blasphemy.

Mr. Sewell had treated as nugatory and absurd the plea of conscience which converts advanced as the motive for their secession to the Church of Rome. This is what Aubrey de Vere says on the subject: "Conscience, we know, is that which has compelled many of the wisest and holiest in the Anglican communion to go forth from it as Abraham left his native land, in many instances renouncing all. We know that they are incapable of falsehood and they are alive and can tell us what they have found, not like Abraham a desert, but from the first moment of entire submission, the House of Faith, the golden Home of Love, the long-lost Eden, the City of God, in which saints in glory and men below, are fellow-citizens in daily communion. It was called the Syren's Island; but they who sought it, included the sternest, the strongest, the saintliest, the men who had *most abundantly used the resources of their native soil*, . . . and their bones are not found bleaching on the Syren's shore. Their act was that which pride abhors—submission. Their learning ended in their knowing in what sense it is our duty to become as little children, and under what circumstances it is possible to continue such, while the intellect is ever advancing and experience deepening. It was conscience which had laid its hand upon them. Conscience commands all who doubt to inquire. And can any intelligent Anglican, who knows that there is a Church upon earth, and has heard the controversies of the last few years, so delude himself as not to *know* that he doubts? The body to which he belongs is separated from the Church of almost all the world. It is condemned by the teaching of the Eastern as well as of the Western Church. It is divided into almost as many schools as exist outside its pale. It cannot decide between them and therefore cannot *witness* to the Truth. It remains the servant of the State, when, if the heart were sound, and the mind were one, it could at any moment be free. It has been in this bondage for more than a century, and in nearly as great for three, that is, for the whole period of its isolated existence. It was while in this bondage that it professed to rediscover a pure and primitive faith, lost or overlaid during a thousand years. Its consent with Antiquity rests on its *own assertion* only, and is flatly denied by the whole of the East as well as by all the Churches in communion with Rome. It admits that it has abandoned Primitive Antiquity in many points, such as Extreme Unction, Prayers for the Dead, Veneration of Relics, &c. It only reverences the earlier Councils, nay the Creeds themselves (see Article 8), because their decisions are attested by Scripture, that is by the Anglican or individual interpretation of Scripture, and therefore it in reality sits in judgment over them instead of recognizing them as an authority."

These remarks upon the ambiguous position and teaching of the English Church commended themselves to me as being most true. Many were the discussions we had on the subject. Oswald and his sister, Mrs. Vyner, spent some time with us this summer at Clifton. Both were much interested in theological questions. I do not think that either of them had any bias towards Catholicism. Oswald indeed had set his heart on becoming a clergyman in the Church of England and *also* on entering the state of matrimony. As the latter depended in some measure on the former, perhaps he was hardly in the best position for forming an impartial opinion on the claims of the two Churches. The life of an English clergyman is an ideal life to a certain class of minds. They have no conception that there can exist a higher or a more desirable state. I have remarked that such minds never have any leaning towards Catholicism. They have their own standard and they are satisfied with it. Oswald's views were by no means those of the ordinary British parson, as will be shown later on. He had an overwhelming sense of the responsibilities of life. He considered religious inquiry to be a duty, but that the difficulties which beset the inquirer were so great that when he had done his best he could hardly aspire to get beyond a position of general uncertainty. "If uncertainty is to be the end of our inquiry, what is the use of beginning to inquire?" I asked. The question was thought a flippant and a senseless one. At all events it was not a hopeful idea with which to start. It probably owed its existence to a very decided vein of melancholy which ran through my cousin's character and influenced all his views.

We did not find this melancholy infectious. Perhaps it was the spirit of contrariness which made us rather extra cheerful when with him, insomuch that he would reprove us and say that our life was a perpetual joke. We considered it a sort of mission to make him laugh, and we much liked talking and reading with him. He encouraged us to think, and not to hold opinions without knowing the reasons for them. Without the jokes and the sense of the ludicrous which ever prevailed, we should have been rather a priggish set of young people.

I mentioned Oswald's sister, Ethel, as one who was interested in our theological discussions this summer. She took the Protestant side, and her advocacy of the English Church gained for her the name of "the champion." Although some fifteen years older than I was, she was my great friend. She became so far interested in the arguments which Mr. Aubrey de Vere brought forward in favour of the Church of Rome that she promised not to put the subject out of her mind, but to give it due consideration. For this purpose she was to study Milner's *End of Controversy*. On leaving Clifton she wrote to me:

"I hope you will remember that the (Anglican) 'cause' depends on you now, and if you want a good sound book on the subject and *not long*, I should recommend *Vindication of the Church of England*, by Bishop Bull. I will tell you what I think of Milner when I have studied him. The Preface rather alarmed me when I saw 'No other controversial work of modern times has had equal success in effecting conversions to our holy faith,' but in spite of that even, I do not think it will effect *mine*; for I do not believe that Romanism will stand the test of impartial investigation and calm thought, however much one may feel influenced by being with those who make *religion* their rule of life. These being my opinions at starting on the inquiry in August, 1852. Where do you think August, 1857, will find me?"

She writes again:

"August 30, 1852.

"You are by this time, I suppose, safely in Ireland, and I hope you got over the perils and dangers of the way without difficulty. I enjoyed your last letter from Clifton very much; but I think altogether it is as well that you are gone away for a time. I *really* began to fear for your Protestantism, and am sure it is a very good thing that you should have time to reflect before allowing yourself to be led away by the eloquence and excellence of your friends. (You see I have not quite given up the championship yet.) I must say, so far as I have been able to pursue the inquiry, I see more and more reason to fear that they are under a delusion, though mind I don't think myself qualified *yet* to give an opinion. It is very difficult to see things as they are, uninfluenced by prejudice and uncoloured by imagination. . . ."

Her next letter is dated,
"September 3, 1852.
" Your letter was delightfully long and 'graphic,' and I am taking an early opportunity of answering it, and at the same time giving you a little Protestant advice. I don't agree with our friend as to the danger of putting off 'submission' for six years. I think the subject important enough to require at least that examination, for how are we to arrive at a 'firm moral conviction' without reading and argument? Of course, let these be carried on in a right spirit, that is with prayer and an earnest desire to be guided to truth, but not with a wish and determination to find Rome right and ourselves wrong. I think that there is so very much that is attractive in the Roman Church, that there is little fear of our not doing it justice in the investigation. The peace converts speak of as so delightful would alone be enough to make us wish to join them, but it may be a peace we have no right to look for on this side of eternity. Do not in your inquiry read Roman Catholic books alone; we are none of us sufficiently acquainted with history or our own

theologians for that, and it would be at least dangerous. I must say, as far as I have yet seen, I find so many contradictions in the decrees of the different Councils, and of the Councils compared to Scripture, that it is difficult to reconcile them with the idea of Divine guidance. It is not sufficient to assume the infallibility of the Roman Church merely because it asserts that there is a necessity for an infallible visible guide on earth. We must try to find proof that such does exist before we believe in it. Such proof we should expect to find at least in *consistency*, but with all due allowance to the doctrine of development, you will find, I think, that in some points the decrees of the Council of Trent directly contradict those of Nice and Ephesus. I am sure *I* shall never be a good Papist until they give up Trent.

"Milner is by no means convincing as far as I have yet read; in fact he advances nothing that has not been refuted over and over again. I am going to send for the other book that was recommended to me—Waterworth—to give the cause a fair chance, for (though P—— would think me a dreadful heretic for saying so) it would require something infinitely more convincing than Milner to convert me.

"I believe what makes P——'s arguments appear so convincing at the time, is his own religious mind, and that he won't stop to go into detail and authority for what he brings forward, but gives you a grand general view of a system, splendid in itself and infinitely attractive, as bringing us into closer communication with the unseen world than any we have been in the habit of contemplating, but of which when you descend to *proofs*, you find they lie far more in our ideas of moral necessity than any of revelation or prophecy. . . .

"How do you like Ireland? you don't tell me a word about it, but I hope you will in your next. Consider too the champion's Protestant views and tell me if you agree with them. I am afraid you will become Papists *involuntarily* at Currah. I don't think you can help it."

From these letters it will be seen that the champion laid claim to an eminently fair and judicial mind. She did not judge the question of the Roman claims to be beneath her consideration as do many who pretend to impartiality, nor would she admit for a moment that it was a question, the study of which was beyond the power of an ordinarily well-educated person. She did not approve of the silencing system so dear to the High Church parson, "women had no right to an opinion."

It may be noticed also that she attributes to the charm of personal influence any predilections she might experience towards Catholicism. I knew that *my* predilections had nothing to do with persons. They began on the day when I first entered a Catholic church. I was attracted to individuals because they were Catholics, not to Catholicism because of those individuals. Nor was it true that all the converts we knew were delightful. There were some who bored me considerably. They were tiresome by their want of tact. One in particular, an ex-parson, in season and out of season would make the remark that there could be but *one* Church. I did not participate in the champion's suspicion that the Roman Catholic claims could not bear investigation. A religion which numbered amongst its defenders St. Thomas Aquinas and Bossuet, to cite two only out of many in different countries and ages, could hardly be contrary to reason. Say that these were pre-possessed from infancy in its favour; in our own century are there not many who could be named for whose submission to the Church of Rome no such pre-possession could be assigned? Amongst these, as we used to remind Oswald, there was his own favourite, Frederick Schlegel, and to come nearer home was there not John Henry Newman? "The poverty of the form of Protestantism he saw around him might account for Schlegel's conversion," Oswald said; "and Newman—well, his greatest works were written when with us. It is not likely he will write anything to surpass the Oxford University Sermons, and after all he may find he has made a mistake and come back." Here I may remark that Anglicans constantly answered appeals to the authority of Newman by assuming that they had had some secret revelation to the effect that he was not satisfied. Newman might repudiate such an idea over and over again, he might declare that "Protestantism is the dreariest of possible religions; that the thought of the Anglican service made him shiver, and that the thought of the Thirty-nine Articles made him shudder;"[1] somehow Anglicans chose to look upon him as a witness in their favour until a conclusive refutation of their hints and inuendoes, if they fell short of positive assertions, was given on his receiving a Cardinal's hat from Leo XIII. To the last, I believe, Dr. Pusey wrote he was sure dear Newman would never accept it!

I did not know on what the champion founded her charge against the Church of want of consistency. Probably it may have been from some muddle between doctrine and discipline, and from ignorance that whereas her doctrine ever remains the same, the Church varies her discipline to suit the needs and circumstances both of places and of times. Perhaps too in the Protestant histories which she had read, the opinions of the heretical Bishops in the East were quoted as teachings of the Church of that time. Their insubordination to the See of St. Peter no doubt appeared to her a convincing argument that the claims of that See were unwarrantable. Once in reading some

[1] *Catholic Letters of Cardinal Newman*, p. 37.

early ecclesiastical history, I asked her to remark how St. Athanasius was constantly appealing to Rome, and that it was always heretics who objected to the Pope's authority. She said she did not think so much of St. Athanasius since she had read more about him. Saints who have been conspicuous in defending dogma do not as a rule excite the admiration of those who are outside the Church.

I do not know what account of the proceedings at Trent the champion had been studying, but I do not think she followed the example of my friend Sybella, who wrote:

"I am reading among other things Donovan's *Catechism of the Council of Trent;* being driven to the perusal of this work by the violent abuse of 'Papists' to which I was a listener at our late missionary meetings. Hearing their Church stigmatized as an enemy of the Christian religion, and yet being sure that there *do* exist many true Christians in her pale, I was determined to see for myself, if the errors of that Church were really so deadly as to cause her to forfeit the very name of Christian. I cannot decide till I have finished the book, which is of considerable size, being intended as an assistance to the clergy in their pastoral duties, but as far as I have gone I can discover no heresy, only some assertions on comparatively trivial points, for which I can see no authority in Scripture."

To return to the champion's letters.

"September 18, 1852.

"I *did* like your letter very much: you write so fully and amply on subjects, that I find yours most satisfactory epistles. I perceive you are decidedly less *Popish* than you were three weeks ago, which I ascribe to the absence of Popish friends and the presence of Oswald. How long will it last, do you think, after you reach Currah? Not many days, I am sure, for it would be impossible but that you should be somewhat influenced by our friends, who of course will be anxious to complete the work they left in so auspicious a state.

"It seems to me just now that the more I think about the question, the less I know what to think; for even supposing one had attained a 'conviction' either way, we have no decided proof that such a conviction is true. Pusey and Manning, both learned and excellent and earnest, must be convinced in their own minds, and yet *one* of the two must be very far from the truth: and then I think that we are so very apt to be swayed far more than we are aware of by our own inclinations and dispositions. You see I have not advanced at all since I wrote to you last on this subject. . . . .

"I am not altogether surprised at Mr. Somers writing as he did, for I think he may fairly have supposed himself to have *some* grounds for fear that your attachment to 'our beloved Church' might be shaken. I suppose he does not in this instance understand by that *his* 'grand universal Church,' so we may hope he is becoming a good Churchman, perhaps under the influence of Robert Wilberforce's book.

"I should like to know *where* you find yourself when you have reduced your reasons to writing. Should you mind telling me? It might help me to the same discovery.

"I was grieved the other day in reading 'Milner' to find him say, that Scripture without tradition is a 'dead letter.' It seemed to me so very irreverent and false, when there is so very much in Scripture that every one can understand and which if they only acted up to it would be sufficient to ensure a holy life. Then I cannot see how the Anglican Church can be said to *reject* tradition, which all the Roman Catholics say we do. I think we hold all that we believe to be Apostolic. There are a few questions I should much like to ask an enlightened Roman Catholic, but I am afraid I shall not have an opportunity. . . . How very nice your expeditions to the mountains must be, and how delightful to be within reach of such beautiful scenery as you describe. I suppose you will astonish your drawing-master by your collection of sketches when you return to Clifton."

"September 29.

". . . Yes, I do fear for you at Currah, for you cannot but be influenced by your friends, and there will be no counteracting influence. I fear you will forget your present intention of giving the question a fair examination and making a search for *truth;* for you are already talking about secondary motives, such as the necessity of giving up Protestant and Puseyite friends, which I think should be the *last* considerations instead of the *first*. Don't be in a hurry, and recollect the six years you have promised to wait, however powerful Mr. de Vere's arguments may be and his earnestness to complete the work. . . . I feel so puzzled sometimes, when thinking of the conflicting opinions of the Anglican and Roman Catholic divines, I am almost tempted to envy Mr. Somers his *extended* views embracing *all* denominations, but then I am sure they cannot be right.

"Mr. de Vere thinks there is a necessity for and must be an infallible visible Church; but supposing, in virtue of our Saviour's promise, we might expect to find such on earth, yet His promise as all other recorded promises were, was *conditional*, and therefore liable to be forfeited, and who can say that the Church at different periods has not *as a body* been corrupt, though some faithful have always been found in it, and if so, is it wrong to imagine that the light of the Holy Spirit has been withdrawn from it (as we might believe from some of the later definitions) in proportion as it has been faithless to the charge committed to it?

"As to the Article you mention, I don't think that it says that the *whole Church* has erred in matters pertaining to God, but that *General Councils* have done so, and if we don't believe that we must all be Papists, at all events if we allow Trent to have been a General Council.

"I may as well conclude this letter by giving you the extracts you asked for concerning the Councils.

"'Nice in the Sixth Canon decrees that every Patriarch within his province hath full and perfect jurisdiction, without any dependence on the Church or Bishop of Rome, and that the jurisdiction of the Church or Bishop of Rome is no less limited than that of the other Bishops or Patriarchs. In the confession of faith, according to the Council of *Trent*, they swear with the same breath wherewith they profess their reception of all the Canons and General Councils that they acknowledge the Holy Catholic and Apostolic Church of Rome to be the mother and mistress of all other Churches, and the Pope to be Successor of St. Peter, the Prince of the Apostles, and to be also the Vicar of Jesus Christ, to whom obedience is due.'"

This profession of faith at Trent is here supposed to contradict the Sixth Canon of Nice! What a confusion Anglicans get into between

Patriarchates and the Primacy! Because the sees of Antioch and Alexandria, as being connected with St. Peter, had more authority than others, therefore Rome, where St. Peter finally fixed his seat, had no greater authority than Antioch and Alexandria. They will not face the fact of the Divine institution of St. Peter's office, nor the evidence that it was always recognized by the Church, and that those bodies which called it in question were invariably heretics, any more than they will take into consideration the fact of the continued existence of the Apostolic See through well-nigh nineteen centuries, depending for its support on the Divine power and Providence that called it into being. That it has been so maintained they attribute not to Divine Providence, but to the ambition of every individual Pope.

Reading the history of the First General Council, I meet with the following passage: "What is actually seen at the Nicene Council is that the three greater Metropolitans (who from the middle of the fifth century were called Patriarchs, but long before possessed their prerogatives), the Bishops of Rome, Alexandria, and Antioch, were in possession of a higher authority than the rest, an authority which had come down to them from the first origin of their sees, and which the Council did not create, but recognize. Though their sees were the most renowned cities of the Empire, the higher authority of these

Bishops was carried back to the Apostle Peter, who had sat in person, first at Antioch and then at Rome, and had placed his disciple Mark at Alexandria. The name of Peter stood at the head of the episcopal catalogue in these three sees, and the local tradition in all of them gave constant witness afterwards to Peter in many various ways. The Nicene Council knew only these three superior metropolitans, recognizing their special rights in the Sixth Canon,[1] which runs thus:

"Let the ancient custom continue in force which subsists in Egypt, Libya, and Pentapolis, by which the Bishop of Alexandria possesses authority over all these, since the like custom subsists also with the Roman Bishop. In like manner also their privileges should be preserved to the Churches, as to Antioch and the other provinces. And in general it is plain that if any one becomes a Bishop without the consent of the metropolitan, the great Council decrees that he do not remain a Bishop. But if two or three, through individual spirit of contention, resist the general choice of all, which is at once reasonable and according to ecclesiastical rule, let the voice of the majority prevail.

"In these terms the Council admitted what were afterwards called the patriarchal rights of

---

[1] Hergenröther, *Photius,* i. pp. 26—30, shows that the Sixth Canon speaks of the rights of the great metropolitans over a complex of provinces.

the Bishop of Alexandria, over the three civil provinces of Egypt, Libya, and Pentapolis, which in the time of St. Athanasius had nearly a hundred Bishops. It admitted a similar right in the see of Antioch over the metropolitans subject to it, in which patriarchate both metropolitans and Bishops were much more numerous than those subject to the Alexandrine Bishop. The Council in this Sixth Canon justified the prerogatives which it thus admitted in the see of Alexandria by reference to a similar right existing and exercised at Rome; and then by force of the same principle recognized the prerogative of Antioch and of metropolitans in general.

"In the previous history of the Church, these three named sees, which were often called in a special sense 'the Apostolic Sees,' exercised a sort of hierarchical triumvirate which the Roman See, ever strenuous in its grasp of tradition, firmly maintained."

Mr. Allies goes on to remark that "from early times the Popes recognized the two Bishops of Alexandria and Antioch as, conjointly with themselves, successors of St. Peter, and quotes the remarkable letter of St. Gregory the Great to the Bishop of Antioch.[1]

The second extract sent by the zealous "champion" is as follows:

"At the Council of Ephesus it was determined 'that it should not be lawful for any one to

[1] *The Throne of the Fisherman*, p. 53.

produce, write, or compose, any other creed besides that which was agreed on and defined by the holy Fathers who were met together at Nice by the Holy Spirit, and those who should dare to compose, produce, or offer any other creed to such as desired to return to the truth from Paganism, Judaism, or any heresy whatever, should, if Bishops, be deprived from the episcopal throne; if inferior clergy, be deprived of Holy Orders; if laymen, excommunicated or cast out of the Church.' You will observe," my correspondent continues, "how very much the *spirit*, if not the *letter*, of the last has been set aside by the articles of faith which the Council of Trent has added since."

It is curious that the obvious interpretation of such a decree does not suggest itself—viz., that it prohibited the substitution of another creed for that defined at Nice. Would it not be absurd to suppose that the Church, whose voice is that of the Holy Spirit, could say that whatever heresies might arise in future ages, there would be no further interference on the part of that same Holy Spirit Whose office it is to guide her into all truth according to the promise of her Divine Founder? Is it not utter folly to maintain that after the year 325 any heretic might teach what he chose, and that the Church should be powerless to contradict him and to proclaim the Catholic doctrine? If the

Church could speak with no uncertain voice at Nice, why not also at Chalcedon and at Trent?

The letter goes on: "I am going to make a long extract from Cave on the subject of the Primacy of St. Peter being asserted at Nice, as *I* thought that one of the most convincing of Mr. Allies' arguments, and it seems *you* accept it. Speaking of the Fifth Session of the Council of Chalcedon, Cave says: 'After this, things went on smoothly till they came to frame the Canons, among which one was that the Bishop of Constantinople should enjoy equal privileges with the Bishop of Rome, and then the Legates could hold no longer plainly telling them that this was a violation of the Constitution of Nice, and that their commission obliged them by all ways to preserve the Papal dignity, and to reject the designs of any who, relying on the greatness of their cities, should attempt anything to the contrary.'

"To prove that this was contrary to the Nicene decrees, they produced the Sixth and Seventh Canons of that Council, beginning thus, as Paschasinus (the Papal Legate) repeated them: 'The Church of Rome ever had the Primacy; let Egypt therefore have this privilege, that the Bishop of Alexandria have power, &c.;' where instead of the first words of that Canon, 'Let ancient customs still prevail,' the Legate shuffled in this sentence as more to his purpose, 'The Church of Rome ever had the Primacy.' And admitting here that this was only the title to that Canon in the Roman copy, yet it is somewhat more than suspicious that Paschasinus intended it should be understood as part of the Canon itself, and if so there could not be a bolder piece of forgery and imposture. But the Fathers were not to be so imposed on. Actius, Archdeacon of Constantinople, produced a copy from among the records of that Church, which he delivered to Constantine the secretary, who read it according to the genuine words of the Canon without any such addition, 'Let ancient customs still prevail,' &c., and in confirmation of that were read the second and third Canons of the Second General Council of Constantinople.[1] And because the Legate had objected that the Canon had been procured by fraud, the judges required *the Bishops concerned to declare their minds, who all readily declared the contrary.* The case having been thus fully debated, and nothing material being alleged against it, the Canon passed by the unanimous suffrage of the Fathers, the Roman Legates only entering their protestation and resolving to acquaint the Pope with what was done, that so

---

[1] This third Canon was an innovation of the order of the Church in its attempt to give precedence to the see of Constantinople next after that of Rome, *on account of* Constantinople being the New Rome and seat of the temporal Government, thus substituting a secular reason for those spiritual laws which had hitherto ruled the Church. The Canons of this Council had not been received by the Western Church.

he might judge of the injury done to his own see and the violence offered to the Canons."

I do not know whether the Anglican authority from which the above is taken went on to detail what followed—probably not. He would have had to mention how the Legates went back to Rome; how the Council sent a letter to Leo, begging him to confirm the privileges of Constantinople; how the Emperor Marcian wrote to the same effect, and Anatolius, the then occupant of the see, made the most urgent representations, hoping to induce Leo to disavow the action of his Legates. Leo refused to innovate on the constitution of the Church. The claim of Constantinople rested on its being an Imperial residence, not an Apostolic see. The Canon, Leo said, would contradict the privileges of Antioch and Alexandria as well as the rights of provincial Primates, the Sixth Canon of the Nicene Council, and all the constitutions of the Fathers, and much more to the same effect. In his letter to the Empress Pulcheria, Leo says: "What has been obtained from the Bishops, disregarding the rules of the Nicene Council, We annul by the authority of the Apostle St. Peter." He wrote very reprovingly to Anatolius, and "confirmed only the decrees of faith as passed in the Council of Chalcedon." Because Anatolius, angered at the censure on himself, would not publish this letter, the Eutychians made out that the Pope disapproved of the Council. Whereupon the Emperor Marcian, in February, 453, begged the Pope "to confirm the Council in a letter which should be read in all the churches."[1] Anatolius in the following year (April, 454) wrote an apology to Leo, protesting that he had no personal ambition, and submitting to the decision of His Holiness.

The Pope explained to the Emperor how he had already confirmed the dogmatic decrees of the Council in the letter which Anatolius had concealed. He now did this again in a letter to all the Bishops who had been present at Chalcedon, approving all the decisions of the Council in matters of faith, but rejecting all that had been passed against the Canons of the Nicene Council.

If this explanation and true version of ecclesiastical history in the fourth and fifth centuries was not forthcoming at the moment, I do not think the "champion's" extracts much disturbed the conviction that was possessing me of the consistency of the Church's teaching. I knew I should find an answer when opportunity offered, and that soon in our projected visit to Currah Chase. Meanwhile we were spending a very pleasant time with our relations, some thirty miles from Dublin. We were within reach of many points of interest, and with the beautiful

---

[1] *The Throne of the Fisherman*, p. 529.

Wicklow mountains to be seen in the distance. A day spent in rambling over one of these, Lug na Quilla, and an expedition to the Seven Churches of Glendalough, I shall ever remember.

My aunt, our hostess, was as original in her way as Mrs. Wrangham. Her three daughters, though very unlike herself, were equally loveable. She had no inclination for intellectual pursuits. She was anxious that people should please themselves in their own way and not be interfered with. Oswald had proposed a visit at the same time as ours, which my aunt said was "a mercy, because there would be some one who could understand him." "What he says is all Hebrew and Greek to me," she confided to us one day. We were reading Miller's *Philosophy of History* to him. This was a proceeding with which she could not be expected to sympathize.

At Clifton, Ethel and I had been much interested in the first volume of Ruskin's *Modern Painters*. I brought the second volume with me to Ireland, for the gratification of one of my cousins who was much devoted to painting. I used to read to her as we drove together in a pony cart on some of these long expeditions. What a quantity of books we got through in those few weeks! Meanwhile my correspondence with the "champion" was going on. I think the fears she mentions in the last-quoted letter, that I should cut short the time of inquiry and come quickly to a decision, may have been caused by the influence on my mind of a book which occupied all the spare moments I had to myself during that visit. This was the second volume of Moehler's *Symbolism*, the first part of which treats of the Church, and contrasts the Catholic with the Lutheran doctrine. I was struck by some remarks in this work on the prayer of our Lord recorded in St. John xvii., where He prays for His disciples and asks that the Visible Unity of His Church may be a proof to the world of His own Divine Mission. We may read words many a time without their import coming home to us. It was now perhaps for the first time that I considered all that this prayer of our Lord implied. He prayed not only for His immediate disciples, but for those also who through their word should believe in Him, "that they all may be one, ... that the world may believe that Thou hast sent Me." Unity was to be the mark—a visible unity. In what body of Christians is this to be found except in that body which reveres the Bishop of Rome as its visible Head? An invisible unity would not be a fulfilment of our Lord's prayer. National Churches at variance with each other, and exercising little or no control over the faith of their members, would not seem to accomplish His intention. Many are found to say that His intention has not been carried out, that His Divine purpose has failed. But in contradiction of this bold assertion there is this fact of one Church to be met with in every part of the world, which claims to be God's Kingdom upon earth, and is in possession of a unity which its enemies cannot and do not deny. It is not a unity they envy. At what a price, say they, is not this unity maintained? It involves a slavery of the intellect, a surrender of the will to which the right-thinking, and free-born Briton, could never submit. Better far the diversity of sects and creeds that we see around us, than that liberty of thought should be fettered in any way.

Oswald's view was that the Roman Catholic teaching was too objective, and made belief too little dependent on the moral state of the individual. He composed an essay, "On the Value of Opinion," which I wrote out at his dictation. This little treatise gave the idea that we were doomed, all our life long, to be searching after truth. We might all come to different conclusions, although since we possess a common human nature, a certain amount of agreement was to be looked for. We must be content with this. We must ascertain that our motives in making the inquiry are right. We must be careful not to be influenced by prejudices and prepossessions, not to give way to indolence and inclination. In fact, we had to be on our guard against so many things and we were in such a disadvantageous position generally, that the prospect of arriving at truth at last did not seem to be very hopeful.

I quote the following passages from Oswald's

essay: "A condition of certainty upon more than the lowest points in the Christian system is plainly impossible. The rest must ever stand upon evidence more or less imperfect, on proofs which shall convey assurance merely relative. Yet much may be attained; enough to act upon, and in some measure to be satisfied with; for nature and revelation confirm each other in the assurance that God is a Being of mercy and compassion."

After describing the arrogance and presumption of some modern sectarians who in their appeal to reason too often appealed to a standard which had never been prepared for more than the simplest exercise, and who were unable, perhaps, to master a single century of history, to explain connectedly a single chapter of the Bible, or to detect a very simple fallacy; and after insisting on that right condition of the moral nature which we find in Scripture universally required previous to the acceptance or understanding of the Christian dispensation, Oswald asks: "Where then is any place for the overconfidence which on all sides is heard, for that daring presumption which ventures upon an inquiry with any assurance but that of insufficiency and weakness, or which would exclude from any hope of truth such as have differed from a conclusion which at all events has resulted from evidence which can be only partial?"

The conclusion is that "a probability, formed

according to the amount of each man's knowledge and the state of each man's moral disposition, must be to him a law. By this he must be content here to be guided and by this hereafter doubtless he is to be judged. That this probability leads men in various directions, does not impair it as a law of action to individuals. Natural diversity of constitutions, and the vast complexity of the world of thought, and the accident of position and experience, require that particular theories must approve themselves to particular persons. . . . Nor can it be said that this very uncertainty is otherwise than in accordance with the known purpose of the present life, where through long and trying exercise we have in some part to gain that habit of thought, whose development will form one element of future happiness. Such a habit of thought requires the qualities of patience, humility, a deep watchfulness learned from the position in which we know ourselves to be never safe, together with the love and fear of the Divine Being. It requires also a great variety of circumstance and of temptation, through which we only learn to know ourselves—in fact, all those habits of disposition which once belonged instinctively to human nature, but to which, since the fall of man, all have to struggle back."

Lest I should have given too gloomy an account of my cousin's essay, I must add the concluding sentences. They are meant to be re-assuring. "To what hope or rest others may attach themselves in the weary passage of the world to its longed-for end, is not of great account to us. We cannot exchange our being and personality; in this we are isolated and alone with our own character, the special result of countless acts and thoughts which have been specially ours, and of which for the most part we have been the authors. Yet some union is to be looked for on the ground of that common nature of moral sentiment and intelligence which all inherit, and much for us individually, in that the last revelation but confirms the assurance that no earthly perplexity can entirely take away the Nature of the Supreme Being as a Person of Infinite Love. This, with our share of that common nature and with our particular differences, must direct to us our own way—leaving us, not to despair through the difficulty, but to act upon hope; not to mourn in dejection over the darkness of the world's course, but to pray that its weary purpose be quickly ended."

Shall I write as the motto of the essay, "Behold we know not anything"? I asked. Oswald promptly responded: "If the essay ever tempts you to doubt, put it in the fire."

I think the greatest evil of these views lies in the wrong idea that they instil of our good and loving God and Father. To represent the attainment of truth as so very difficult as to be well-nigh impossible, suggests either that He must be indifferent as to whether His children possess the truth, or that He has not cared enough for them to provide them with an unerring guide whose credentials it is within the power of all to recognize.

St. Paul's view of his own mission was, that he preached " to *enlighten* all men, that they may *see* what is the dispensation of the mystery which hath been hidden from eternity in God. That the manifold wisdom of God may be *made known*, . . . through the Church."

Was the Church nowadays powerless to make the truth known? Were we never to rise above probability, were we never to possess the certainty of faith? Why should we be worse off than were the people to whom St. Paul wrote? I used to read this Epistle to the Ephesians, which speaks so much of light and love, and the unity of faith and union with Christ, and to compare it with what I read in Moehler about the Catholic Church, and then to compare it with the uncertainty and contradictions outside, till the suspicion was not long in arising that if our religion is to be a Scriptural religion that religion will most certainly not be Protestantism.

CHAPTER IV.

Misgivings excited by Protestant calumnies. Their effect on the imagination. Mr. de Vere's advice on the importance of attending only to the one question: Is there a Divine Teacher in the world? This question can never be a subordinate one. Difficulties to be surmounted. Necessity for perfect sincerity.

Visits in Ireland. Newman's book on Anglican difficulties. The effect it produced. Why the principles of the Oxford movement made it impossible for those who would retain them, to remain in the English Church. Lessons learnt from the first seven lectures. The difficulties dealt with in the second part of the work. The superiority of Protestant states in material prosperity. The world and the Church have different standards of right and wrong. Protestants cannot understand that faith may exist without works. That there is perfect unity of doctrine throughout the Roman Catholic Church, an undeniable fact. A parallel to the position of the Greek Church to be found in that of the Nestorians. It is no argument in favour of Anglicanism. Consoling reflections with regard to those who have been brought up in heresy and schism. Arguments derived from ecclesiastical history in favour of the Church of Rome.

Return to Clifton. Depression of spirits. Mr. Manning's Lectures giving the reason for his secession. Oswald's remarks about them. Reflections about Faith. Two letters from Mr. Aubrey de Vere. Our Lady of La Salette. Analogy between the manifestations of God recorded in the Old Testament and those which take place in the Catholic Church.

MR. DE VERE had impressed upon us that we were not to take fright at any of the scandals that we might hear in Ireland about electioneering priests, &c. I do not remember what it was that occasioned the following letter from him, but at that time, when secessions to Rome were comparatively a novelty, most extraordinary stories used to be circulated. We were continually hearing tales of the "deterioration of character" which was to be observed in converts.

"Mount Trenchard, Foynes,
"September 14, 1852.

"Thanks for your little note and for being so *good* as to tell me of the misgivings which you are so *naughty* as to feel on no better authority than a newspaper paragraph. I have already written for information on the subject, and till I receive it I had better say only that in the reports circulated to the discredit of eminent Catholics just now there is generally no truth, and seldom more than just enough to give a foundation for an enormous mass of exaggeration and calumny. For this there is no help. Such 'hearsay' is the very food on which Protestant prejudice lives; and in such matters the rule is a simple one, viz., that the *supply* corresponds with and equals the *demand*. The misfortune is that the imagination remains oppressed even when the mind is disabused.

"But who shall contend with legion? One report confuted, a thousand new ones take its place; and in this species of warfare, retaliation is not a weapon which Catholics are permitted to use: for with them *detraction*, even where there is nothing of untruth or distortion, is considered one of the gravest offences against charity. Since the plague of locusts there never was anything like the swarm of rumours, reports, and falsehoods, intentional or unintentional, with which the air has been darkened during the last two years. I often wonder how through such a cloud it should ever be possible to direct one's steps in the right way, and reach that only place of refuge in which truth and peace are found at once, and from the eminence of which we see the utter *irrelevancy* of the innumerable trifles by which our attention was so often withdrawn from the essential and directed to the accidental. What is impossible with man is possible with God; and it is through His grace only, and by the gracious leading of His Spirit that we are enabled to *advance* in the way of salvation. Except through His aid not only are we unable to find, but even to seek. Our very inquiries lose themselves in a labyrinth of paths which cross each other every moment and lead no whither. It is by the leading of the Spirit that we distinguish between these and the one path which conducts us through the forest, and issues forth into light.

"I will not attempt to tell you, my dear friends, how much I sympathize with you in the difficulties which beset you. I know them by experience, but I should be sorry to think that your experience of them was to be as various and to last as long. How many years, gone alas! for ever, did I not lose by not keeping steadily before me that *one* question upon which yet I could not but have sufficiently known that all depended: the question as to whether God has or not, commissioned a Divine Authority to teach us authentically His Truth and His Will, and, if so, what community upon earth stands forward thus as His Prophet and the expounder of His Word. Be wiser, I beseech you, than I was, and do not allow your attention to be distracted from this one inquiry which God has given us the means of making effectually. If we were competent to sit in judgment on this or that doctrine in detail in our individual capacity, God would not have constituted a Church in His beloved Son, and filled it with His Holy Spirit that it might guide us to our Heavenly Home. If there be a Church and if we be external to it, is it not self-evident that we must, from the disadvantage of that position which we have inherited, see its doctrines and its practices alike in a false perspective, as Dissenters do those of the Established Church, and so condemn what we have not apprehended aright? Is it not certain also that in such a position we could not possibly decide for ourselves what Christian doctrines are or are not essential, what required to be defined and on what difference of opinion is allowable? Let us never forget that such a question, as which of the various religious communities around us is the Messenger and Apostle of God, can never be a *subordinate one*. It is all or nothing. If we have ever realized the idea that this is the question indeed at issue, a great grace has been accorded to us. Let us be faithful to this, and light will be given us in proportion as the eye can bear it.

"All this sounds dry and hard, and unlike the discussions which we used to have at Clifton and which we shall have, I trust, at Currah, for one never can say what one wants on paper. Yet it is suggested even more by what I have fancied (for you have been very much in my thoughts) must be your position and trials in Irish Protestant society, and in the excitement that succeeds an election, than by anything that you tell me. You must have many difficulties, more even than you know, for the spirit of delusion weaves snares most carefully round those whom he fears to lose. But you have one sufficient security in the aid of Him through Whose grace alone you have been led to take a real interest in the one question worthy of our serious consideration. You will, I am sure, be sincere with yourselves. Perfect sincerity will preserve you from falling into innumerable entanglements from which extrication is difficult. It will make you use the means at your disposal and co-operate with grace. It will make you distinguish between vague impressions on matters upon which we can have no accurate information and solid opinions; and again between the firmest opinions attested only by human judgment, and the clear and definite certainty of convictions founded on the witness of God and His Church, and communicated to us by faith. I do not fear for you, for I am sure you are sincere and I know that you will always pray for light and that the prayers of others will support your own. In the meantime do not be astonished at finding perplexities in your way, and remember that it is in the spirit of hope, not of fear, that we must seek the truth; for we are in the hands of a loving Father, Who loves us most when we need Him most, Who watches the steps of each of His creatures and counts the beating of every heart in which He has a place.

"God bless you, my dear little friends, and guide you aright in all things. Remember me most cordially to your mother and your cousin and to his sister when you write to her. Accept once more my best thanks for your little note, and believe me ever most truly and kindly yours,

"AUBREY DE VERE."

If Ireland had had a charm for us when we were staying with our Protestant relations; if there was a peculiar fascination in the blueness of the mountains and the rich brown of the moors and the intense crimson of the sunsets, the charm and the fascination were increased when we found ourselves at Currah Chase with Sir Vere and Lady de Vere. I think this visit was one of the happiest times in our young lives. We had never been in a more congenial atmosphere. We had never had such an opportunity for becoming acquainted with all the arguments for Catholicism. I spent a good deal of time alone in the house when the others were out, and had a feast on the works of Newman and other Catholic writers. Any difficulties we had were answered fully by our friends. Personally I had but few difficulties, and would have asked nothing better than to be received into the Church there and then. The Protestant service at Adare to which we went was very miserable. The preacher read out a passage from the Bible which he said did not *sound* Scriptural. He hoped, however, to show us that it was capable of being interpreted in a Scriptural sense. How I longed to be getting out at the Catholic chapel and hearing Mass with our friends instead of "going further to fare worse," as they expressed it. Catholicism was the religion of the country. The Establishment was an intruder, that was evident. It was a question I sometimes asked High Church people like Mr. Cleveland. Which Church should one attend in Ireland. On the Continent, Mr. Cleveland maintained, it was the duty of an English Churchman to go to Mass. It seemed to me that the same rule ought in consistency to apply to Ireland, Catholicism being the religion of the people. No, Mr. Cleveland was inclined to think that the *Established* religion was the right one to follow there. Could he mean—

established by Act of Parliament, or did he mean —established by Christ?

We had a good deal of reading aloud at Currah Chase. Newman's *Anglican Difficulties* was one work we read, also *Loss and Gain*, a story I never tire of reading again. It is a characteristic of Cardinal Newman's writings that one can read them many and many a time. One always finds in them something fresh and something adapted to one's present frame of mind. They appeal to me now as forcibly as they did in youth or middle life. Many authors that are favourites at one period lose their charm later. Authors that were less appreciated formerly are seen to have great merit when the judgment has become more matured. The charm of Cardinal Newman's writings remains. It does but become intensified with time. His words read to us, as he has said, our "wants and feelings, and comfort us by the very reading," "opening a way to the inquiring and soothing the perplexed."

Perhaps it was not till I read these lectures, *On the Difficulties felt by Anglicans in Catholic Teaching*, that the reasons why Anglicans ought to submit themselves to the Roman Catholic Church, and ought not to be content to remain where they are if they accept Catholic teaching, presented themselves in a very definite shape to my mind. The Roman Church had always had an attraction for me. I had, moreover, failed to see on what grounds doctrines which were spoken of as "corruptions" were to be rejected. But might we not hold these doctrines and go on very well as outsiders? Was it not more humble and more becoming to remain in the form of Christianity in which we had been born? No one would find fault with us for that. No one indeed would know that any other course had been suggested to us. It *seemed* eminently the safe thing to do. Safe indeed so far as this world was concerned, but what about the next? Could it be safe if, as was here asserted, the Roman Catholic Church was the Kingdom of Christ upon earth, a claim which no other Church could in any way substantiate?

Newman addressed himself to the Oxford religious party of 1833, and assuming that the principles which that party advocated were true, he insisted that there was no consistent course open to the holders of such principles but to submit to the Church of Rome. Now we had always been taught these principles, but we had also been taught, that they were held by the English Church. We were told that if they were directly contradicted and preached against by nearly all the clergy whose ministrations we attended, this was the fault of those clergy. It was said to be an accident which arose from the circumstances of the times, the want of discipline and the interference of the State. Newman proved conclusively, so far as I could see, that this was not the case. The reception those principles had met with in the English Church, showed how utterly foreign they were to the nature of that Church. In the first place, the main idea of the movement was to destroy Erastianism. Erastianism was so inherent in the very constitution of the Established Religion, that, "to destroy Erastianism was to destroy the religion."

Again, the impossibility that those who would retain the principles of the movement should remain in the National Church was evident, because now, in direct contradiction to those principles, they would be obliged to appeal to their own private judgment as a basis for the religious doctrines which they professed, instead of appealing to an external authority. They had no authority. The Bishops of the Established Church were against them. Its divines were against them. Its law-courts were against them. Its Prayer Book could not be made to sanction all their doctrines. These doctrines were as entirely the fruit of their private judgment as were the doctrines of any of the sects in England.

The Branch Church theory Newman demolished. He showed that a Branch Church must be a National Church, and that a National Church must be necessarily Erastian. It is the Catholicity of the Church which frees her from the jurisdiction of the State. It enables her to fulfil the purpose of the Incarnation, to found a Kingdom that should be independent of the kingdoms of this world. The existence of such a Kingdom—an isolated Church without any visible Head, and at the same time without any centre of unity apart from the Temporal Sovereign—would be impossible.

Those who despise dogma, and who look upon religion as merely a matter of opinion, and who advocate religion only so far as it conduces to civil order and to the service of the State, are consistent in denying the authority of the Church. If the Church has no Divine message to deliver, and no Divine work to do, what need is there for its existence? The Church to be intelligible, must have both its dogma and its sacraments. She must have truths to teach, and spiritual benefits to bestow which cannot be gained without her. She must be "built upon facts, not opinions; on immemorial testimony, not on private judgment." It is her consciousness that God has given her a doctrine to deliver and a work to do, which makes her so bold and so uncompromising in the assertion of her independence. The supernatural doctrine which she has received from Jesus Christ and the supernatural powers which He has bestowed on her priesthood, are her justification for the position which she has always assumed in face of the civil power.

The Tract-writers had set forth Catholic doctrine and the reality of priestly power with the firm conviction that such truths had only to be clearly stated to be recognized at once as doctrines of the English Church. They were, as the writers considered, incontestably the teaching of the Apostles and of the early Church. When, however, the voice of the English Church was heard through her Bishops, who one and all of them were opposed to such an interpretation of her Articles and her Prayer Book, consistent members of the party could not but feel that the ground was cut from under their feet. They might hold this or that doctrine, but they must hold it on private judgment. Authority they had none. The English Church disavowed that authority with which the Tract-writers had invested her. There was one Church only on the earth which even claimed such authority. To that Church they must, if they would be true to their principles, betake themselves.

Such is, in brief, what I gathered from the first seven of Newman's lectures. The five lectures which constitute the second part of the series, deal, not with the difficulties of the Anglo-Catholic in the Established Church, but with certain objections against the Roman Church, which might tend to deter Anglicans from joining it lest they should find in it difficulties as great or greater than the difficulties in their own communion.

The first of these objections commends itself very much to the ordinary British mind, viz., that Protestant countries are superior to Catholic countries in material prosperity, in secular progress, or in what is called civilization. There are more railroads in England, she is superior to other nations in mechanical inventions, her ships are better built. Admitting for the sake of argument this to be the fact, Newman asks, What has this to do with the question? The Church has her own distinct work. She does not profess to invent steam-engines and build ironclads. Her one aim is to save souls. Her interest in these material things is only so far as they may conduce to some spiritual good. Mechanical inventions are not necessary to salvation, so it is not reasonable to reproach her with not having made any.

Again, there is a perpetual and a necessary antagonism between the world and the Church in their altogether different standards of right and wrong. Virtues which are considered essential by the Church, such as the virtues of faith, of purity, and of charity by which the soul is united to its Creator, are not made much of by the world. An outward respectability is all that the world recognizes. The judgment of the Church is that of her Divine Master: "I judge not according to the look of man, for man seeth those things which appear, but *the Lord beholdeth the heart.*" Worldly people, whose standard is not His, are shocked and scandalized. They have no knowledge of Divine principles. They cannot, therefore, be fair judges of a Divine Church and of her work. It is a more difficult work than is that which the world has to perform. The Church has to contend with the inclinations of fallen nature instead of ministering to them. Her work is moreover a hidden work, and the good which she does is of necessity in the most important of its results secret.

Another difficulty which Protestants feel is what they consider the levity and the want of reverence which seems to them apparent wherever Catholicism is the religion of the people. The reason is because they *are* Protestants. As Protestants they have no conception of faith as Catholics understand it. Faith is a certainty, a spiritual sight of the unseen. It can and it does exist without love, and without obedience. It is quite possible to have faith, as real as is the faith of a martyr, and yet not to act upon it. It is quite possible to know with certainty what will be the consequences of sin and yet, for the sake of an immediate satisfaction, to commit sin. Individuals will be good or bad in a Catholic community, as well as in a Protestant community. In the former, however, in spite of their being bad, they will retain the knowledge of revealed truths as facts. They will have them before their minds as facts, not as mere matters of opinion. Hence the phenomenon which is so puzzling to Protestants, of Catholics who believe in supernatural truths leading bad lives. Protestants have no idea of faith as distinct from hope, and love, and obedience. If faith does not show itself in works, according to them, faith does not exist. God in His mercy has ordained that it should be otherwise. By means of this gift of faith many a soul which has lived for years in sin is brought back to Him at last, to Him in Whom it has ever believed at least, even if it has neglected to obey His commandments.

The objections to Catholicism which are stated by Jewell and others, that there are as many varieties of opinion among Catholics as among Protestants, seems to Newman almost too futile to call for a serious reply. It is to him evident that no one who chooses to inquire can have any doubt as to what the teaching of the Catholic Church is about any one article of faith. Let the inquirer but ask one of her priests in any part of the world, and the answer will be the same. If there is this undoubted unity with regard to all revealed truth, why may there not be differences with regard to questions which are mere matters of opinion? The history of the way in which the Church has dealt with and has finally eradicated heresies within her pale, furnishes irrefragable testimony to the unitive power of the Apostolic See. The history of the Monophysite heresy and, in modern times, the action of the Church in repressing the wide-spread heresy of Jansenism supply abundant evidence.

Anglicans find great comfort in dwelling on the antiquity and the imposing claims of the "Greek

Church," and the number of souls it includes within its pale. They consider that the separation of such a large religious body from the See of St. Peter must somehow make their own separated position safe. It is nevertheless a fact, and a fact which Holy Scripture teaches us to look for, that truth is ever opposed. It is opposed not only by direct contradictions, but by pretences and impostures which are often so specious as to mislead the many. The Epistles of the great Apostle are filled with warnings to this effect. His warnings seem to point to the emergence of such phenomena as the Greek Church and Mahometanism. In ancient times the heresies of the Novatians and the Arians were far more widely spread than is the Greek religion now. A parallel to the *national* character of the latter may be found in those various tribes of Goths which took possession of the Empire. They had all learned their form of Christianity from Arian preachers.

All the facts that can be alleged in favour of the antiquity and the authority of the Greek Church are to be found in the history of the Nestorians. The rebellion of the Greek Church against the supremacy of Rome is no more a true objection to that supremacy than was the rebellion of the Nestorians and the Arians.

Newman's eleventh lecture suggests some most consoling reflections on the irresponsible state in which we may hope many individuals to be who, whether in England or in Greece, have been brought up in heresy and schism. Many in the Greek Church may be in invincible ignorance of those truths which that Church rejects, and they may nevertheless have Divine faith in those truths which she teaches. They may also receive an abundance of grace from Masses and from Sacraments. In our own country great blessings may be derived from study of the Written Word of God and from the Catholic prayers which still find a place in the Anglican Prayer Book.

The case is different with regard to those whose eyes have been opened to see the heresy and schism in their own communion, but who resolve to shut their eyes, or who at all events delay to act upon the light vouchsafed to them. A great grace has been given to those men which has not been given to others. The pages in which Newman appeals to these men with all the force and with all the tenderness of his eloquence, I wrote out in order that I might always have them by me to refer to. Never could I put his words for very long out of my mind. Many years were, however, to go by before I was to find the safe resting-place in "the true home of souls, the valley of peace," and to receive the fulness of faith which makes its possessor almost "see invisible mysteries and touch the threshold of eternity."

It was, however, from the concluding lecture in Newman's volume that I made the most copious extracts in my note-book. There the argument from ecclesiastical history in favour of the Church of Rome is drawn out. Newman describes the impression made on him by finding that the general theory and position of Anglicanism as a *via media* was no novelty. It had always had its counterpart, and that an heretical counterpart, in ancient history. It was as a *via media* between the extremes of Popery and Protestantism that Newman had so strongly advocated the claims of Anglicanism in his work, *On the Prophetical Office of the Church*. To find, as he had found in studying the history of the ancient heresies, that there had always been an intermediate moderate heretical party, and that this party in principles and practice bore an unmistakable resemblance to modern moderate Protestants, gave the death-blow to his theory. In the history of Arianism, for instance, we meet with the Eusebians (called after Eusebius, Bishop of Nicomedia), who professed to agree neither with St. Athanasius nor with Arius, but to take a middle and a safer course. They insulted the Pope and they gained the favour of Constantine, and still more of his son and successor Constantius. Newman compares the historian Eusebius of Cæsarea, who belonged to this semi-Arian party and whose writings are characterized, not by an Arianizing, but by an Eclectic spirit, with certain Anglican divines. Constantine's letter to the Bishop of Alexandria and to Arius he cites as an example of the indifference which the State shows to religious dogmas, even as regards so vital a question as is that of the Divinity of our Lord. He then tells us how he found any defence of Anglicanism would form an equally cogent defence for primitive heresies, and that all objections urged against the Council of Trent were available equally against the primitive Councils. "It was difficult," he says,[1] "to make out how the Eutychians or Monophysites were heretics, unless Protestants and Anglicans were heretics also; difficult to find arguments against the Tridentine Fathers which did not tell against the Fathers of Chalcedon; difficult to condemn the Popes of the sixteenth century, without condemning the Popes of the fifth. The drama of religion and the combat of truth and error were ever one and the same. The principles and proceedings of the Church now were those of the Church then; the principles and proceedings of heretics then were those of Protestants now. I found it so—almost fearfully; there was an awful similitude, more awful, because so silent and unimpassioned, between the dead records of the past and the feverish chronicle of the present. The shadow of the fifth century was on the sixteenth. It was like a spirit rising from the troubled waters of the old world with the shape and lineaments of the new. The Church, then,

[1] *Difficulties felt by Anglicans in Catholic Teaching.* Fourth Edition, p. 338.

as now, might be called peremptory and stern, resolute, overbearing, and relentless; and heretics were shifting, changeable, reserved, and deceitful, ever courting the civil power, and never agreeing together, except by its aid; and the civil power was ever aiming at comprehensions, trying to put the invisible out of view, and to substitute expediency for faith."

The more learned Anglican divines evidently sympathize with ancient heretics. Jeremy Taylor does not hesitate to express disapproval of the Nicene Council. He also commends the Letter of Constantine to Alexander and Arius. On such a doctrine as that of Jesus Christ being the Eternal God or a mere creature, he says, "If the article had been with more simplicity and less nicety determined, charity would have gained more, and faith would have lost nothing." Jeremy Taylor is but one of many. The tendency of the supporters of the *via media* is towards latitudinarianism. The position of the *via media* is heretical. The essential idea of Catholicism is the infallibility of the Church. The essential idea of the *via media* is that the Catholic Church has fallen into error.

The Roman Catholic Church, moreover, in its ceremonial and its ritual, its devotions and its ways of acting, is the only living religion which can pretend to be a representative of the Christianity of antiquity.

The history of the doctrinal definitions of the Church affords a still more striking argument. Definitions are not accidental, but are governed by laws. The very same laws will be found to rule her definitions in every century of the Church's history.

This argument is more fully worked out in the famous book on *The Development of Christian Doctrine,* from which Mr. Aubrey de Vere read to us some passages. The honour which is due to the Blessed Virgin Mother of God, was a difficulty to one of our party. Newman shows the effect which the Arian controversy had in manifesting the prerogatives of Mary. The Nicene Council determined that "to exalt a creature was no recognition of its divinity." "The highest of creatures is levelled with the lowest in comparison of the One Creator Himself. . . . Arius or Asterius did all but confess that Christ was the Almighty; they said much more than St. Bernard or St. Alphonsus have since said of the Blessed Mary; yet they left Him a creature and were found wanting. Thus there was 'a wonder in Heaven;' a throne was seen, far above all created powers, mediatorial, intercessory; a title archetypal; a crown bright as the morning star; a glory issuing from the Eternal Throne; robes pure as the heavens; and a sceptre over all; and who was the predestined heir of that majesty? Since it was not high enough for the Highest, who was that Wisdom, and what was her name, 'the Mother of fair love, and fear, and holy hope,' 'exalted like a palm-tree in Engaddi, and a rose-plant in Jericho,' 'created from the beginning before the world' in God's counsels, and 'in Jerusalem was her power'? The vision is found in the Apocalypse, a Woman clothed with the sun, and the moon under her feet, and upon her head a crown of twelve stars. The votaries of Mary do not exceed the true faith, unless the blasphemers of her Son came up to it. The Church of Rome is not idolatrous, unless Arianism is orthodoxy."

I wrote out this passage and various extracts from the lectures ere the sad day came when we were to say good-bye to our dear friends at Currah Chase, and to be left once more to our own resources to free ourselves from Protestantism as best we might. How depressed we felt on our journey home! On arriving at Dublin, we met some of my mother's ultra-Protestant cousins. It was a sudden and a startling change. Olivia was hardly in spirits to make a suitable rejoinder when one of these ladies inquired: "Was it not *very odd*, dear, to be *staying in a house* with Roman Catholics?"

Protestant prejudice was much stronger in those days than it is now, and Roman Catholics were looked upon as an altogether different breed. I suppose it was acknowledged that they were human beings. Catholic Emancipation, however, was still too recent for it to be generally admitted that Roman Catholics were entitled to the same privileges as are the rest of their fellow-countrymen. I remember when we first went to Clifton, a lady, speaking of Catholic priests, said: "There ought to be a law to prevent them from walking about." Popery seemed to be considered infectious. The mere sight of a priest might suffice to convert a man in spite of himself. It was an unwilling deference to this feeling and to the opinions of sound churchmen which led mother to ask Mr. Neve, the Catholic priest at Clifton, not to come and see us. He had been at Currah during the first days of our visit there. We hoped to see more of him when we returned to Clifton.

On our arrival he sent to each of us a note and with it a book. To Olivia he wrote:

"November 5, 1852.

"Is not this almost like a romance? or is it one of the stern realities of this world as when human beings, instead of living in charity, watch each other and are afraid of each other as mutual foes? I mean the fear you have of seeing me; why you are a captive, without freedom and yet not happy in your captivity. What intolerant masters you have!

"I will not believe that you are quite satisfied in your present state. You have a right to make inquiries; if I can render you any assistance, I shall be most happy to do so. I will answer any question you may wish to put.

"I enclose a letter which I sent to my friends seven years ago, it may touch some chord in your own feelings. I hope you pray for guidance, it is the only way."

This is his note to me:

"I take the liberty of sending a pamphlet of Mr. Northcote's, published some time ago. It may interest you to read some of the opinions of those who were on the point of joining the Church of Rome. You ought to read both sides, as you are making inquiries on the subject. Pray believe that I shall be happy to be of any use to you in the way of lending you books or answering questions which are within my capacity. Your greatest help though in all doubts will be in prayer for guidance."

I was pleased with this note and with the expression of interest which it contained. It was a comfort to know there was one person who "cared for my soul"—cared for it with that supernatural love which comes straight from the Sacred Heart of the Good Shepherd, Who carries on His Divine Mission of seeking the wanderers through the priests whom He has consecrated and appointed to be His representatives on earth. But, because Mr. Neve was a *priest*, we were not to see him. It did seem hard that a friend with whom we had had such pleasant walks and talks in Ireland, and whose society we had found so congenial, should now be as a stranger to us, simply on account of Mrs. Grundy. I always resented the sway of that chattering female. Her power is most pronounced in provincial towns. Mother had fits of setting her at defiance. Unfortunately these fits did not last very long.

Mother talked freely on Church questions and difficulties with the easy-going Herbert Graham. He was of opinion that there would be no harm in our going *once* to hear a French sermon from the Abbé Miot. We must not, however, make a practice of it, and we had better come away without taking part in the service. The visit of a colonial Bishop was impending, who in the course of the winter was to preach sermons for the benefit of his mission in the neighbourhood of Clifton. The clergy of the Clifton churches, I fancy, regarded him as too much tainted with Puseyite errors to allow him to occupy their pulpits. " Dear Robert," as we had always heard him called, had been mother's friend since she was sixteen. She intended to have a talk to him when he came, about " Rome." I hoped something might occur to prevent the visit of the Right Reverend Robert. Till he should appear mother was not averse to the reading of Catholic books. She procured the four lectures published by Mr. Manning explaining the reason of his secession. These she read to us and afterwards handed them to Herbert Graham. I remember feeling indignant when Lady Millicent said, "Herbert did not wish her to read them." The prohibition, however, seemed to imply that they did not make the comfortable Herbert more comfortable. It implied also that they might suggest to Lady Millicent questions which he might not find it altogether convenient to answer.

Two characteristic letters from Oswald arrived about this time.

"October 19, 1852.

"I was most pleased with your letter, chiefly, I think, that it told me of your preserving so kindly a remembrance of our meeting in Ireland, otherwise it brought but few happy thoughts. It was not very definite as to your state of mind in respect to the painful question that must have often tried the faithfulness and patience of you all whilst at Currah. However, it is now in some measure withdrawn, and in place of pity, and perhaps perplexity, at the sympathy which has been proffered so abundantly, is the calm tribunal of retrospect and conscience in the quiet moments of the day, or the watches of night, weighing the varied sources of pain and pleasure during your late visit; perhaps, too, temptations under the garb of such bold decision, to waive the difficulties in the way of the step to which you have been invited, by some shorter consideration and less earnest application of all your moral and mental powers, than will secure even a human measure of assurance. If such have been your thoughts, tell me, I entreat you. At least you are certain I can feel for you each and all, wheresoever your trial in this weary state of probation may visit you. It is not I believe the act itself in the perplexity of these times which is of so great and fearful consequence as the spirit and the motives."

"November 6.

"I have been of late distracted by many things to do and think about, and so have been unable to read Manning's new book. I trust, however, I shall never be so overburdened as to forget you and your cares, or any whom I have once known as yourselves. Whilst here alone, I often think it a great happiness to own some living interests, though the objects be out of visible reach, but this introduction is not to the purpose, although uppermost. The extracts you have quoted seem to me so vague in argument and altogether empty, that I cannot but say the opinion of Festus about the result of learning being madness, seems sometimes probable. I do not speak in bitterness, but in pity.

"Faith is said to be identical with certainty. Where faith begins uncertainty ends, is the general account supported by appeal to Abraham, Moses, and others. Now the very simple history of these characters in the Epistle to the Hebrews, and the definition there of that faith by which they were strengthened in their pilgrimages, should be enough to correct this. In the very idea of hope, it is there said, is the idea of possible failure and uncertainty. Besides the history of many of these same persons—Abraham in three instances, Moses in one, Elijah in one, and others—almost all in various instances shows how their faith did at times fail, and that it was not a certainty; that the evidence on which their probation was based was not even to them, at all times, sufficient to guard them from misgivings as to the continuing mercy and watchfulness of God. Yet in the main it was enough; enough to guide them in patient expectation to a general course of life which was pleasing to God, and which no doubt led them to the land which seemed to them while on earth very far off, though there is hardly one, excepting perhaps Samuel and Daniel, of whom some occasional declension is not recorded. And this might have been expected in them by those who will calmly think of the nature of faith, and is to be looked for still by such as believe the present dispensation to be still a probation state. For faith is to be considered objectively and subjectively. Thus the objective is the revelation of God's will, at present imperfect, yet containing assurance of things so awful and important as will urge any one to act upon. The subjective is the mind which receives these suggestions. Whether they are received and acted upon depends upon the moral condition, and if they are so acted upon this result is faith which therefore is the test of the condition of the subjective proving its earnestness and patience, a disposition to realize the dependence of man upon the Creator, the Redeemer, and Sanctifier, together with all those affections and relations which fill up the Christian life and have the value of faith. For if it were not seen as an active and living principle, there would be the absence of this essential of our life towards God; if our present position were one of certainty, there would be no room for the exercise of watchfulness against the lower influences that distract our judgment, of passion, pride, and self-will, and the whole design of our present dispensation would be lost, which represents man as ever trembling on the verge of an eternal decision which each act, word, and thought must affect. Thus a position of general uncertainty is the only one in which the affections whose expansion will be the happiness of a future state can be acquired. It is therefore not only a virtue to act upon probability, but it is the only way in which patient, earnest virtue is expressed and perfected, and the habit of so acting is faith, and those who would gain its promised end must bear with patience and self-denial its life-long burden.

"I hope you have understood me about faith generally, as I have not intended to speak of faith in any particular system, but you must tell me. I cannot agree with the denial of connection between the Christian Church and the Jewish. The last was indeed a shadow to ours, and ours is again to the future, but of this connection I think we wrote something which if it does not seem satisfactory after your consideration, you must also write and tell me. Let me lastly entreat you not to take up such armour as Manning offered you, without proving it to the best of your power, and may God keep you from any sinful judgment in these trying dangers, is ever my prayer for you all."

Vague, misty, and disheartening, were these remarks of dear Oswald's. Why was faith to be a life-long burden, requiring patience and self-denial to bear it? That was not the Catholic idea of faith. Father Faber has written, "Heaven must indeed be beautiful if the saints can part there with their gift of faith and not pine to have it back again." *Our* faith was to be a burden so long as life should last. Oswald confuses the certainty which God means us to have with regard to the truths which He has revealed, with the uncertainty in which it is His will we should live as regards our future, and what He may require of us in this life.

Tennyson writes:

> We have but faith: we cannot know
> For knowledge is of things we see.

Aubrey de Vere used to say these lines expressed the idea about faith which obtained largely in the present day. Men had lost not only faith but even the very meaning of the word. Faith *is* knowledge.

That was the conclusion which I longed to arrive at. Those Catholic devotional works, adapted by Dr. Pusey, and which I so much appreciated, were based on that certainty which comes from Divine faith, *i.e.*, belief in a truth because God has revealed it. When the soul has once got a glimpse, however imperfect may be its glimpse of that inestimable gift, it cannot choose but wish to see more. "Knowledge is of things we see." Did not Newman say of those to whom the grace of conversion had been given, that they "almost seemed to see invisible mysteries"?

Our visit at Currah had been so happy, it was provoking that Oswald should assume a commiserating tone respecting it. From a note of his, it appears I was in no hurry to answer his previous letter. It was perhaps because I could not honestly say anything about my state of mind in regard to what he calls, "the painful question," that would please and reassure him.

Meanwhile we received the following letters from Mr. Aubrey de Vere.

"Currah Chase, November 12, 1852.
"My dear little friends,—I believe that the real reason I am writing to you is because I miss you

very much, and think it better to have you near me in imagination, than not at all; however, I have found an excellent pretext for adding a postscript to my packet of fifty sheets (I hope it arrived safely), for I am sending you a couple of relics which even Exeter Hall could not complain of. One is a memorial of Milton, which I gathered years ago, when I was as enthusiastic as you can be, though not so young. The other is a really good autograph of Alfred Tennyson, a poetic, not a prose one, like that which you already have. I send a second for Mrs. Vyner, as I remember she was one of the three competing parties that pleasant summer evening as we walked home from the Downs.

"We miss you horribly, and I think it was very unkind of you to run away from us just as the leaves were falling from the trees. You are only 'summer friends,' is not that all?

"I am so glad you have made the acquaintance of the Northcotes, they are good and clever people. You are very naughty not to let Mr. Neve visit you, or rather your mother is, for I must not give a scolding wrongfully this time. The last time I sent one to Olivia about Sir J. Stephen's works, though I see she only *threatens* to read them. Tell your mother that she must not expect the greatest of all blessings without being willing to *dare* something; for courage is now, as in the early times of the Gospels, one of the chief attributes of *Faith*. I have just stumbled on an interesting note from Manning on this subject, written very soon after his conversion. If she likes to have it, I will send it to her. . . .

"Ever affectionately yours,
"AUBREY DE VERE."

"Currah Chase, November 30, 1852.
"Thanks for your notes, my little friends. I *think* that both 'the children' are growing very good; but if I had to bet—which has so long been thought a wise way of solving difficult questions—I would bet that Minima is the better of the two, or at least that Olivia oscillates most, like that useful and ingenious scientific instrument on the summit of church spires, which stands giving useful information, where the cross stood in those 'dark ages' of ignorance and superstition shown by Dr. Maitland to be only the ages concerning which 'men are in the dark.' There is a scoff at Olive for saying that she sometimes feels very Sir-James-Stephenish, and that it is a great hardship that one cannot see one's way at once to certainty in these matters. However, I am not impatient, for I believe that you are *in earnest* in your search after Truth, and that is more than half the battle. You know, also, that neither sooner nor later can certainty come through *opinion*. Certainty comes through Faith, and Faith comes by Grace; and Intellectual Inquiry is, in sacred matters only, *instrumentally* and

subordinately useful, though in its proper province it is *essential*, since if we shrink from doing our part, God will not do His. Intellectual Inquiry tells us, with an evidence at least as strong as that on which we act in the common affairs of life, whether God has given us a guide or not, and who that guide is—what are the *functions* of the Church, and what are the marks or *notes* by which it may be known. Faith is then at once challenged and directed; and the rest must depend on the degree in which we co-operate with grace. Every difficulty in our way is sent to us, or permitted, by One Who knows exactly what we can bear; and if we but use such hindrances aright they will be turned into blessings, forcing us to cultivate whatever virtues we most want, in the absence of which not even Catholicity would avail us—such as patience, resolution, *courage* (for every age of Christendom is a crusading age), and, above all, love for One Whom we must think of as bleeding ever on the Cross for us, and counting by the drops of His Blood the moments that pass until we comply fully with whatever grace He has given to us. He is not impatient if we be but sincere and single-hearted, and allow no unworthy feelings to counterbalance supernatural duties. He gives Grace in different degrees, and requires us only to co-operate with what is given, and then He will give more. One step at a time, and that will give us light for the next. Have you not observed how much, in mounting a hill, your view is extended by a very few paces in advance, provided they are in an upward direction? Such a hill is truth. We may wander round and round for ever, but from the moment we begin to face the difficulty, instead of contenting ourselves with wandering in the pleasant paths, or in those we are used to, our progress is rapid in most cases, and sure in all; only in these matters we must take great pains to be as superior to the temptations of self-will, or individual taste, or personal predilections and associations, as we are to self-interest in its more vulgar forms.

"I am disposed to be a great believer in your patience at least, my dear Minima, for it must have required much to copy out that long Essay.[1] Had I known what a task lay before you, I would have tried to make it shorter. I am very glad you liked it; and I would write twice as much to give any one of you (including Mrs. Vyner and Oswald) the best assistance. I hope that your mother will write to me again on the subject, now that she has finished it, and that she has found in it some help towards contemplating the matter from a *Catholic point of view*. I do not know how much more is possible, while we occupy a position external to the Roman Catholic Church, than to see clearly with respect to a particular contested doctrine, that our difficulty results mainly from the point of view which our Protestant or

---

[1] This was an essay on the *Veneration of the Saints*.

Anglican antecedents have hitherto made ours, that from the Catholic point of view, disorder and confusion become at once harmony and proportion; and that whether the doctrine be right or not, the *main* objections brought against it, those which are most relied upon, and which have *done work* for Protestantism, are unfounded calumnies and superficial. Other objections or difficulties may still remain, for in such matters scientific demonstration is impossible. These difficulties may also weigh much with our feelings, our nerves, or our imaginations: but, so far as intellectual belief goes, it seems to me that as soon as we have seen clearly as much as I have just described, and *realized* what we have seen, the question at issue becomes resolved into the question, 'Which is the right *point of view?* Which is the true analogy or proportion of theology?' Thus we arrive again at the question, 'Which is the One Catholic and Apostolic Church sent by God to be our Guide?' According as this question is decided, the question of the Saints must be decided, so far as *certainty* goes. But in the meantime a great obstacle is removed, which might otherwise have hindered us from looking steadily at the great cardinal point of all discussion, from the moment we perceive that the Protestant doctrine about the Saints, however confidently or plausibly urged, is after all but a 'view' and 'tradition,' like the Dissenting theory respecting the Sacraments, Episcopacy, and the

Invisible Church, by many unhappily associated with the Scriptural and the Spiritual, but in reality negative only, and narrow.

"Poor Dr. Hook! I know the *Nonentity and Inanity*. It is very sad, but it will do work for Protestantism better than Bishop Hall's *via media*. Those who believe with him that the Saints see what is going on here, in the mass, will come to ask themselves whether the same faculty must not enable them to see things in detail, and those who really wish to honour them will discover that such honour is a practical thing, and not an abstraction. Dr. Hook's tone is faithful to the Protestant tradition, and it will have its effect, alas, even with those who do not accept his opinions on the subject. I should like to read the 'loose thoughts.'

"So Herbert Graham believes in Convocation and Lord Derby.

> Ah! that a Conqueror's word should be so dear—
> A *gift* of that, &c.

"What say you of the Bishop of South Carolina's submission to Rome? He, indeed, must have had some difficulties to contend with! I hope the Bishop of Brechin will also erelong be at rest.

"Now I must say good-bye, and God bless you both. Remember me most kindly to your mother, and tell her that I am not likely to forget our walks, as I still walk to the rock in the dusk of almost every evening. I hope I shall get her promised letter soon.

"Yours very affectionately,
"AUBREY DE VERE."

Mr. Northcote, mentioned in the preceding letter, whose acquaintance we had just made, had been an Anglican clergyman in the diocese of Exeter. He lent us an interesting correspondence which he had with Bishop Philpotts before resigning his office. He wrote some interesting articles in the *Rambler* about Our Lady of Salette. This story was exciting attention at that time. It was a grief to me that my mother could never understand the Catholic doctrine about the Blessed Virgin and the Saints. She thought that to invoke the saints was to invest them with Omnipotence. She could not see that we had any warrant for supposing the saints could hear us, or could know anything at all about our affairs. Occurrences such as the apparition of La Salette or the conversion of Alphonse Ratisbonne were very distasteful to her. I could not feel shocked at them myself. I wished that it was not thought wrong of me not to be shocked. The same sort of things happened in the Bible. In the Old Testament God is represented as constantly giving warnings and manifesting His will to His servants, much in the same way as He does now in the Catholic Church. Protestants believe that angels interfered in olden days with the dwellers on earth. They are sure that angels can have nothing to do with us in these enlightened times. Dear mother used often to say how blessed it must have been to have lived under the Jewish Dispensation. Then people could go and inquire of the Lord and receive an answer! How wonderful to have seen the glory of the Lord dwelling upon Sinai and covering it with a cloud, and to have talked with Moses after he had gone up into the mountain and remained there forty days and forty nights!

To those who are outside the Church it may well seem as if the Jewish people were more highly favoured than are Christians. Could this really be the case? If Almighty God held familiar and direct intercourse with the prophets and saints of old, why should He not vouchsafe the same favours to His servants now? We were to believe that the angel of the Lord spoke to Elias and bade him eat of the heavenly food which was to strengthen him for his forty days' journey to the Mount of God. Why might we not believe that angels could speak to us and we to them? Why might we not believe that there were still on earth chosen souls who need no other food than the Living Bread that comes down from Heaven? We were taught that the Lord spoke to Elias in his cave on Horeb; why should He not have spoken also to Francis on the mountain of Alvernia, and to Ignatius in the grotto of Manresa?

Thoughts such as these were suggested to me by our Latitudinarian friend, Mr. Somers. "If you believe the Scripture miracles," he used to say, "you have no choice but to believe the ecclesiastical miracles. Newman shows that plainly in his Essay on Miracles." In like manner, if we believe in the constant intercourse of God with man as related to us in the Old Testament, we must cease to have any difficulty with regard to that which is supernatural in the lives of the Saints.

I considered that the Bible might be God's way of writing history. I thought that if the account of what was going on at the present time were put on record by an inspired writer, a very different view would be presented of it. Many people and many incidents which the world ignores would be brought into prominence. Much that we think of vast importance would be little accounted of in such a narrative. As great an element of the miraculous and of the supernatural might be manifested as in the books of the Old Testament. The contents of the Old Testament do not surprise us because we have been familiar with them from childhood. I said "as great," but surely there would be a far greater element of the supernatural nowadays. The relations of God with man are so much nearer and more intimate since "the Word was made Flesh."

CHAPTER V.

Letters from Mr. de Vere. God's action through secondary agencies. The intercession of God's Saints and the one Mediator. Holy Scripture and the honour due to the Saints. A question for the Church, rather than for private judgment. The functions of the Church. Our duties towards the Church.

Doctrines not defined by the Church until definition is necessary. Many examples of the cultus of the Saints in the first centuries. Their intercession referred to in the ancient Liturgies. The Roman Liturgy. Explanation of certain prayers *for* Saints. The Notes of the Church in their plainness.

The old Cathedrals of England, and some thoughts which they suggest.

Protest of the High Church party at the time of the Gorham judgment. If the Church of England did not proclaim her faith in Baptism because she had no power of making her voice heard, she found power of voice to pronounce judgment against the Papal Supremacy. On that doctrine her members were agreed.

Authority found only in the Catholic Church. Her "Notes" easily perceived even by the unlearned.

The point really at issue. Are the difficulties greater now than they were at Pentecost?

MY mother appears to have written a letter about the essay on the veneration of Saints mentioned in the preceding chapter. To this the following letter from Mr. Aubrey de Vere is a reply.

"Currah Chase, December 13, 1852.

"I think still that you are *pretty good* in those matters—better than you think yourself in some respects—and what if worse in others?

"Let me begin with the good. You say that you see clearly that at least one objection to the cultus of the saints is illusory—that which supposes that in the Catholic system they stand *between* the Christian and his Redeemer so as to *separate*. They must then be intermediate, as the sacraments, the ministry, &c., are, that is, *as bonds* to *connect*, not as bars to *sever;* for in things Divine nothing can be indifferent. The saints are idols, or they are actually the channels and instruments through which, as through other bonds, Christ gives us His gifts and gives us Himself. St. Thomas Aquinas puts this clearly. This is so, he says, 'not because there is anything lacking in God's mercy, but that His foreordained *order* be preserved in all things'—the order, namely, by which He commonly acts through *secondary* agencies, making men the instruments to each other of His Providence in the order of *Nature;* prayers, preaching, sacraments, saints, &c., &c., in that of *grace*. You have taken in then the great Catholic idea, and that is half the battle. Nor can Bishop Hall and such writers be very great authorities to you, since it is plain that so far from having fathomed the mighty matter concerning which they wrote as confidently as if they had had half the existing Church to back them, they actually reversed the great *principle* upon which all depends, as the Dissenters do when they affirm that the doctrine of the priesthood puts a man between the Christian and his Saviour.

"Those who have not grasped the *idea* have no faculty for understanding Scripture aright on the subject. Let me give you one instance out of a hundred. How many of the 'great divines' quote, against the Catholic doctrine, the text, 'There is one Mediator between God and man, the Man Christ Jesus!' yet the very next verse might have opened their eyes: it is, 'Who gave Himself a *ransom* for all'—pointing out that the mediation here spoken of is the incommunicable one of *expiation* and *atonement*. That it *cannot* refer to the mediation of *intercession* is equally clear from the three preceding verses commanding men not to forget that to take their share in Christ's office of intercession is not only a privilege, but a duty. See 2 St. Timothy 2—5. Alas! that to understand what no Catholic child, rightly taught, could stumble at, should have been so difficult to learned men out of the fold that it was comparatively easy to attribute to nearly the whole Church of East and West an utter ignorance of the fundamental verity that Christ is our Redeemer!

"Well, but you say Holy Scripture does not *command* us to give religious honours to the saints, as it commands us to 'love one another,' &c. But this depends wholly on the *interpretation of Scripture*. It does tell us to honour God in His saints, to give honour to whom honour is due, not to speak of countless other passages alluded to in my essay, which are not more vague in their nature than the texts you refer to. The question is whether all such texts alike are to be taken in their *larger* meaning, or in some *restricted* sense. That again depends on who is to interpret Scripture—the individual or the Church. Only ask yourself seriously, Are we or are we not to hear the Church? If she has *any* function, must it not be to judge in such cases? Who can understand Holy Scripture so well as she to whom it was given, and she who has the Spirit that inspired it? Who can witness respecting antiquity so well as she who did not *succeed to* the Primitive Church, but *is that Church,* living through all the ages, in the *Eternal Present of Him in Whom she stands?* The real and sole mode of solving such questions must be the inquiry: 'Has God still a witness on earth or not; and if so, which of the claimants is that witness? Have we or have we not the means of exercising faith and obedience?' We may be strongly moved to put this question aside when we seem to ourselves to have some strong *moral* or *spiritual* intuition into the *sinfulness* of an essential Roman doctrine or practice: but that stumbling-block removed, to insist on having a perfectly clear *intellectual comprehension* of the doctrine in all its bearings—to know why a practice is expedient as well as without offence, and why it was defined in later Councils rather than in earlier, and what is the real meaning of a particular canon in a particular Council which no one pretends to be a General one (like that of Laodicea), and why early writers confessedly not always *explicit* on the Trinity were not explicit on the saints—surely all this is *utterly and fatally* to mistake the province of the individual Christian! It is *conceivable* that there should be *no Church*: but if there be one it is not *conceivable*, much less *possible*, that the individual should, while out of her fold, have that very knowledge which she was constituted to give him, if she was constituted at all. Were such the case a Church would have been needless as a teacher; and submission to her creeds or their interpretation could not possibly be an act of faith. At most it could be but an act of acquiescence, our individual *approval* of the decisions of the Church of Christ.'

"Such would be but one more form of self-deception, and private judgment under a mask. If we do not see this *clearly*, and resolve *finally* to act on that perception, a moment's reflection will show us that we are in a forest in which to us there can be no path: for of such critical objections in detail there is literally *no end*. As long as we like to read new books on all sides of all subjects we must necessarily find a fresh crop of such objections; and even if we do not read them, we know that they exist. We have then to decide whether God did or did not command the Gospel to be preached to the poor, and give them the means of knowing what is His *authentic* Word. I am not urging any one to precipitation; it may often be dangerous, as to trifle with grace or outstay the 'acceptable time' may be, and so often is, fatal. I only say that we should propose the subject of inquiry to ourselves in such a way as to admit of a possible answer, and not in one which after a thousand years of inquiry would end, like a game of cat's-cradle, where it began.

"You believe in a Church. This is an infinite mercy. It is not from 'flesh and blood,' but from grace that we are enabled even to grasp the *idea* of one. Now, then, be quite sincere with yourself, and ask yourself: 'If there be any Church, has it *any functions*, and if so *what are they;* and if I owe it any duty, what is that duty; and if I am not sure *which* is the true Church, how is that knowledge which includes all others (as when of old one decided between the claims of Simon Peter and Simon Magus), accessible *to me?*'

"I am almost doing you a wrong when I go into mere matters of detail, for in so doing I seem to sanction a false principle: but I will do so a little, *under protest*, and assuring you that this is not the way either to truth or peace.

"1. The statement of the book you speak of that certain definitions were not made till later times is, as you will observe at once, wholly irrelevant, for there is no necessary connection between the time of the practice and the time of the definition. Definitions are made by the

Church simply as occasion demands them, and commonly avoided, not sought, because the Church teaches as a mother and as far as she may, avoids the character of a mere Dogmatist. The Creed of Pope Pius, like the Athanasian Creed, was made when circumstances required it: and the doctrines of the Trinity and the Incarnation were not the less primitive because the definitions on the subject belong to the fourth and fifth centuries, not to the first century.

" 2. If any one has the least doubt as to whether the cultus of the saints arose in the twelfth century or in early times, he has only to get any book of Catholic citations from the Fathers, beg of his Protestant friend to strike his pencil through every passage of which he thinks the authenticity even doubtful, and then try how he can explain the rest. Waterworth's *Faith of Catholics* has hundreds of pages consisting of such citations only, and not from the later Fathers, but from those of the classical ages in which all the greatest Fathers lived—the ages of the first four General Councils. You will see at once what admissions have also been made on this subject by some of the more learned *Anglican* divines by turning to the chapter on the saints in Challoner's *Catholic Christian Instructed*, in which you will find much to interest you. Now, if any one is likely to know the sentiments of the first three centuries, whose records are but few, must it not be the Fathers who immediately succeeded them, and who in their works and Councils professed to retain the *traditionary* faith? If they are not to be trusted in this matter, how can they be trusted in others? If they did not know what their forefathers thought, how can we?

"3. The statement that the ancient *Liturgies* do not contain *invocations* to the saints is absolutely and wholly beside the question, for the Roman Liturgy is equally void of them. The *Liturgy* is the Mass or "Tremendous Sacrifice" of the Church, and that is offered to God only. Prayers to the saints never occur in the Liturgy, but in special Litanies, &c.

"4. But so far from its being true that, as Bishop Bull says, the *Intercessions* of the saints are not referred to, the opposite is the fact, as any one can see by referring to Waterworth, or to the work on the *Ancient Liturgies*, by Dr. Brett, the Anglican Non-juror. Prayers to God, beseeching Him to help us by the 'Intercessions' of 'Blessed Mary ever Virgin,' &c., are a prominent part of almost all of them. The form is nearly the same as that in which the references to the ministrations of the saints are now made in the Roman *Liturgy* and in all other prayers addressed to God.

"5. There are also a few *exceptional* prayers in the records of early times, *for*, not to the Blessed Virgin and the Apostles. They did not proceed from any doubts as to their salvation, and they may be understood on that principle on which we pray for things certain, as 'Thy Kingdom come,' 'Thy will be done,' not as endeavouring to move God to what He would not otherwise grant, but as expressing the consentaneousness of our will with His will, and making our prayers an instrument through which He does what He pleases to do. Apparently such prayers gradually ceased (while the other class was continued), because of two views of the saints perfectly compatible, the Church attached herself more and more to the more prominent and special one. It is also very probable that the doctrine of the saints rose into greater *clearness* as the doctrine of the Trinity did so. Those who object to the 'theory' of development, entirely forget that their counter-opinion on the subject is also but a 'theory' of their own. But the change in this instance does not necessarily involve the theory of development at all. In the meantime one thing is certain: namely, that if the prayers *for* the Blessed Virgin, the Apostles, &c., were inconsistent with the practice of *invoking* them (that is, asking them for their prayers), it would be equally inconsistent with a belief in their *intercession* for us. But *that* is a doctrine admitted by all the learned, and what proves too much proves nothing. Protestantism is always the victim of the sophism called 'false antithesis,' or imaginary opposition. If the saints did in any sense *need* our prayers for them, which is far indeed from being the case, how would such a circumstance prove that we did not need theirs? Do we not pray for those on earth whose prayers we in turn invoke?

"What is that book on the Church of which you speak? If it is small enough for you to send it over with a guard of half a dozen stamps, I will gladly read it, and do anything I can to adjudicate between him and Dr. Klee.

"But, alas, I must end as I began ... and you must not be angry with me. *These are not the points really at issue;* and if they were, every pebble in the road to Paradise would be a fresh stone of offence. The question of the Church, and the *nature* and *rule of faith*—that is all in all. By God's grace we can find God's Prophet and Apostle. The simplest can find his guide if he will: the wisest cannot, without that guide, find his way. How, for instance, could you ascertain with the certainty of faith whether my quotations from the Fathers or those of a Protestant friend gave you most of their real mind? whether the books I would recommend for study or those that he prefers are the best? But the 'Notes of the Church' are so plain that he who runs can read. Our 'point of view' is then determined: other evidence then falls into its proper *subordinate* place, helping us to *direct* and *apply* a faith which can live and act because it has a fixed outward object, as well as an inward root.

"Are you not very happy now that you have your friend the Bishop of N—— with you? Pray tell me whether he gave you a great scolding, or was well pleased with you. He might well have feared, because you *almost* touch the 'Church of Rome,' as he would perhaps call it: he might well take courage, for between 'almost' and 'altogether' the distance is *infinite*. Yet a moment can carry us across it—the moment in which we exercise faith and rise above opinion and criticism. What is hardest to man is easiest to God; and in Him is our might. Let us try to train faith through love, and shake off fear once and for ever, by learning to exult in and love every sacrifice, great and small, by which love can be proved, tried, and strengthened. Exultation is easier than resignation, and the whole is easier than half, in these matters.

" Pray write to me *soon* again. Inquirers cannot guess how much more anxious about them their Catholic friends *must be*, than their Protestant or Anglican friends (even though older and better friends) *can be*. But I will not go into this; for I greatly object to what may be called indirect invocations, as substituted for honest arguments—as when one says, 'This at least you must hold!' 'You *cannot* be so unfaithful to your own experiences,' &c. We can but put forward naked truths, and leave the task of suasion to the Spirit of God. By the way, I had not time even to glance over the MS. I sent you the other day, so pray correct all errors in it, and do not be angry with any hard sayings. It is a bad compliment to file down such. With love to 'the children.'

"Ever yours most truly and kindly,
"AUBREY DE VERE.

"P.S.—Pray remember that though letters of Manning's or others that I may send you are for yourself alone, and that in this age of 'scandals' I can trust them no further, anything that I write on theology you are at perfect liberty to show to any one who will take the trouble of reading it. If my remarks are sound, they can do no harm to any one—if unsound, the sooner they are exposed the better. Every Tractarian (one must use names, however imperfect they may be) of a manly and candid mind will perceive that what I cannot but regard as the extremely weak points or incoherencies of Puseyism, I attribute to the necessities of an impracticable *position*, not to any conscious insincerity. Others are now passing through the same process which those whom we converts most revere passed through in their turn, a little time ago. All is well as long as inquirers continue to advance, rapidly or slowly, and register the progress they make from day to day, so as to keep what they gain, and avoid the fate of Penelope's web."

Anglicans of the present day have almost forgotten the Gorham case, and the excitement which it produced. The conduct of the Bishops and the clergy who abstained from protesting against the decision that Baptismal Regeneration was in the Established Church an open question, was excused by some on the ground that the Church of England had no means of making her voice heard. How loudly that Church could make her voice heard when its members were agreed, is a fact which is commented on in the following letter:

"Currah Chase, December 29, 1852.

"I am quite unhappy to hear that you are so far from well. I am also sorry (though perhaps I ought not to be so) at what must have been a great disappointment to you, your not having been able to go to the Cathedral on Christmas Day! Now that is very kind of me, is it not, considering that these Cathedrals are in fact great Roman Catholic monuments turned against the Church that built them, and which alone knows how to *use* their long-drawn aisles ('linked sweetness long drawn out') by an opponent who never will stand on his own ground, or fight with his own weapons. However, I cannot help being sorry that you did not hear the faint echo of the ancient anthem. Pray forgive me. After all I do not know how far this regret proves that I am only an easy, good-natured, not a real, truth-telling and truth-working friend like Mr. Neve. There is something to be said on the other hand, too. The Anglican fair shadows, it is true, are to many but a delusion and an opiate dream, theological blandishments keeping people from perceiving their need of the great realities which in the Roman Catholic Church are the solemn, soul-satisfying *substance*, symbolized by ritual and ceremony. But with others, and even with the same people at a moment of higher grace, they have an opposite effect. They wear a character of unreality, and at the same moment they point to what is real. Do you remember some lines from Shakespeare which I once quoted to you, altering but a word?

> Ah me, what thing is Faith itself possessed
> If but Faith's shadows be so full of joy?

" Now, some feeling of this sort occurs to the High Churchman in the midst of all the borrowed beauty of a worship which up to a certain point has been favourable to his spiritual growth, but has become a *limit* to it, just as what is good for infancy is bad for childhood. Suddenly he asks himself, why should external Types develope aspirations which have no corresponding objects, and elicit ideas which lack a counterpart in reality? Patriotism could be but a name if we had no country; the affections but a worry and weariness if, like the raven loosed from the ark, they found nothing solid on which to alight. And what more is an altar if there be no sacrifice, or but a phantom one flatly denied by nine Englishmen out of ten, as to the nature of which even those who retain the term cannot agree, and which in the end of the discussion commonly turns out nothing more than the sacrifice of 'ourselves, our souls, and our bodies,' or else of 'alms and oblations,' or 'praise and thanksgiving'? Now, these are all excellent things. They are among the 'first principles,' and are *included* in the Roman and in all Christian worship. But these things constitute at most but a terrestrial or a figurative sacrifice; and these things are claimed equally by *all the sects that denounce the very idea of the altar and of priesthood*, and who fancy that the Sacrifice of Calvary is made of none effect if the Church on earth offers to God the same Sacrifice which her Divine Head offers ever in Heaven. Why, then, the Anglican asks, have we altars like the primitive Church, if that 'dread and tremendous, unbloody Sacrifice,' which the primitive Liturgies proclaim to be the very centre and soul of Christian worship, be wanting? What can candles, or no candles, signify to us; and may it not be very true that essential forms *become* formalities when they cease to be supported by corresponding realities? What does it matter whether the font be of wood or stone, placed at the door or in the transept, if the highest tribunal to which the Church submits asserts that it is consistent with Anglican doctrine to maintain either that infants are regenerate at the font, or that it is a soul-destroying error to believe that we are thus 'born again of water and of the Spirit'? It is now nearly three years since a document was put forth by the chief leaders of the High Church school, and signed, among others, by Dr. Pusey, Archdeacon Wilberforce, and Mr. Bennett, asserting distinctly that 'the *Church of England* will eventually be bound by the said (Gorham) sentence, unless *it* shall openly and expressly reject the erroneous doctrine sanctioned thereby,' that 'to admit the lawfulness of holding an exposition of an Article of the Creed, contradictory of the essential meaning of that Article, is in truth and fact to abandon that Article.' 'That any portion of the Church which does so abandon the essential meaning of an Article of the Creed, forfeits, not only the Catholic doctrine in that Article, but also *the office and authority to witness and teach, as a member of the Universal Church,*' and that 'by such conscious, wilful, and deliberate act such portion of the Church becomes formally *separated from the Catholic body, and can no longer assure to its members the Grace of the Sacraments and the Remission of Sins.*' Three years have nearly passed, and what has been done? Absolutely nothing. The High Church body cannot pretend to say that that sentence does not *compromise the Church of England;* for they protested against it on the very grounds that unless repudiated *by the Church of England* it must represent *its judgment,* and that to maintain the contrary was but a quibble of the lawyers, contrary to good faith, to common sense, and to the verdict of all Christendom. Neither can they say that *their protest* represents that of the Church of England, for their utmost efforts did not procure the signatures of one-fourth the number of the Anglican clergy. They tried once to get a better Court of Appeal, and the Bishop of London's suggestion, though so inadequate as to have been pronounced at the time *worthless* by the leaders of the Tractarian party, was scornfully rejected, and has never been brought forward since.... The Gorham judgment then stands — that judgment respecting which Mr. Gladstone asserted in his pamphlet, that the Church had only 'to choose between the mess of pottage and the portion of the bride.' And what has happened in the meantime? The Archbishop of Canterbury has proclaimed that Episcopacy and the Apostolic Succession are not necessary marks of the Church; and that the German bodies which possess neither are true Churches notwithstanding. Seventeen hundred clergymen of the High Church school signed a document which declared that they could not and would not admit the Queen's supremacy in spiritual matters, or matters affecting doctrine. Yet the Queen's supremacy remains just what it was, and continues to define, in matters of doctrine, that Baptismal Regeneration is an open question, and most of these signatories remain just where they were.

"The Church of England, it was urged, did not proclaim the faith on the article of Baptism only because she was deprived of the power of speaking and acting. It seemed a very sufficient answer to this to remark that her chains were chains of gold, such as even the little Free Kirk of Scotland had shaken off 'like dew-drops from the lion's mane' when a mere point of discipline was in question; that to remain in such bondage is simply to abdicate the *primary* office of the Church, that of *witnessing to the truth;* and that Christianity would never have spread beyond Judea if the clergy had not been willing, not only to live without State assistance, as the Irish clergy do now, but to live in constant peril of death, as the English and Irish Catholic clergy did during a large part of the centuries after the Reformation. But, as if to supersede all doubtful considerations, Providence itself stepped in, and permitted the Church of England to pronounce its mind more fully and unequivocally, without Convocation, than it had ever been able to do in the days of Convocation. The same mighty See which sent Augustine to be Archbishop of Canterbury or to be a martyr, like those who bleed every day in China, sent Dr. Wiseman to be Archbishop of Westminster. I will not say whether it had a right to do so or not, for that is not the question. The same Crown which decapitated Cardinal Fisher and Lord Chancellor More, because those illustrious representatives both of Church and State in England believed the novel Royal Supremacy to be an impious error, subversive of the whole organization of the Christian Church—the same Crown which in Elizabeth's reign and in Victoria's reign, appointed Bishops during *the royal pleasure*, which, by the *admission of High Churchmen*, prohibits the exercise of such discipline as is necessary to secure the sacraments from sacrilegious profanation, and imposes on the Church doctrinal decisions which are simply heresy—this same Crown was aggrieved by the so-called 'aggression.' Now I will not assume either that it had, or had not, cause of complaint, for that is not the question. I only want to point out that these apparent accidents gave rise to a circumstance the most surprising since the Reformation. In spite of its bondage, and its absence of representation, *the Church of England rose up like one man*, and with a degree of unanimity hardly ever witnessed before, which could not be hoped for in Convocation, and which would be marvellous even in a General Council, *pronounced judgment, and that in a matter of faith*. Unchallenged by the State, and not waiting for Parliament to meet, its Bishops, its clergy, its Universities proclaimed that wherever the 'unity' of the One Church may reside, it does *not* reside in the Apostolic See. From the great elder brother who, sitting in Peter's chair, has in all times of perplexed doctrine, or tyrannic oppression, fulfilled the great charge and 'strengthened his brethren,' the Anglican clergy appealed—and to *what?* To that very Royal Supremacy of which they had so lately seen the fruits, and which but a few months before had fastened the mill-stone of heresy (by the confession of High Churchmen) round the neck of their Church. No one can say that this all but universal declaration did not include doctrine. It distinctly negatived that of the *Papal Supremacy*, not to speak of all those others which are involved in that doctrine, such as the *organic unity* of the Church, the permanence of the *Apostolic authority* respecting doctrine and discipline in the Apostolic Church.

Now observe. If it has the *external* means of denying the Papal Supremacy, it must have the *external* means of denying the Gorham heresy, and asserting Baptismal Regeneration as the exclusive truth. Why then has it not done so, when, according to the High Church manifesto, *all* was at stake? Because it had not the *internal* means of doing so, viz., one mind, one will, or even a predominance of mind and will in favour of the truth, and in favour *of asserting that truth to the formal exclusion of the opposite error;* in other words, *not* because of the oppression of the State, unquestionable as that is, but because of its own internal unsoundness.

"And now the very people who signed the Tractarian manifesto, asserting the *fatal* consequences which must result if *the Church* (not a school in the Church) did not repudiate a decision which it never has repudiated, and which, after the lapse of years, has almost faded from men's remembrance, like that on the Hampden case, or the Jerusalem Bishopric, denounce as unfilial, perhaps as schismatical, the conduct of men like Manning, H. Wilberforce, Dodsworth, and James Hope, who signed the same manifesto, but who meant what they said, and had courage both to know what they meant and to act upon their convictions. These men had declared that, under given circumstances, a certain Church would be proved to possess neither a teaching authority, Church-membership, or the grace of the sacraments. Accordingly, when they had done all that they could do, and *all that has yet been done*, to make the Church of England repudiate that judgment, and found that the *all* was *nothing*, these men submitted to a Church which, by the confession of all their old friends, possesses and has ever possessed in their fulness those attributes of the Church, not to speak of others of which she claims the *exclusive* possession. And yet to act as they have done is now pronounced schismatical or wrong, even by those some of whom, before the Gorham judgment had taken place, spoke of Dr. Newman's secession as the result of God's gracious acceptance of Catholic prayers, and described him as simply labouring in 'another part of the same vineyard.'

"My dear friend, only think sincerely with respect to *the point really at issue*, and you cannot be perplexed long by statements so contradictory.

There are those who can *reckon* arguments but never *weigh* them; such persons are in danger of never seeing their way (though Divine grace may in a moment remove any difficulty), for there are innumerable arguments to be found on every side of every question. But you, by God's mercy, have been enabled all along to see that the question of the Church, and the *true authority* in faith is *all in all*. You are, therefore, close to the truth; and almost a single act of courage would enable you to close with it and be at rest. *You* never have *believed* in private judgment and never will. You have not the necessary unreality or presumptuous daring, and you have the noble instinct of loyalty. Obedience is not only intelligible, but natural to you. You have only, then, to find the true *object* for it. You know that nothing human or mortal can be that object. It can only be God's Church, as filled with His Spirit, and plainly declaring His will and His truth.

"You speak of 'your Pope' being to you what Manning is to many Catholics. If he *really is* you can have no other course than that of submitting to the one infallible guide; for it is only as representing her that Manning has the weight of a feather with any Catholic. We have confessors and directors of conscience, but in theology no guide at all except the Church. Our teachers agree upon all that she has defined as belonging to faith. If one teacher denied what another asserted in the region of faith, we should be in a position the opposite of that in which we actually stand. If her most famous Doctor denied her lightest definition, he would be excommunicated, like the Abbé Lamennais.

"Only bring the matter really to issue, and ask yourself by *whose authority* you determine your course. The Bishop of ——? Well, but how does he chance to be an *authority* to you? Because he is a Bishop? But may not the Bishop of Carolina be as right in advising all persons to follow his example and submit to Rome, as the Bishop of —— in advising the opposite course? Because he is an Anglican Bishop? That gives him no external authority over you unless you were in his diocese. Supposing you were in the diocese of Canterbury or of York, would you submit your judgment to that of those Primates rather than to that of Bishop ——? Or is it that he is your early friend? But why should your early friend be more of an *authority* than the early friend of any other person? Or because he is wise and good? Very likely he is. A Catholic may readily assume this, and I am delighted to do so; but even if this be so, you have no reason to know this except what is founded on your own judgment of wisdom and goodness. The clergyman of your own parish, or the Bishop of your own diocese, and much more that final Court of Appeal to which the whole Church of England practically submits—

these have, at first sight, a claim on you; but their authority, too, vanishes when you ask them whence it came to them. But no other individual can have any. And in obeying any one you would simply be *choosing* your *authority*, which is a contradiction in terms. As well create a Church, or first invent a religion, and then receive it as revelation.

"Do not deceive yourself. Any one, the beggar in the street, may *advise* us, and a good *suggestion* may come from the meanest. But *authority* belongs only to him whom God has plainly commissioned relatively to us, and who can show his credentials. Dr. Pusey has at least a large following and a very great name. Yet, if you said to him, 'How am I to know, except by private judgment, that all you have been telling me is true?' he could only answer, 'Because I speak in the name of the Church of England.' If you were to rejoin, 'Does not the greater part of the Church of England, and especially of her chief pastors, disown you as her interpreter; and does not the greater part of Christianity disown the Church of England; and how then, except on private judgment, can I side with a small minority?' you would find that he had come to the end of his dogmatic theology, and that nothing remained except mysticism and a purely arbitrary interpretation of the signs of the times, of which the newspaper is the calendar.

"There is no *Authority* for us except the Church; and her 'Notes' are made plain in order that the simplest may see them. The least learned cannot but see that Unity and Catholicity, where there exist many competitors, can belong but to one claimant; and that *she* cannot be to us a sure guide in religion who asserts, as the Church of England does in her 'Articles,' that every Church may fall in turn, and that General Councils may err. Only think patiently for a very little time on the point really at issue; and you will see that between a *complete* authority and *none* there is no possible compromise. We have no authority if we sit in judgment over our Authority. If the Bishop in whom you have confidence told you to submit to Rome, would he be an authority? *No.* Then how has he *authority* when urging you against this course? Why are not Manning and Newman authorities also—men who speak of that which they have tried, and who assure you that till they were Catholics they were but groping with dim eyes and feeble hands about the outer walls of Christianity?

" Let us beware of self-delusion. Let us call things by their names. Authority is authority, and friendship is friendship. Both involve duties, as do all good things. Our duty to authority is to obey it if we have found it consistently attested, and if not to find it. *In the search only may we exercise private judgment.* Our duty to our friends is to love and serve them, to honour them and abstain from judging them, nay, to hope that they *may* be high in grace under circumstances in which we possibly, with our special opportunities might not, if we were untrue to those opportunities, even be in the way of salvation. But we are not to be *servile* to our friends or even to our benefactors. In making them our masters we do a wrong to them as well as to ourselves, and deprive them of all the solid good God might ultimately have given them by our hand. Yet how great a snare is this! How it gratifies the affections, seems for the moment to give one rest and shuffle off responsibility; nay, how it tempts one to make promises, which, if unlawful, ought of course to be openly withdrawn from the first moment that we know them to have been wrongly made, and which may eventually, if we fail to do this, force us to be false to all our earliest and most sacred engagements and obligations. Be true to yourself, and you will be true to your friends. Be true to God and to His Church, and you will be true to yourself. . . .

"Good-bye, and God bless you.

"With all the good wishes of this most holy and blessed season,

"Yours most cordially,
"AUBREY DE VERE.

"P.S.—Above all things beware of irrelevances in discussion. Mark well the difference between what is really theological argument—whether sound, or fallacious argument—and theological statements which, though of high interest, and with important practical bearings, yet constitute literally no argument at all. Mere theological rhetoric and declamation are the most insidious foes to all real theology. They only draw you into a boundless and unhealthy forest, out of which escape is often difficult when you have once entered. I will give you one suggestion by which you may avoid the snare. When pressed by irrelevant arguments ask yourself, 'What would these allegations prove, relatively to the *point at issue*, whether they be true or not?' Consider only the arguments that remain after this sifting process has been gone through; and then, depend on it, you will have time enough for books of devotion and those spiritual exercises which say so much more to the soul. These last are all that we *need* when we have once found a true and authentic authority in matters of faith; but to throw ourselves exclusively even upon these, holy as they are, in order to avoid inquiry, would be but an evasion.

"On reading over my letter it seems to me very cold, dry, and hard.... However, it is sincere; and sincerity, which is so much in all things, seems to be almost all in all in what concerns souls. One should always shun all except Divine considerations in Divine things. I would not, if I could, tell you how deeply I sympathize with you. The spirit of delusion tries us most when he sees that we are escaping from him. He knows that when our faces are once fairly set in the right direction our feet are brought to the distant shore and planted on the rock, almost instantly, as if by angelic aid. The moment you bring yourself to look your opinions in the face and confess to yourself and others that you have doubts as to the Church of England, it is probable that more than half your trial may be over. Your doubts will be finally settled almost as soon as they are fairly acknowledged. I beseech you to side with all that is strongest and noblest in you and against whatever is weakest. Do not think it unfilial to inquire whether she who alone claims you with a mother's authority and a mother's love may not indeed be your mother—or disloyal to ask whether the earth still contains a real object for loyalty in the highest sense of the word.

. . . . . .

"I often wonder whether the difficulties as to entering the one Fold are greater or less now than they were when St. Peter opened the commission of the Gospel, first to the Jews and then to the Gentiles. *Now* it is difficult to believe that bodies clad in the venerable raiment they carried off with them from the Church's stores, and preaching many doctrines either hers or like hers, are but in appearance what they claim to be. *Then* it was difficult to believe that the Church of God was a thing of yesterday, without a history save that of a few persons ignominiously put to death!"

CHAPTER VI.

High Church friends. Mr. Allies' book on *St. Peter, his Name and his Office*. Ethel's opinion on the danger of a hurried inquiry. A Colonial Bishop points out the danger of any inquiry at all. *Margaret Percival*. Her uncle's advice.

A long letter from Milly. Her views. Her fears. Her desire for the restoration of the godly discipline of penance. Her appreciation of suffering, mental and physical. Description of the death she wished to die. How her wish was realized.

Archdeacon Wilberforce's Sermons *On the New Birth of Man's Nature*. Dr. Arnold's opinion of the English divines. Wrong ideas about the Sacramental system.

Charles Kingsley's novels. First visit to Oxford. Ethel's letters from Scotland. Her description of the Presbyterian service.

Extracts from Diary on religious difficulties. Letters from Mr. Aubrey de Vere. The "Church of our Baptism." Mr. Manning comes to Clifton. Interviews with him, and the effect of them.

WE had a High Church acquaintance at Clifton, Mr. Linlithgow Scott. He used to have long talks with mother on Church matters. I remember that soon after our return from Ireland he invited us to a select party of persons who were supposed "to think alike" on those subjects. Here we met Mr. Woodford, afterwards Bishop of Ely, who had already made his mark in Bristol as a preacher. He had the church of Lower Easton, then in the suburbs of Bristol.

His sermons and choral services attracted many to his church. Although he was an Anglican parson, we liked him very much. He was sympathetic and attractive through his originality and his simplicity. His sermons were decidedly striking. After we came to know him better we used to have arguments with him on the Roman question.

To Mr. Linlithgow Scott we were indebted for a perusal of Mr. Allies' book, *St. Peter, his Name and his Office*. If one of our convert friends had offered to lend my mother this work, probably the offer would not have been accepted. But Mr. Linlithgow Scott was a thoroughly good Churchman. He said that he had been surprised to find how very much there was about St. Peter in the Bible. Mr. Allies had collected all the texts and facts which bore upon that great Apostle. It really was a very fair work, and very instructive. We should be interested in it, and as members of the English Church we might at all events recognize the *Primacy* of St. Peter. When the book came I found that Mr. Linlithgow Scott had left off reading it just at the place where the demonstration of the untenableness of the Anglican position began. The leaves of that portion of the book were not cut. I took care that they should be cut before the volume was returned. Some instinct must have warned good Mr. Linlithgow Scott that it was better for his peace of mind that those pages should remain uncut. Had he read them, he might have had some scruple in placing arguments so cogent within reach of young people with inquiring minds. Unfortunately, or fortunately, that idea did not seem to enter into the heads of our elders. They were so sure of the impregnability of their religious position, they were so utterly impervious to any attacks on Anglicanism, and they were so attached to their own "incomparable Liturgy," that they failed to perceive that ours was a totally different frame of mind. Moreover, their theory was that those who had been brought up in sound Church principles were cased in armour that could withstand all attacks. They were impervious to Popery on the one side, and to Rationalism on the other. They said that only those whose training had been Evangelical became converts to Rome. Evangelicals were so fascinated when first they grasped the true idea of a visible Church, that they did not know where to stop. We had been familiar with this true idea from our childhood, and therefore we were not likely to be deluded by Popish arguments.

Ethel Vyner was more correct in her judgment. She writes:

"I only read Oswald the parts of your letter that you intended for him, for as he has not been looking or talking in a melancholy way lately of you, I thought it was well not to make him uncomfortable by telling him of all your doubts and waverings ... He is very glad to hear that Olivia is so industrious upon her picture of the seven churches, more particularly as he presumes she intends it for him in compliance with his request. I *am* glad to hear of your acquaintance with Mr. Woodford, that is, if he is not likely to follow the example of Mr. Pollen and the St. Saviour's clergy. He will doubtless supply all you find wanting in Herbert Graham, whom I have considered as a good and earnest rather than as a learned man, since his confession to me that he could not himself answer a Romanist, but knew that there were those who could. His advice may be very good for most people, but for those who *have* doubts, to tell them to believe and not examine, is almost a confession of the weakness of their cause. Nevertheless, I believe that it is Rome which would not stand the test of examination, and I do not understand what you mean by saying that 'if Rome is wrong, Anglicanism must be wrong also.' Explain this, please, in your next.

"I have not read Newman's *Anglican Difficulties*, nor do I feel myself at all prepared to read it yet, but I hope I shall some day.

"So you have already given up your resolution of the five years' examination, as you say you do not intend to *renew* it. I am sorry for this, and more especially for the reason you assign for this change of determination, *i.e.*, the possibility of conviction coming without much reading. I believe such a conviction would be nothing more than the influence of the minds of others upon yours, and that the only conviction we should be right in acting upon would be that resulting from long and patient study, which if pursued as a search for *truth* must alone end in conviction. This to a humble and religious mind would always be accompanied by an internal evidence. But if you fancy you have this beforehand, call it conviction or what you like, how do you differ at all from the hundred and one different sects, who all believed they had it, and built their systems upon it, disregarding all evidence, save that which supported their own imaginations?

"Of course our Papist friends will tell us to profit by their experience, and urge upon us the danger of delaying to submit to a system they have to themselves proved true, without going through the tedious task of examination for ourselves, but this would be nothing more than conceding to them their pretensions to infallibility and acting under personal influence.

"I do not see that the fact you mention regarding Trent raises it much in my estimation, or improves its claim to be called a General Council. Do you know exactly of what it *was* composed? If not, I will tell you in my next. I wish I could have a long talk with you. . . . Now I must say good-bye, wishing you a merry Christmas, and that the New Year may indeed bring with it blessings to you all."

The New Year found us paying a visit in a country house full of young people, where we had a gay and festive time. Milly was of the party. In our more serious moments I had the solace of telling her about our Irish visit, the books I had read, and of all that was in my mind. She was always sympathetic, even if she might not agree. She could understand that to see the comic element in grave matters was not necessarily to be un-serious and irreverent, so that I was quite at my ease in her company. I knew there was no fear of shocking her, as I did sometimes shock Oswald, and even Ethel.

Our return to Clifton was followed by an unpleasant time. The threatened visit of the Colonial Bishop came off. I remember feeling very low-spirited as I drove with him and mother to Henbury Church. A conversation was going on between them which would certainly lead to tiresome restrictions in the future, and perhaps to a cessation of intercourse with our Catholic friends. The Bishop had no hesitation in deprecating any line of conduct which savoured of disloyalty to the Church of England. How could he do otherwise? How could he encourage any inquiry into the claims of Rome? Who were we that we should not be satisfied with that which satisfied wiser and better people? Was it not the height of presumption, a manifestation of self-conceit, that we should take upon ourselves to decide that we should be better elsewhere than in the Church of England, where Providence had ordained that we should be born? At first sight the Bishop's view certainly seemed to have humility to recommend it. On the other hand, to accept and act upon his view made the practice of humility difficult, if not impossible. Some people may rest content not to trouble themselves about doctrine at all. They hear one clergyman preach a doctrine and another clergyman preach the direct contradictory of that doctrine from the same pulpit on the same day. They think, or perhaps not *thinking* at all, they act as if they thought both doctrines were equally in accordance with the mind of God. To those who do really reflect, such a view is not possible. They must make a choice. They are compelled to sit in judgment on their teachers. They must otherwise be prepared to change their beliefs to suit the parish in which they may find themselves. Consequently the position in which they are placed is not conducive to the growth of humility. It is all very well to say that this is an exaggerated statement of the case. It was a real practical difficulty to me personally, and I have reason to know that it is so still to many thoughtful Anglicans.

Poor Margaret Percival, in Miss Sewell's interesting but very provoking story, had difficulties such as these. The arguments which her uncle, the model clergyman, brings forward to solve her difficulties, could hardly, in real life, be found efficacious. The Papal Supremacy, he said truly, was the one and only point to be determined, but it could not be determined except by a person of immense learning, a learning to which no young woman could aspire. Margaret had no right to have any doubts at all. The Church of England had the Apostolic Succession, she taught the Apostles' Creed, *and* she appealed to Scripture. Dissenters appealed to Scripture, but rejected both the Creed and Episcopacy. Rome possessed both the Creed and Episcopacy, but she forbade you to test her doctrines by Scripture. In the Church of England alone was safety. She possessed both the Apostolic Succession and the Creed, and she required you to believe nothing that was not contained in Scripture. To doubt the word of the Church of England was an act of the gravest disloyalty and presumption. If her ministers taught contrary doctrines, that was not her fault, but their fault. Her children had their Bible and their Prayer Book. The real teaching of their Church was quite plain and it was not to be mistaken.

Miss Sewell's clergyman did not see that acceptance of articles of faith on authority and acceptance through our private judgment on Scripture are incompatible. No one can receive any doctrine on both motives at once, which is what he asserts to be the prerogative of members of the Church of England.

Why Anglicans felt so sure that all their own doctrines are contained in Scripture and that those which they are pleased to call the Romish corruptions are not therein contained, I never could understand. No doctrine appeared to me to be more plainly taught in Scripture than that of the Supremacy of St. Peter, unless it be the Catholic doctrines of the Holy Eucharist, and of the place of Mary the Mother of God in the Kingdom of her Divine Son. Yet these we were told are corruptions and cannot be found in Scripture. "What am I to do if I find them there? May I not believe them?" I have asked. I was told, "No, such a discovery can only be made by one who has a perverse spirit, and much self-conceit. Bull and Beveridge, Barrow and Stillingfleet, never found such doctrines in Scripture and therefore they cannot be there."

I did not mean to imply that my own or anybody's private interpretation of Scripture ought to be a reason for believing a doctrine. It only seemed to me that those who appeal so confidently to Scripture should allow others an equal right to do so.

But this is a digression. I must go back to our friend, the Colonial Bishop. I fancy that what he said was very much what Margaret Percival's uncle said. Whatever he said had a great effect upon my mother. She became for the time being very Protestant. In this disposition she was encouraged by the fuss which the newspapers were making about the *Madiai* case.

The Bishop was not wholly responsible for the depression I experienced during that function at Henbury. It proved to be partly physical and to be accounted for by the imminence of a severe attack of measles. This illness put a stop to talking, reading, and all active occupation for some time. How miserable I was both in mind and body! When I was at last well enough to write, I poured forth my whole soul to Milly. She appears to have thought the communication very interesting. She sent the following reply:

"February, 1853.

"I feel overwhelmed: there is so much I want to say and must say, come what will of this letter as to age. As to length, I feel I could without much difficulty, make it like the sermon of a certain minister of the Kirk who had seven parts, divided each into fifteen heads, each head with about six improvements; so many remarks could I make on every point of your letter. Dearest, I never had a letter from you which I loved so much. How I longed to read it when it arrived, just as I was rushing into the carriage to start for church! How virtuous I was and wouldn't read it till after the service, lest I should be unable to give heed to Mr. Robbins' exhortations, and oh! how I did read and delight in it as I rumbled and jolted home over ruts and stones, getting much shaken, but struggling through my letter in spite of all. . . . I can't tell you the happiness and comfort it is to me that you should write to me as you do now about your thoughts and feelings. I had been longing to know what you were about mentally, by this time. How often I think of our last New Year's eve and how we talked during those few precious minutes while the rest were dancing. I sometimes wish I were more like you, more anxious and restless in my search after truth, for I don't think I have ever troubled myself very much about my belief, on important points at least; but perhaps it is better for me not to have done so, for I don't think my mind is strong enough to bear much, safely, in the way of various arguments. This, however, I don't ascribe to the weakness or badness of my belief, but to *my* weakness and badness *in* it. I hope you won't think I *ought* to question my belief in our Church. I don't think you will, for I know, with you, it is as you say that you *cannot*, not that you *will* not be satisfied without inquiring. Oh! how earnestly I do long that you may be led into the right way, wherever it is. I don't think you would be angry at what I do ask for you, for though, as you know, I can't help feeling sure—as sure as we poor ignorant things can be—that our Church has the right faith, and consequently that in so far as others differ from her, they are, so far, wrong, yet I never ask unconditionally, that you may be kept in this branch of the Church Catholic (though I do trust, oh! how earnestly, that you may), but rather that to the truth, wherever it is, you may be guided. One thing I feel sure of, that even though we be to a degree divided by these sad, sad barriers of discord and schism, the separation can only to a great degree be outward; for there are things, the highest, deepest of all, on which we are still one and shall be ever I trust, whatever you may come to, my own darling. And then at times I am tempted to think that these divisions must be nothing *really*, only shadows as it were, which confuse our dim eyes and *are not* before the clear vision of our one Lord, and that they are of importance only so far as they are sinful in raising bitter feelings in us, one towards another. And yet I do not think I really believe this, I don't think it can be true. There is so much said about the Church and its reality and visibility, that it *must* be important to what form we belong. There must be right in one, and wrong in others. Yet when we go to seek that one right one, there seems to be so little to guide us, such conflicting beliefs, such various evidence, good men all teaching differently, and the Church—oh! *how* shall we be certain what is her voice and what she says? So at times I feel almost despairing, and then the only thing is to turn to practice and give up speculating. 'If any man will do His will, he shall know of the doctrine.' But this I don't think my darling's thoughtful, searching mind will let her do, *without* inquiring also. It is a trial appointed to some which is not given to others, to be unsatisfied and unable to rest till they have inquired into the grounds of their belief. Only, dearest, don't be anxious, don't be in a hurry to leave us. Think of Dr. Pusey's speech at the Union. (Do you remember it?) Oh, dear! it *would* be a sad parting to me, though my love seems to grow more and more as I think of the chance of it even. I don't like to think of its possibly occurring, though I should feel it less than many others, such as Mama and Sybella would. I wish I could talk to you. I hate only writing about this. I can't say a bit what I feel, and what I do say sounds not at all like what I mean. . . . But perhaps you know what I feel better than I can tell you. How I like to think you believe I can sympathize with you!

"I wish I could read those sermons of Archdeacon Wilberforce's *On the New Birth*. You know that subject of Baptism is always a little difficulty with me, and I never yet had a book which entirely freed me from doubts, though now I have but few. I could not bear the idea of giving up High Church doctrines, of finding them unwarranted. They are to me so full of help and comfort. I should lose so very much by having only the meagre faith which I can't help feeling Low Churchmen have.

"I am beginning to like Lent better than I did, now that I am fairly in the midst of it. And as to abstinence, the daily consumption by me of mutton chops and other luxuries excludes the very idea of such a thing, alas! We enjoyed Ash Wednesday, inasmuch as we walked down to Durnley in a snow-storm to the church there. We had a very good service, done, I mean, *con amore*, and a sermon on fasting. Surely it is only *sham* Churchmen who talk of restoring the godly discipline of penance without really wishing it. I believe the true ones do wish it. *I* do. I wonder if I should be bad enough to be excommunicated and go to church in a sheet! Rather cold just now, but I dare say such outward humiliations would tend to make one feel more ashamed and sorry, if done in a right spirit. Only I can't help having doubts if such penances are according to the spirit of the New Testament, or do not rather pass away with Jewish rites. I wish I could think otherwise, for I should so like their revival, if I could but be persuaded that they are right...

"What you said about your dread of bodily pain and weakness rather surprised me. I should not have fancied you would have had it. I wish I could feel about *mental* suffering as you do. It is just this which I dread with an intense cowardly fear. I have no noble sense of the greatness and blessedness of such trials, as prolonged anxiety, loss of friends, the daily suffering of the sorrows or faults of others. Or rather though I *do* see such suffering may be and is great and blessed, if rightly borne, yet I would do anything to avoid having to bear it. I shrink from the prospect of such being one day my lot, and this makes me long to be near death, to be pretty sure of dying *soon*. I feel that would make me so happy. And yet there are times when I feel, like you, the extreme interest of life, its beauty and greatness; but this is more as connected with others (such as you especially), than with my own part in it. I seem myself to be so simply a clod of earth, and as though my only chance of being anything better were to get away altogether from eating, drinking, and fussing about self.

"Your thoughts about death interested me. I can't feel though that I should like at all a sudden death, for several reasons. Were I given my choice, I should choose that it should come very gradually, that I might have plenty of time to look at it, consider it, and prepare calmly for it. It is something so wonderful. At times it seems rather horrible and frightful, merely, I believe, from dwelling only or chiefly on its mortal and earthly effects; or from seeing it represented in a revolting and wicked way in books. But more frequently, my ideas of it are rather beautiful, though confused, and of course it is always awful. I fancy that when quite close to it the more earthly feelings will lose their sway, with the gradual failing of the bodily powers; that is one reason why I want rather a slow dying, so that I may have time to become gradually spiritual before I lose all connection with body. It is strange that, considering we are only living *to die*, we should think so little generally of death, and be so startled when it comes anyhow suddenly before us, as if *we* had personally nothing in the world to do with it, instead of its being ever awaiting us silently, 'the shadow with the keys,' such a real thing, although a shadow.

"I must now bring this long letter to a close, but I must just tell you, that mama had a nice letter from Mr. Somers the other day, in which he said he had been having an argument with you, and you seemed quite up in all the Roman Catholic arguments. Of course you are! Now good-bye.

"Your ever fond,
"MILLY."

In reading this letter, well-nigh forty years after it was written, I like to think how entirely Milly's desires for death were realized. She had plenty of time to look at it and prepare for its approach. How gladly she welcomed it! How patiently she bore the pain and weariness of her long illness! To her was given the grace to die within half an hour of receiving the Holy Viaticum, on the morning of that blessed day on which the Church celebrates our Lord's Presentation in the Temple. Truly might she say with holy Simeon, "*Now* dost Thou dismiss Thy servant, O Lord, in peace. For mine eyes have seen Thy salvation."

When in the February of 1853, she wrote her fears and anxiety about me, and expressed a dread of the barrier difference of religion might possibly raise between us, how little did either of us imagine that she was to be the first to find her way into the One True Fold!

The sermons referred to by Milly in the preceding letter, *On the New Birth of Man's Nature*, I had found very instructive. Since I studied Archdeacon Wilberforce's works, and thought about all that the doctrine of the Incarnation involved, the poverty of the Protestant system, as it was ordinarily taught, came before me very forcibly. Protestants dwelt on the doctrine of the Atonement to the exclusion of every other doctrine. The Death of our Lord as having effected our redemption, was insisted on, as though nothing remained for us to do. His Life as it is the model for our imitation, the lessons to be learnt from the Annunciation, the Nativity, the Presentation, the Flight into Egypt, the Hidden Life at Nazareth, were not put before us. There was an incompleteness and a want of harmony, even in the more advanced of the High Church writers, which I did not find in Archdeacon Wilberforce. He went deeper down, and taught us to regard sacraments, not as arbitrary rites, but as "an extension of the Incarnation," the means by which we became partakers of the Divine Nature. Jesus Christ did not take our flesh merely to die, and through His Death to effect our redemption. Our human nature was to be renewed and sanctified. His Sacred Humanity was the principle by which this renewal and sanctification was to be effected. The grace given through sacraments is the means by which His Human Nature acts on ours, and by which we are united to Him. In the sermon on *The Sacramental System*, Robert Wilberforce maintains, that to deny the efficacy of Baptism is a virtual denial of the Incarnation and of the necessity of the mediation of Christ. Such a denial implies that there exists a principle in human nature which is capable of raising and purifying it, without the necessity of supernatural assistance. Rationalism supposes that the cultivation of the natural powers and faculties of man will suffice for his renovation, whereas the Church teaches that it is through the introduction of a higher influence, the union of the Divine with the Human in the Person of Christ our Lord, that the race is to be raised and ennobled. Each member of the human race is bound to the Divine Head of that race by the Holy Sacraments, and becomes as truly a child of the Second Adam through his new birth in Baptism, as he is a child of the first Adam through his birth in the natural order.

I have thought that in Protestant countries like England, it is the utter ignorance of these relations of God with man, as manifested in the sacramental system of the Church, which has made many of the more intellectual and thinking of the minds amongst us sceptics. The religion which they reject is not in reality the religion of Jesus Christ. It is something which has usurped its place, a mass of incongruities and falsehoods. Could they but have had the teaching of the Catholic Church, such as it really is, put before them in its harmony and coherence, they would have seen its adaptation to all the needs of the soul; its capability of satisfying the highest, as well as the lowest, of human intelligences. They would have gladly recognized it as the truth for which they had been craving.

"If any man be in Christ, he is a new creature." How many unsatisfactory Low Church sermons have I heard on that text! Archdeacon Wilberforce showed us that this renewal was not effected by any mere feeling of our own, by any inward conviction that we were "in Christ," as Mr. Robbins taught, but by a real union with His Sacred Humanity effected by the Sacrament of Baptism, and preserved through the partaking of His Flesh and Blood in the Holy Eucharist. If it were objected that it was quite incredible that such a change could be brought about by Baptism, Wilberforce answered that it was not more wonderful than that certain mental qualities should be transmitted from father to son in the natural order. Again, as "that common nature which we inherit from our original parent is transmitted through the continuity of the flesh, it was not inconsistent with the order of the Divine economy, that our Lord's Flesh and Blood mysteriously and supernaturally communicated, should be the principle of a higher life to His brethren."[1]

I think Mr. Woodford told us he considered Robert Isaac Wilberforce the greatest theologian the Church of England possessed. His were great works.

Speaking of the English divines in general, Dr. Arnold asked, "Why is it that there are so few great works on theology, compared with any other subject? Is it that all other books on the subject appear insignificant by the side of the Scriptures? There appears to me in all the English divines a want of believing or disbelieving anything because it is true or false. It is a question which does not seem to occur to them." This at all events could not be said of Archdeacon Wilberforce.

In this sweeping condemnation of English divines, Dr. Arnold excepted Butler (the one amongst them whose writings I much studied) and Hooker. The latter was however a puzzle to him. "I long to see something," he writes, "which should solve what is to me the great problem of Hooker's mind. He is the only man that I know, who, holding with his whole mind and soul the idea of the eternal distinction between moral and positive laws, holds with it the love for a priestly and ceremonial religion, such as appears in the Fifth Book" (of the *Ecclesiastical Polity*). After thus excepting Hooker and Butler,

[1] *Doctrine of the Holy Eucharist*, p. 100.

Dr. Arnold goes on to say of the English divines, "Their language is delightful to my taste, but I cannot find in any one of them a really great man. I admire Taylor's genius, but yet how little was he capable of handling worthily any great question. And as to interpreters of Scripture, I never yet found one of them who was above mediocrity. I cannot call it a learning worth anything, to be very familiar with writers of this stamp, when they have no facts to communicate, for of course even an ordinary man may then be worth reading."

These opinions of Dr. Arnold's I wrote out in one of my juvenile note-books and added at the same time the following reflections of my own. "I can *understand* the dislike and contempt with which Dr. Arnold regards High Church principles, and if, as it seems to me, he takes an erroneous view of the real tendency of those principles, may it not have been more the fault of those who advocated them than his own? His objection to the sacramental system is, that it places the Church in Christ's office as Mediator between God and man, and puts outward rites in place of the one Sacrifice once offered.

"Now I find that Archdeacon Wilberforce raises a somewhat similar objection to Dr. Arnold's own views. The Anti-Sacramental system, Wilberforce says, substitutes for the work of Christ the actions of the individual mind. Proclaiming that our redemption from sin *has been* effected by the Death of Christ, it leaves with the individual the power of appropriating to himself the benefits of that redemption. Its tendency is to overlook the present mediation of Christ and to forget that the gifts of grace are bestowed through the communication of His Human Nature in the means which He has appointed. It treats the Sacraments lightly because it fails to recognize their real character. Thus Baptism and Holy Communion are represented as forms to which the disposition of the receiver can alone give value: not, the one as the way by which we become partakers of the Divine Nature by being engrafted into the Body of Christ, so that it may be called a new Birth—the nature of the Second Adam becoming ours as truly as by our natural birth the nature of the First Adam was transmitted to us: nor, the other (the Blessed Eucharist) as the nourishment of this new nature, the means by which that Body which was slain and that Blood which was shed for us should become indeed our food. The real objection to this estimate of the Sacraments arises from a forgetfulness that Christ being the 'One Mediator between God and man' Who unites these two natures, 'must be approached through that Manhood whereby He allies Himself to our race,' and from a wish 'for such communing with the Spirit of the Universe as may be maintained by each individual in the separate temple of the heart.' Not that there is any conscious design of rejecting Christ. He is present to the thoughts, and no doubt in this way is supposed to be the means of access to the Father. 'But this is to forget,' Archdeacon Wilberforce declares, 'that the principle of His mediation is not that His Man's nature is the ultimate object of worship, but that it is the sole road of approach to His Godhead. And when the Church system is opposed to that of Rationalism, the actions of His Manhood are in reality opposed to those of our own spirits. The channel of union which has been provided through grace is opposed to that which existed by nature. What is needed, therefore, is some real agency on His part whereby this merciful intervention may be effected. Adam is not merely an object to men's thoughts like the angels of God: he is bound to his descendants by the true but unknown tie of paternity: if Christ our Mediator be the Second Adam, there must be as real an influence, by which all His members must hold to *His* Man's nature. And if this union is not brought about as Rationalists suppose, through those means which had their existence through Creation, it must be effected through *media* which are beside and foreign to nature. That spiritual power whereby His Humanity becomes the seminal principle of His Body mystical, must act through such supernatural agency as it pleases Him to adopt. So that the ancient writers, as Bishop Taylor says, speak of the Blessed Sacrament as *the extension of the Incarnation*. . . . Therefore, to maintain that the outward means of grace whereby we are united to the Manhood of Christ, are not less necessary than those emotions of our own which have their seat within, is not to put the Church in the stead of Christ, but to protest against men's putting themselves in the place of their Redeemer. To speak of inward seriousness as necessary, is only to testify the truth of each man's separate responsibility; but to speak of it as superseding outward means, is to do away with the office of the One Mediator.'[1]

"Surely if these principles were rightly *understood*, there would no longer exist the same prejudice against the sacramental system in the minds of thoughtful and earnest men. But that system is regarded by too many as something which supersedes and overlooks the mediation of the Second Person of the Blessed Trinity, and not as the system which He Himself instituted in order that men might become partakers of the Divine Nature. Those who have believed in it and acted on their belief know how untrue is the idea that it must draw away their thoughts from Jesus Christ. They feel that without this sacramental union the passages in the New Testament which speak of Christ dwelling in them and they in Him, would have no meaning for them, that they would lose the one great proof of His love to them individually. His presence would be no longer a conscious reality, Himself no more their strength, their support, their life.

[1] Wilberforce, *On the Doctrine of the Incarnation.*

"Yet I am not surprised that those to whom these doctrines are a novelty should experience great difficulty in comprehending them, and should denounce them as unscriptural. Their language teaches me how entirely we may misjudge the opinions of others, and how very much we should guard against prejudice and a one-sided view. That there are difficulties in the sacramental system few know better than myself. It seems also to involve consequences which I hesitate to admit. Undoubtedly it confers responsibilities from which all who are not really in earnest must shrink.

"It has been well remarked that the belief in Sacraments as conveying supernatural gifts tends to turn men's minds so completely to their Almighty Author, that in times of doubt they afford a stable comfort without in times of steadfastness ministering to pride. 'Their advantage in time of doubt is, that their ground is *God's promise*, and not man's confidence: so that they supply some fixed external standing-place in those hours of dejection, when men's own feelings are in most need of succour. In such seasons comfort must come from without, for how are inward doubts to be solved by the mind, whose very complaint is doubtfulness? In such moments, then, how inestimable that gift, whereby our God assures us of His favour and goodness towards us!'"

This somewhat lengthy extract from my note-book shows something of what I learnt from R. Wilberforce's works *On the Incarnation* and *On the New Birth of Man's Nature*. His treatise *On the Holy Eucharist*, which appeared in 1853, taught me a good deal more.

I shall always feel grateful to Oswald for having encouraged us to study these books. He said that Robert Isaac Wilberforce had done as much as any single man could do. He had put the whole controversy on the deepest grounds. Those who really grasped his argument, must, Oswald thought, agree with him.

I made notes in my diary this summer, of counsels given to us by Oswald with regard to our reading. He was very urgent that we should study some standard author such as Butler, and put into our own language the principles which we had learned from him. We were to give our whole attention to what we read, and to make notes if possible, otherwise our reading would leave little more than an impression. If we read in this way for a certain time every day, the listlessness and frivolity to which we were so much inclined would be kept in check, and we should be doing something to prevent our minds from sinking to the level commonly found in the world!

I think we profited by these wise counsels, and made it a rule to do some serious reading every day.

Under the head of "serious reading" could

hardly be placed the novels of Charles Kingsley. These novels were making a sensation at that time, and they possessed a great fascination for us. *Alton Locke* had been published some years before. It is associated in my mind with pleasant evenings at Bath, when Mr. Burton read it aloud to us. *Yeast* we delighted in still more, but *Hypatia* was the one which interested me by far the most. In looking through it now I am at a loss to see how I could ever have tolerated this book. I not only tolerated, but was intensely absorbed in it. We began the reading of it aloud, but my mother did not think it was a book we ought to read. We put it aside, and did not go on with it till we went to stay with my aunt. She insisted on our reading *Hypatia*. She was very enthusiastic about Mr. Kingsley's writings, in spite of his not being quite "orthodox." There was a freshness and an originality about them which appealed to a mind like hers—a mind which retained the characteristics of youth long after the season of youth had passed. Her interest in Philammon and Hypatia, in Synesius and Raphael Aben Ezra was as intense as if they had been living persons of the present time. In fancy she was dwelling in the Alexandria of St. Cyril's day, and taking part in its theological and philosophical discussions. As matter of fact she was inhabiting a quiet country home in the England of the nineteenth century, where her occupations consisted of expounding Scripture at the parish school, and carrying cans of broken meat and pudding to the poor of Lystone. *Hypatia* is much associated in my mind with walks through this village. I used to read it on my way when my aunt deputed me to take her place in giving religious instruction to the school-children, and in visiting for the same purpose the old or infirm. It was hardly the best preparation for such work—work for which I felt myself most unfitted. It was, however, useless to be humble and plead inefficiency. My aunt insisted on our expounding as she did. Olivia utterly refused to do so, and took with her Jowett's *Christian Visitor* or Barnes's *Notes* on these occasions. It *was* rather hard, when I was feeling much bewildered by Kingsley's perplexing theology to be ordered to spend half an hour in explaining Christian doctrine to old William Brown. On one occasion Mrs. Wrangham informed me that she was going through the Creed with this worthy man, and I was to continue the explanation of it from where she had left off. I was obliged to represent that till I myself had clearer ideas with regard to the meaning of the words, "I believe in the Holy Catholic Church," it would be quite hopeless for me to undertake to enlighten the aged Mr. Brown!

I had come to the chapter where Raphael Aben Ezra exclaims, "I am sick of syllogisms, and probabilities, and *pros* and *contras*. What do I care if, on weighing both sides, the nineteen pounds' weight of questionable arguments against, are overbalanced by the twenty pounds' weight of equally questionable arguments for? Do you not see that my belief of the victorious proposition will be proportioned to the one overbalancing pound only, while the whole other nineteen will go for nothing? . . . No, I want a faith past arguments: one which, whether I can prove it or not to the satisfaction of the lawyers, I believe to my own satisfaction, and act on it as undoubtingly and unreasoningly as I do upon my own personal identity. I don't want to possess a faith. I want a faith which will possess me."

A faith past arguments—a conviction that could not be shaken—a certainty that had for its warrant the word of One Who cannot deceive or be deceived—this was what I too was longing for—the faith of the great Saint and Doctor of the Church, Augustine, from whom eventually Aben Ezra is represented as receiving the grace of Holy Baptism. I did not want the modern imitation of that faith which is portrayed by the Rector of Eversley.

As I said before, it is difficult for me now to comprehend the attraction which Mr. Kingsley's works certainly had for us. It was an attraction felt by many. His biography shows that he exercised an immense influence over a vast number of minds. He despised conventionalities. He hated what he considered shams. He was thoroughly in earnest according to his lights, and I do not think he ever had a suspicion that

Catholicism could be the religion by which Almighty God willed that the souls of English men and women should be saved, although he seems to allow that for Italians it might be a Divine institution.

During our visit to Lystone this June we went to the Commemoration at Oxford and saw that city for the first time. It fascinated me much. It was unlike any place I had ever seen, and possessed something of the charm which attaches to the old cities of Italy. And there were the associations of our own times which made it dear to me. Here Newman had lived. Here was the church where he had preached his wonderful sermons. Here those Tracts were written which were still influencing so many minds. The Oxford Tracts and the Oxford Movement belonged in 1853 to the immediate past only.

I wrote my impressions to Ethel, who was paying a visit in the west of Scotland. She in return sends me her experiences of that country and of the religion by law established there.

"June 17, 1853.

"You do not know how much I enjoyed your long letter up here in the wilds. What a delightful time you must have had at Oxford! I am very glad you met Oswald there. Here we have plenty of 'creature comforts,' *i.e.*, fresh air and scenery, to enjoy, but as yet we have not seen a person to speak to, not even the 'minister,' who we thought of course would call on his parishioners without delay. I suppose he is afraid of an attack from 'the champion,' whose fame has doubtless reached him.

"I send you a sketch of the view we have from our drawing-room window. The fearful specimen of ecclesiastical architecture that figures in the foreground is the Presbyterian Church, which is within a few yards of us. There is another within a quarter of a mile—a Free Church. *Where* the congregations come from I cannot imagine, as we have not hitherto been able to discover a village anywhere, unless three very small cottages can be dignified with the name. We are told that when the congregation is very small the minister, instead of a sermon, makes a short address to those who are *absent*, saying how sorry he is not to see more at church, and how much he hopes it will not be the case next Sunday, &c., and dismisses those who *are* there without any comment. Singing they have when there are any singers, and at other times he reads what ought to be sung. The great disadvantage of this place is being so far from an Episcopal Church. There is a clergyman at Oban who has service in a room above a grocer's shop, but that is eight miles off, and I do not expect ever to be able to get there on Sunday. Last Sunday we were in Oban, so we attended it, and the Sunday before we were at Ardrishaig, where there is a perfect little church attached to the Bishop of Argyle's house, and the service is beautifully performed.

"I ought to tell you something about our journey here. You know York, I think, so I need not expatiate on the beauty of the Minster; it fully came up to my expectations. From York we went to Edinburgh, which I liked immensely; there is so much to interest one in the buildings and antiquities. Roslin is delightful, and Holyrood, though it makes one very melancholy tracing the scenes of poor Mary's misfortunes. From Oban we went to Dunstaffnage, where the early Scottish kings found their last earthly resting-places, I believe, *before* Iona was made the royal burial-place. We have still in view a visit to Iona and Staffa, which will be the most interesting of all, and then I am afraid we shall have seen all the lions of the neighbourhood.

"We are within ten minutes' walk of a loch, and are surrounded by hills. What I do not fancy is being so completely cut off from all society, as I anticipate we shall be all the summer. K―― and L―― rather rejoice in it, as he is quite happy with his fishing, and she with looking after domestic arrangements, but these, you will agree, are very unproductive sources from which to draw ideas."

Ten days later Ethel writes again:

"June 27, 1853.

"Your letter was most acceptable and amusing—a great relief to a very dismal Sunday evening, for the letters here always arrive in the evenings.

"I am sorry I cannot furnish you with a copy of your interpretation of the *Ancient Mariner*, the valuable manuscript being carefully locked up at my home. I dare say you recollect that the hero was N——, who with his 'cross-bow,' *i.e.*, 'private judgment,' shot the albatross, *i.e.*, 'destroyed faith,' and the explanation you gave of the terrible consequences which followed to him and his shipmates when they justified the act,

> 'Twas right, said they, such birds to slay,
> That bring the fog and mist,

and that it ended in N—— being safely landed on the shores of Rome. It might have been rather wicked but not worse, I think, than many things you say and write!

"You do not seem to have a very correct idea of the Presbyterian Church when you associate it with Anglican forms, to which I am quite as much attached as ever. I will just give you an account of last Sunday, and I am sure you will not accuse me of attending Presbyterian meetings from any liking to them. They do not occur at any of our church hours, and we hold our own service first, merely attending these because we were told that we should be considered heathens if not seen at church, so we thought it might be setting a bad example if we absented ourselves. At twelve o'clock the bell rings for about a minute, and the Gaelic congregation previously assembled about the church go in.

"Before the service began the minister came out twice and looked round to see if any more were coming, and when satisfied with the number commenced. Of course we did not attend that service. About half-past one the bell gives a few more tingles, when the Gaelic audience are expected to depart and the English to come in. Not being prepared for so very short a summons, I missed the first Psalm, and when I went in all the congregation were standing, the minister holding forth what I, at first, thought was only an exhortation, but afterwards found was a prayer, which lasted about a quarter of an hour. He then invited us to a meditation on the first Psalm (which was the sermon), and it lasted about half an hour; at the end he told us he had 'got no more.' Then followed another long extempore prayer, all the people standing as before, which concluded with the Lord's Prayer. Then they sat down, and the minister proposed to sing a 'paraphrase,' which he read all through, and gave an *imploring* look at us, as if to say, 'Do pray sing,' and he sat down. An exceedingly melancholy man, who had been heard to sigh deeply several times, got up, and with a very weak, cracked voice sang nearly through the first two verses before any one supported him at all. It was quite impossible for us to take the minister's hint, as we neither had the words or knew the tune, and it was extremely difficult to look grave during the performance. After this we were dismissed, and I certainly never *wish* again to attend such a meeting. It is lamentable to see to what a length the spirit of opposition has carried these people, and even more lamentable to think that such is the Church of the land established by an English sovereign. I miss an English church more than anything here, and never can look forward to a Sunday with pleasure."

"July 9, 1853.

"We have been in Scotland now six weeks without having any society whatever. Can you fancy that state of things? I sometimes feel very much inclined to envy you, meeting so many interesting people, for you generally have a *hero* in every letter. They never come across *my* path. I quite agree in Mr. B——'s view; it always seems to me impossible for any but Papists to find out that the Church ever had better days, or days so good as the present, a conclusion which has been much confirmed since the perusal of Socrates' *Ecclesiastical History*, for one is naturally willing to believe that the *early* ages must have been the most perfect, and it does not appear that Christians were at all more united in his days than they are at present, and that there was even a remnant left seems little less than a miracle.

"What are you, Minima? You don't approve of High Church or *sound* men. I suppose you are not quite a Latitudinarian, are you?"

No, I was not a Latitudinarian, not at least by conviction, however much the worst part of me may have been attracted in that direction. Perhaps Ethel's question as to what I was might have been answered in Tennyson's words:

> An infant crying in the night,
> An infant crying for the light.

From a little diary I wrote at intervals this summer, the following extracts are taken, written at Lystone, where we were seeing a good deal of Mr. Dean:

"*June*, 1853.—We had a long conversation with Mr. Dean, discussing our difficulties, but arriving at no conclusion. A talk with him on religion generally makes me very unhappy, although I feel certain he will understand and sympathize in the perplexities which distract me. This can't be said of most of the people with whom I associate. Inclination leads him to remain where he is, reason indicates a different course. He says he has long ago left off trusting to reason in these matters! Perhaps he talks on these subjects in a light manner. I know he does not feel lightly. I wonder if he will ever be a Catholic. He will never be settled till he is a

Catholic—of that I am sure. At present he doubts whether the Papal Supremacy can be proved historically, and whether to accept it you must not admit the theory of development.

"Mr. Allies, Mr. Dean says, is one of the closest arguers of the day, and in his last work he has brought together all the Scripture proofs for the Supremacy and has arranged and commented on them so as to leave no doubt to any impartial person that the Supremacy is clearly contained in Scripture. But if this is the case, why does it appear to have been imperfectly apprehended by those who lived with the Apostles? Why are there passages in their writings which seem to contradict the idea? These are difficulties: that there are some and perhaps more difficulties if we reject the Supremacy is also true, but these must be examined lest we should receive as Divine that which is only human.

"My difficulty is that I cannot reconcile the Catholic doctrines and principles I have believed for so long, with those of the Church of England. I must either abandon them (which I *can't* do) or carry them to their legitimate conclusion, *or* continue to hold them without being faithful to them. None of these three courses is agreeable to me: I won't be in a hurry about deciding which to pursue. I only hope I am not running the risk of becoming indifferent or getting into an unreal state of mind.

"The Roman Catholic religion is much more suited to my spiritual wants than is the Anglican, and that seems an argument for its truth. When the conviction that Catholicism was true first took possession of my mind, it appeared like a bright light illuminating the darkness. I welcomed it as the satisfaction for which my soul was craving. Catholicism seemed so harmonious, such a contrast to the discordant doctrines that we were in the habit of hearing. It was unlike any other system of religion. Apparent contradictions, when more closely examined, vanished. Intellectual difficulties which had perplexed me for a time were removed. Hardly a doubt was left in my mind that Catholicism was God's revelation to man. Catholicism was the inheritance of which we had been deprived. Why should I hesitate to embrace it? Would not one strong effort of the will put me in possession of the truth, and silence doubt for ever? May God forgive me if I was wrong in hesitating, and if unworthy motives were the cause of my hesitation. I do not think they were. I might well distrust my own judgment. I was so inexperienced and so imperfectly informed. Was it not right to test the strength of these convictions before acting on them?

"Several months passed. My perplexity did not lessen. I could not pretend to take an interest in English Church matters. Discussions on these subjects appeared to me very tedious and dreary. I felt less good, less in earnest than I had been. The dreadful idea that I might be trifling with grace pursued me. This state of things is still going on. How long is it to continue?"

Various good resolutions followed. I write that Clifton seemed flat and dreary when we returned there that July. Mr. Woodford preached on the feast of St. James, taking for his text those words of the two Apostles, "We are able." I applied to myself the concluding words of his discourse—"A strong will and a sure confidence, these will lead you through the dark waters to the haven where you would be." That haven to me was Rome. Yet I wrote in my diary shortly afterwards: "I don't know whether the certainty that the Roman Church is true would bring me greater happiness or misery. There is the impossibility almost of acting against my relations, the fear of ridicule and contempt, the great submission of will required if I join the Church, on one side. On the other there is the peace and rest which those who do submit to the Church never fail to obtain, the joy of obedience to God's will, the help and guidance afforded to the soul in its battle with the world, the flesh, and the devil, and in one word the sacraments of Jesus Christ."

. . . . . .

The following letter may find its place here, from Mr. Aubrey de Vere to my mother.

"25, Chapel Street, Grosvenor Square,
"August 2, 1853.

"It seems to me ever so long since I have heard from you or of you, and I want very much to know how you are all getting on: so pray open that writing-desk in my favour at which you used sometimes to sit so indefatigably at Currah, writing to wicked people who wanted you to run away from the infected house, and tell me a little about your proceedings of late. Have you been well and strong, or have you been weak and suffering from this changeable weather that never is the same for two days together? You see when the outward elements blow *hot and cold*, what inconveniences result! Now you can easily draw an inference as to certain *inner* elements, and so learn to 'be good.' I did not think your last letter sounded good at all; on the contrary, I thought I could trace in it all sorts of alarms, the inspirations doubtless of provincial Popes. It is not, however, any of your dear Popes that I am afraid of so much as something in yourself. I have made a discovery about you. Did you ever observe that we sometimes discover something about a friend's character by observing how, in a *dream*, we have made him act, and accordingly what qualities our half-instinctive knowledge of his character has made us attribute to him while our active faculties were exerting themselves with all the impartiality of unconsciousness? Well, in the same way we get indications of character by observing what are the little trivial incidents or sayings which we recollect most often in connection with our friends, and then analyzing these so as to find out what they *indicate*. Now, I find I have been often remembering one little incident which you mentioned to me, viz., that you were so fond of the place in which you had passed your childhood that, when it passed into other hands, you used constantly to drive *to the gate*, look in, let your fancy be wafted along with the linden odours through remembered bowers, allow your affections to rest a while under the green shadows of the old beeches, and then . . . *drive away!* Why not drive in? Why not plant your *foot* amid old mosses? Why not touch the stems graven with old names? Why not enter the dusky aisles of the woods and breathe the air which the violet only, and the spirits of the past, had breathed before you? Why not let the old meadows have you again for an hour and the woodbines detain you? Is it not that you are too easily satisfied—a phantom satisfied with phantoms, and a shadow to whom shadows are substances? Now, do not be a phantom or a shadow. Do not drive to the gate of Paradise, or be contented with looking in at the entrance to a heavenly home—the home of a Heavenly Father. There is no rude porter there at the gate to drive you back, or to think you linger long. It is yours by Baptism, though, like so many of us, you were stolen from it in childhood. In returning to it you but return to old loves and old laws, and the old and holy allegiance, and the first fidelity of regenerate souls

> Though spoused yet wanting wedlocks solemnize.

"Of all the wretched sophisms by which those who would fain follow the Truth, 'whithersoever He goeth,' are perplexed; of all the voices muttering in our ear which tempt us to turn our head and look back while mounting the hill of wisdom (cloistered with God in the firmamental region of light and love and endless peace), there is none more obviously idle and *evasive* than that which frightens back so many, 'keep to the Church of your Baptism.' There are no local Baptisms into local Churches. There is but one Church, and a whisper or a sigh is heard at once in all regions of its infinitude. So there is but one Baptism, through which we were originally consigned to the one Church. The font is the pellucid and peaceful bosom of the one Virgin Mother of souls. Whatever or wherever the true Church may be, to her the Baptism belongs; and in returning to, or abiding with her, one returns to or abides with one's Baptism. We cannot be *unfaithful* while we go to the Truth; for the Truth is the first of all things, and to Him our first allegiance was plighted. Truth is eternal and immutable, the beginning and the end. Consequently in Truth, and therefore in the true Church, our past as well as our future, our fidelity as well as our hope, must be involved.

"Now, are you not inwardly saying, 'What are you driving at?' I will tell you. First, you are easily contented with imaginary things fairly adumbrated, things

> Hanging like a picture fair
> In the rich and shadowy air,

and so I am uttering my *Protest* (may I not too be a Protestant?) against phantoms, and making my *Confession* that Religion is Substance and Reality, or nothing; for Poetry, not Religion, is the world of thoughts, visions, aspirations unembodied, and unfulfilled loves.

"Secondly, you are a lover of the Past. In your shadowy land Reality comes more near to you through the Imagination and the Memory, than through the Senses. In cold weather it is the far horizon, where heaven seems to meet earth, that is seductive, not the flowerless foreground, or the cold spring beds whose buds look as if there was not heart enough in them to make them flowers. Now, you too have something of this chilliness and timidity about you, and while your fancy plays with present things, it is in the past that you seem to yourself to find your safest asylum. This circumstance exposes you especially to one particular danger, that, namely, proceeding from the sophism 'old times,' 'allegiance,' 'loyalty,' 'Church of your Baptism,' 'unfilial,' &c., through which so many orphaned souls are deprived for ever of their Mother, and kept in ward to Tutors, Guardians, the Lord Chancellor, or mere self-elected Guides, blind leaders of the blind, and through which the mighty Mother is deprived of souls who would have been the most lamb-like in her fold, who would have crept nearest to her side for warmth, and who are least able to find their way alone over the snowy and nocturnal wolds. And so I have told you that your real and earliest Past belongs to the Church, and in returning to her there is nothing which you will feel more strongly than that you have *returned* to the 'Church of your Baptism.' It is with the individual as with nations. Protestantism is the heady Hobbledehoyhood of communities that have lost the former and not reached the latter. Nationalism must end like a school-boy's 'barring out.' But as we must, as individuals, end first, let us not wait till the turbid stream runs by.

"I heard such a beautiful sermon yesterday from Manning. He has been staying out of town for a few days; but his home in town is this house (Mr. Monsell's), which is mine also.

"Have you got the *Hours of Sarum*, published by Mr. Chambers? I have been reading a number of your Puseyite books lately—one little one called *Rosaries*, Palmer's *Dissertations on the Orthodox* (Eastern) *Communion*. An odd book called *The Counter Theory*, tossed into the wind as a counter-attraction to Newman's great book *On Development*, and (last and best) Archdeacon Wilberforce's admirable book *On the Holy Eucharist*. It is said to be the best book ever put forward in the Church of England, and I should think it probably is the best book on that great subject. Great indeed may a subject be called which involves not only so great a *Doctrine*, but as you may say, the whole *Worship* of Christianity. It is immensely learned, and though deep, not difficult, except in a short part; and the views that it discloses ought to be to many as a new world from which the veil had been removed. Yet any one may soon see that the whole of this sublime doctrine was really involved in that of the Incarnation, and that whoever *really* held the latter ought to have held the former also. Pray lose no time in reading it if you have not done so already, and tell me what you think of it. I should like to know what Oswald Middleton thinks of it also. Is he married yet? . . . How lovely Clifton must be looking now—that is the downs' and river's 'wooded walls.' Do you take walks and do 'the children' go out sketching?

"Do you ever think of Currah? This year you must see it in its summer or autumn dress, not in its bleak and dreary undress. Yet even in its grey ascetic garb you could see beauty in it. How well I remember our pleasant evening walks to the rock, and all our readings and fifty things beside. Do pray write to me at once. With much love to 'the children.'

"Ever most truly yours,
"AUBREY DE VERE."

To the same month belongs another letter from the same writer to Olivia.

"East Sheen Lodge, August 29, 1853.

"This book was to have been taken with the little Puseyite volume of *Rosaries* which I sent your mother this morning, but it arrived too late to share the honour of being taken in charge by such a bearer. Pray make up to it for the loss it has sustained by reading it and liking it. It is full (if I may venture to judge) of passages worthy of being remembered.

"I was delighted to see your handwriting again, but, O Sophist! what am I to say to you? You are growing what you used to call "Sir James Stephenish," I almost fear; for contradictions in terms you cannot swallow, and you have not faith enough to trust that Divine element of certain truth, strong as the sea, though like the sea capable of frowning as well as smiling, over which the Mystic Ark alone can float. Well, I must not scold you. One should only pray for one's friends that they may have the same merciful opportunities which were so often accorded to us, and may have grace to use all the grace given.

"You will soon, I hope, see one whom you have all often wished to see. You must write and tell me how you have liked him. I am so really grieved at not having seen you. Had I known in time that you were leaving Clifton so soon, I would certainly have gone to see you. What pleasant walks and rambles we should have had, and what disputes.

"And so Oswald is married! And is he a clergyman too? Some wicked people would say that the only safe hands into which a young clergyman can be placed in these dangerous times are those that belong to—— but you shall finish for yourself, lest it might turn out a scandal added to the thousand and one. I could say a good deal about the *Counter Theory* which you name, but I should weary you. It belongs to the region, not of argument, but of *Evasion*. The author does not sit down to the problem like a man, but plays with it as Spanish ladies play with their fans.

"I am delighted with All Saints (the new church in Margaret Street). It is *very* fair among the fair shadows.

"Good-bye and God bless you both, my dear little friends, and God bless your sweet mother too. But do not say 'I am very far from being good.' The near may be far; then why should not the far be near.

"Affectionately yours,
"AUBREY DE VERE."

The "bearer of the little volume on *Rosaries*," "the one whom you have all often wished to see," mentioned in the preceding letter was Mr. Manning, who came to Clifton this August for a day or two, on a visit to Lord and Lady Charles Thynne. He was already a Catholic priest. We had two interviews with him. Mother said she considered it right that we should hear what he has to say. This however was to be said to us three collectively. We were not to see him privately, and it was taken for granted that we were not to be influenced by him in any way. It was embarrassing to be put as it were upon one's honour to disregard his arguments however convincing they might be. On those terms I would rather have declined seeing him, only it seemed possible that as mother had always had such a reverence for him, he might be able to effect a real change in her views. His arguments, however, had no effect on her.

In my diary I note that the first day we saw Mr. Manning he talked about the Supremacy. With regard to the opposition to it in the early ages of the Church, he said that this very opposition was a proof of its existence. The claim of the Roman Pontiff would never have been disputed, had it not been asserted, and as a matter of fact it was only disputed by heretics.

The next day he made an earnest appeal to our consciences. I know that my mother in her conscience could not accept doctrines which she had always regarded as unscriptural. Therefore this appeal did not touch her. It was different with me, and Mr. Manning probably saw this. He said that no man could deliver his brother nor make agreement unto God for him. In God's sight we were all equal. Each of us would have to answer for her own soul. He told us very distinctly that there was no safety for our souls outside the Church of Rome, and urged us to join it at once. "I go away to-morrow," he said, "but there is time first to see you all safe in the One Fold." Olivia and I did not know what to do. In the position in which we were, refuge in the One Fold did not seem a possibility. We were on the eve of starting to pay a round of visits to various country houses. Plans for many weeks to come would be upset, if it were known that we had renounced Protestantism. Thoroughly uncomfortable and miserable as we were, we had to content ourselves with determining that nothing could be done till we returned to Clifton. When that time should come we must and would make up our minds to act as our consciences dictated.

Mr. Manning said he should not despair of us. There was one way of obtaining the grace of conversion which he had never known to fail. He should remember us in the Holy Sacrifice of the Mass. "You may go on for long as you are," he said, "clinging to a person, to a theory, to a book, but come at last you will, in spite of yourselves, drawn by that Unseen Power."

When he pressed us with the question, "What would you do if you knew you should die to-night?" I could answer, "In that case I would be received, because it does seem to me most probable that the Church of Rome is right, but if I am not to die just yet, and taking into consideration the circumstances in which I am placed, perhaps it would be better to wait a little, and not to be in so great a hurry." This did not appear an unreasonable answer. I wish it would have satisfied Mr. Manning. Much perplexity and misery would then have been spared me. A young person of sixteen, acting against the wishes of all her relations in such a matter, has many difficulties to contend with. To begin with, there was no opportunity of seeing a priest alone. Girls were not so independent in those days as they seem to be now. I had a horror of acting in an underhand and deceitful manner. I could not satisfy myself as to what I ought to do. Whatever course I should take seemed to be a wrong one. For the moment, however, when we started on our travels, there appeared to be nothing to do but to wait, and to hope that all would be made clear, the mountains and hills be brought low, the crooked ways be made straight, and the rough places plain.

CHAPTER VII.

Visits to Protestant friends. Vexation. Oswald's collection of books.

Archdeacon Wilberforce's *Treatise on the Holy Eucharist*. Its definite teaching. This doctrine the key to Christianity. The Sacred Humanity the appointed channel of grace. St. Augustine's testimony.

Lessons learnt from study of Archdeacon Wilberforce's book. Practical difficulties that it suggested. Milly's letters on the subject. Her doubts and perplexities.

The Holy Communion, by Father Dalgairns. How Christianity satisfies the yearning of the human soul for union with God. Jewish saints contrasted with Christian saints. The sixth chapter of St. John's Gospel.

WE had a glimpse of Mr. Manning at the Bristol Railway Station. He was going in one direction, we were going in another. He had provided himself with a copy of Macaulay's essay on Ranke's *History of the Popes*. In this essay, he remarked to us, Macaulay endeavours to account on natural grounds for the indefectibility and the ever-renewed vigour of the Catholic Church. "I wonder if we shall ever meet again in this created world," Mr. Manning said, on taking leave of us. When we did meet again, it was in Rome.

Our first visit was to the Burtons. Of course we could not help letting Milly see how perturbed was the state of our minds. Of course Milly was perturbed because we were perturbed. She poured out all her fears and anxieties about us to her mother. She in her turn became disquieted lest we should imbue her daughters with our Popish ideas. It was suggested that we should promise not to talk of religion. Milly said, "This would be quite impossible. How could we bear to be together and not to speak of that which was nearest to our hearts?" What line Sybella took I do not remember. At any rate there was no fear of her being persuaded to relinquish that privilege of private judgment which she so much valued. I was distressed at my mother's vexation. She did not realize how unsettled we were. She considered, therefore, that Mrs. Burton showed a want of confidence in us for which there was no warrant. Her vexation was much increased a little later. Letters came from officious people at Clifton, who thought it necessary to tell her that they had heard reports of her having received a visit from Mr. Manning. They could not believe it. They begged her to authorize them to contradict all such ill-natured rumours!

Amongst our visits this autumn was one to Oswald Middleton's family. He had recently married and was not at his former home. He had left there, however, his small collection of books. This included the Ecclesiastical Histories of Socrates, Sozomen, &c., translations of which had been published at Oxford. These histories I read with interest. I read also Newman's *University Sermons*. From that one on "Implicit and Explicit Reason," I wrote several extracts in my note-book. Schlegel's *Lectures on Modern History*, and Ruskin's *Seven Lamps of Architecture* were also amongst the number of works which Oswald's library afforded for our perusal.

Meanwhile Olivia and I were studying a book which perhaps influenced me more than did any other book in my early life. This was the treatise by Archdeacon Robert Wilberforce *On the Holy Eucharist*. This volume contained the definite teaching on the Holy Eucharist for which I had been longing. It was a theological treatise which was unlike any that had hitherto appeared in the English Church. It was free from that vagueness and evasion which are the characteristics of Anglican writers in general. The Catholic doctrine was boldly put forward. In the last chapter, entitled "Practical Conclusions," it was shown how far the English Church had in her existing practice departed from the teaching of our Lord on this great Sacrament, as His teaching was understood by the Universal Church.

This treatise carried to its legitimate conclusion the principle which had been insisted on in Archdeacon Wilberforce's former works. The Sacred Humanity of our Blessed Lord is the means by which we are to be sanctified and saved.

When the words of consecration are pronounced, His Body and Blood become really present on the altar, and are given to us, according to His promise, in order that we may have life. This supernatural presence is effected by the words of the priest who represents Christ, and not, as Protestants hold, by the disposition of the receiver.

The Catholic doctrine regarding the Holy Eucharist, like that of the Incarnation, must be either true or false. It seemed curious that many Anglicans do not see this. They say that it may be true, or it may not; and that it does not much signify what we believe concerning it. They shrink from asserting that there is a Real Presence of our Lord's Body and Blood in the consecrated elements. They say that although "He is verily and indeed taken and received by the faithful," He only becomes present at the moment of communion. The sacred elements are not therefore entitled to Divine worship. Those who thus speak have similarly vague ideas with regard to the Incarnation itself. Ask them whether the Infant in the manger at Bethlehem was God, press them with the fact that either He was God or He was not God, and they will answer that we were not intended to go into such subtleties, and that it is better to be vague in these matters. When our Lord said, "Unless you eat the Flesh of the Son of Man and drink His Blood you shall not have life in you," He did not intend that we should take His words literally, or inquire too closely into the meaning of them.

Often had I been silenced and perplexed; almost had I been made to fancy that it was wrong to yield a simple belief to these words, and to be certain that our Blessed Lord meant what He said, and reiterated so solemnly. Now at last this book of Robert Wilberforce's justified me in the belief which I had implicitly held. Its clear enunciation of doctrine satisfied me. The doctrine was the same—so it seemed to me—as that of the Church of Rome. Numerous passages from the writings of the early Fathers were cited by him in support of it.

It was not the authority that could be adduced for this great doctrine, however, which most impressed me. I learnt to understand that it was the key to the whole of Christianity, "God manifest in the Flesh." The Incarnation was not a thing of the past, and of historical interest only. It was a living, energizing fact. "The Bread which I will give is My Flesh, which I will give for the life of the world." Protestant "objections vanish when it is shown that our Lord's Real Presence in the Holy Eucharist is a natural sequel to the doctrine of the Incarnation; that it immediately connects itself with those truths which are revealed to us respecting God, Christ, and mankind; and that it supplies the medium through which the merciful actions of the Mediator are brought home to His creatures."[1]

And again. "The strong antipathy which our reason entertains against the notion of an unnecessary miracle, vanishes so soon as we see that the agency introduced only occupies it's natural place in that chain of causes by which the acts of God above are linked to those of His earthly servants. No theist feels repugnance at admitting a spiritual influence of God upon the minds of His creatures, because the mind of man appears to be an instrument which is naturally adapted for the reception and perpetuation of intellectual and spiritual impulses. The knowledge, therefore, that we possess this door, whereby we can hold intercourse with spiritual beings, inclines men to allow the reality of their influence. And in like manner, when it is discovered that our Lord's Humanity is the appointed channel through which we participate in heavenly blessings, and that the Holy Eucharist is the medium through which it is imparted, His Real Presence in that ordinance is discovered to have its fitting place in God's dealing towards mankind."[2]

There is another passage or two on which I thought that those would do well to reflect to whom this doctrine is a difficulty.

"Our Lord's mediation not only implies that

---

[1] *Doctrine of the Holy Eucharist*, p. 109.
[2] Pp. 107, 108.

He condescended to be a sacrifice and intercessor on man's behalf towards God, but likewise that He made His Manhood the channel through which the perfections of the Creator extended themselves to the creature. There is 'one Mediator between God and man, the Man Christ Jesus.'"

"Grace is never spoken of in the Gospels, except as associated with the Humanity of God the Son."

"Hence it may be seen why the Holy Eucharist is so important, and how it is (as St. Augustine observes) that 'no one may say that the road of safety lies in a good life, and the worship of one God, without participation in the Body and Blood of Christ.' 'For the statement that God will have all men to be saved, is not to be understood as taking effect without a Mediator; and that Mediator is not God, ... but the Man Christ Jesus.' There must be some means, then, by which we must be put into relation with the New Man, even as we have a natural relation to the flesh of the old one; we must be united by grace to Christ, as we were united to Adam by nature. Neither should it surprise us that the processes should present some analogy; that if the poison of the one is transmitted through his flesh, so His Flesh shall be the medium through which is transmitted the virtue of the other. For that which constitutes our earthly being is not only a separate personality (however derived and in whatever consisting), but likewise that common nature which we inherit from our original parent. This nature is transmitted, according to the most mysterious of all earthly laws, through the continuity of the flesh. It was not inconsistent, therefore, with the order of the Divine economy that our Lord's Flesh and Blood, mysteriously and supernaturally communicated, should be the principle of a higher life to His brethren.

"This, then, was the truth which our Lord declared in the institution of the Holy Eucharist, a truth which, whether or not fully understood by His Apostles at the moment, was certainly explained in those statements, which the Holy Ghost afterwards recalled to their memory, as it was confirmed by the practice and belief of the Church which they established. 'Take, eat, this is My Body.' What was this but the explanation of that mysterious prediction, 'I am the Living Bread, which came down from Heaven; and the Bread which I will give is My Flesh, which I will give for the life of the world'? The Holy Eucharist, therefore, is the carrying out of that act which took effect in the Incarnation of the Son of God. So that when the one is thought strange, we shall always find that the other is imperfectly appreciated. It was by the Incarnation that God and man, the finite and the Infinite, were brought into relation; and that the graces which were inherent in the one, were communicated as a gift to the other. Now, the medium through which these gifts are extended is not the Deity, but the Manhood of Christ. 'The Bread which I will give is *My Flesh*, which I will give for the life of the world.'"[1]

I read the book very carefully, and I took great pains to master its argument. That it had been so strongly recommended by Mr. Aubrey de Vere gave me confidence that it would not contain anything which was materially at variance with the doctrine of the Roman Church. Archdeacon Wilberforce, by reason of his acknowledged learning, piety, and solidity of judgment, occupied a position which was indefinitely superior to that of the ordinary Anglican writers of the day. He took his stand on the teaching of the Universal Church. The Church of England claimed to be part of the Universal Church, and to agree in all things with the Fathers, and therefore he assumed that the Catholic doctrine on the Holy Eucharist must be the doctrine of the Church of England. He appealed also to her having retained the act of consecration as evidence that she believed in the efficacy of that act.

Certainly the Catholic doctrine of the Blessed Eucharist gives a completeness to the work of our Divine Lord which is wanting without it. Were it not for the continual presence of His Sacred Humanity in our midst, the Christian religion would become a thing of the past.

[1] Pp. 99—101.

Many Protestants indeed consider that the chosen people of the Jewish dispensation were in a better position than are Christians. They were invited to a closer intercourse with Almighty God. Through His Prophets they were more fully taught His will.

That the worldly and the unthinking should seize on any pretext for rejecting a doctrine which condemns their selfishness and their indifference is intelligible. But how can those reject the Catholic doctrine of the Blessed Sacrament who really love their Creator, and wish to serve Him? Is it the very greatness of the gift that He bestows on them which tempts them to incredulity? Do they doubt because they cannot believe that God can love them so much? Is it indeed an invention of man that his Creator should condescend to so close a union with him? Who could have dared to invent it? "The Word was made Flesh and dwelt among us, and we have seen His glory," and He Who implanted in the heart of man the craving for the Infinite, has vouchsafed to satisfy that craving in a measure, even in this life.

This doctrine was, indeed, the mariner's compass that kept my frail bark from foundering, and at last steered it safely into port. Oh, that those to whom it is now, as it was to the men of old, "a hard saying," could learn to receive it! Then would they understand the religion of Jesus Christ in the fulness of its truth.

Then would they perceive how possible becomes the attainment of the most heroic virtues, how natural are those acts of humility and self-denial which appear to worldlings unreal and exaggerated, how abundantly a convert to Catholicism is compensated even on earth for all the sacrifices that he may be required to make. Does not the Blessed Sacrament unite earth to Heaven, and unite the worship of the Church Militant with that of the Church Triumphant? The Lamb that was slain is adored on the altars of the Catholic Church, and is presented before the Eternal Father from "the rising of the sun to the going down thereof." The vision of St. John is fulfilled, "The Tabernacle of God is with men, and He will dwell with them."

In two ways my practical difficulties were much increased by the lessons that I learnt from this book: (1) In the first place it was clear that the Sacrifice of the Holy Eucharist was the one act of worship of the Apostolic Church, whereas in the Anglican Church people could not take part in it till they had been confirmed. In the majority of Anglican churches, moreover, it was celebrated only some twelve times—in the country perhaps only three times—in the course of the year. In the Catholic church which we passed every Sunday, there was not only a weekly but a daily celebration. Could it be right to be debarred from going there?

(2) The second difficulty was this. In St. John the Baptist's, where we ordinarily worshipped, the Communion Service was reverently performed. One might conclude that the officiating minister believed in his own power to consecrate and that he had the intention of exercising it. But if for any reason we attended a Clifton church, or went to the ordinary churches in the country, it was certain that any idea of there being a peculiar sacredness in the consecrated elements after the conclusion of the service never entered the clergyman's head. In disposing of the elements afterwards he would talk familiarly with his parishioners: " Very glad to see you here to-day, Mrs. Brown ;" or he would leave them as the perquisite of the clerk. In an English chapel on the Continent, I remember the chaplain coming into an adjoining room where we were putting on our cloaks, bringing what was left over of the bread and wine, and asking those present to assist him in disposing of it. I felt it incumbent on me to kneel down (the rubric in the Prayer Book does say something about reverence on these occasions), though painfully conscious of the tactlessness of such a proceeding, when the Rev. Mr. B—— was chatting casually with my elders and betters, the representatives of British royalty in the city to which I allude. On another occasion I remember an uncle of mine, after returning into the church to fetch an umbrella, coming back chuckling. He said that he had

interrupted the clerk in his enjoyment of the wine that had been left. Such incidents were common enough.

To judge from Milly's letters which remain to me, we had a good deal of correspondence about Archdeacon Wilberforce's views. She had been greatly impressed by those discourses of Faber's, "On the Blessed Sacrament from the writings of the Saints," which had had such an effect on me a year or two earlier. She writes:

"What you say in your letter, and various other thoughts working together, have combined to set my stupid brain in a whirl of doubt and mystery. I *long* to believe one thing, but I fear being presumptuous. Now what I long to believe is your doctrine, and Faber's. But it seems to me that the system called Sacramental is *more* than we have in the Bible. It seems very philosophical, and my faith would not shrink from it, did I feel I had any *right* to believe it. It appears to be a system made by man. Not that by this I mean to say it is either false or incredible, but have we any warrant for taking as an article of certainty and faith anything which is not revealed to us? *Why* do we believe this system? It is most beautiful and very possibly may be true, but is it safe to decide that it is true, and so act on it? Don't be angry with me. I am very tiresome, I know, but these things perplex and make me anxious, and I *must* talk to you about them. I can't help it, unfortunately for you.

"On the subject of the Holy Eucharist I am again thrown into a sea of doubts. Questions arise which reason can't decide, and which it seems wrong and daring to start, yet they *will* come. On such a matter doubt is sad, for it touches one's inner life too closely to be put aside as a thing of slight importance which will come right of itself. I wish I could see you and tell you my thoughts. I can't write them, for sundry reasons. Perhaps it is better for me not to tell them, great as would be the comfort of so doing. I might come to be where *you* are! And then what would it be to my friends at home? What would Sybella say?"

A few weeks later Milly continues: "Now I am coming to the great point of your letter, the Sacramental System. It was a new idea to me, but very beautiful, that re-making of our nature by the Incarnation of Christ, and I feel as if it must be true though so awful in its very blessedness. Only I don't see why sacraments are the exclusive means of union with our New Head. Why not also prayer, faith, reading and believing the Bible? These are all means of grace, and by *grace* do we not really mean receiving Christ into our souls and being united to Him? And don't all the means of grace help as well as the sacraments to do this? We are said to be 'born again' of the Word of Truth as well as by Baptism, therefore is not this as great a means, if used in faith, as the sacraments themselves? Expound to me all this matter, my wise one! I feel you do seek the real truth, and I never fear you won't satisfy me honestly as to what you think. Another difficulty (not first started by *me*) is this. If the Holy Eucharist be so infinitely superior a means of grace as this doctrine of the sacraments would make it, how is it that it is so little made of in the Bible comparatively, that it is not said to be the only means of uniting us to Christ? though of course it is said to be *a* means of doing so, and this is enough to fix its unspeakable blessedness for ever. This perplexes me. You see there is no end to my questions and doubts.

. . . .

"Your letter was very interesting, and I perfectly understand all about Wilberforce, for you do write very clearly whatever you may think. Now I am going to talk about it to prove that I understand, though probably *you* won't be able to understand *me*.

"I quite see the fundamental difference between Wilberforce's and my ideas, as to our Lord's Incarnation and Death, I making the first subordinate and chiefly preparatory to the last. I like Wilberforce's ideas about the Incarnation so very much, I want fully to embrace them, but that very desire of mine makes me fear to take them for granted as true, lest it should be a merely earthly desire, not love of truth. What my way of considering the doctrine is founded on is, I suppose, the prominence which seems to be given in the Bible to the work effected by the Death of Christ, the Atonement, the reconciliation between God and men, as if that was the chief reason for our Lord's becoming Man, viz., that '*by death* He might destroy him that had the power of death.' In the Body of His Flesh through death we are reconciled. By His Death He becomes our Mediator, our Redeemer, the satisfaction for our sins. Of course this could not be without His Incarnation, but is not His Death His chief work, His great act, the object of His Incarnation, the foundation of our hope in Him? Supposing a good man, who does *not* look on the sacraments as means of uniting him to Christ, as anything more than *signs* of an *effected* union, supposing such a one earnestly believes that in that Death is *all* his hope of pardon *and* of grace, can we doubt that the pardon and grace will be given to him, independently of the sacraments, to which, coming not with a full faith, he would not, I suppose, be capable of receiving their full benefit? Yet can we doubt that such a man, living by faith in Christ, is in Christ a new creature? I quite see the force of Wilberforce's argument from analogy, and of the reasonableness and credibility of his doctrine, only—are we in the Bible *expressly limited* to the Sacramental System? How were the Apostles made partakers of Christ before the sacraments were ordained? Are we told that man cannot be brought into union with God except through sacraments? I quite feel and believe that they *are* means of union and communion with Christ. This is their value and blessedness in great measure, but I do not see that, as a system, they are made the only means of union. By living faith we are joined to Christ, our humanity to His Holy Humanity. Sacraments are only the tangible and outward means, so to speak, of that union, but is not that union sometimes effected (not of course in any who wilfully despise or neglect the outward means) without them? I feel, of course, it would be both foolish and wicked to neglect obeying any one command of our Lord, and sacraments *are* ordained by Him, and are therefore most blessed, yes, unutterably precious as His gift and ordinance, so that it seems to me impossible that any one who loves Him should not love and use them. But some do not feel this, some do neglect them, yet, we trust, believe in and love Him, doing it somehow in ignorance or misunderstanding, or having a low idea of their efficacy. Are such without Him? severed from Him in Whom alone is Life? How is this? Do we not try to make too much of a regular system of the doctrine of sacraments? more of a regular system than the Bible does? You'll think all this very horrid, but forgive me, for I am undecided and want conviction, so I am obliged to tell you my worst difficulties in their worst form."

Milly's difficulties were not difficulties to me. I told her she was right in thinking that it was grace that united us to Christ, and that sacraments were valuable as means of grace, but that she was wrong in supposing that the Church taught that sacraments were the *exclusive* means, and that no one could be saved without sacraments. Grace was given before the sacraments were instituted. Sufficient grace for salvation is given to all who have no opportunity of knowing about and receiving sacraments, but this did not prevent sacraments from being "generally necessary to salvation," as the English Catechism said. Sacraments were certainly not inventions of men, because they were instituted by our Lord, and I denied that there was not enough said about them in the Bible to warrant the veneration in which the Church has always held them. On this subject, Newman, in one of his *Tracts for the Times*, had written:[1] "If obscurity of texts . . . about the grace of the Eucharist, be taken as a proof that no great benefit is therein given, it is an argument against there being any benefit. On the other hand, when certain passages are once

---

[1] *Scripture and the Creed*, "Discussions and Arguments," p. 118. Pickering.

interpreted to refer to it, the emphatic language used in those passages shows that the benefit is not small. We cannot say that the subject is unimportant, without saying that it is not mentioned at all. Either no gift is given in the Eucharist, or a great gift. If only the sixth chapter of St. John, for instance, does allude to it, it shows it is not merely an edifying rite, but an awful communication beyond words. Again, if the phrase, 'the communication of the Body of Christ,' used by St. Paul, means any gift, it means a great one. You may say, if you will, that it does not mean any gift at all, but means only a representation or figure of the communication; this I call explaining away, but still it is intelligible; but I do not see how, if it is to be taken literally as a real *communication* of something, it can be other than a communication of *His Body*."

I suggested to Milly that what she said about making a regular system which did not seem explicitly set forth in the Bible, would apply equally to the Creed, and that because there were many good people who thought it their duty to believe only that which appeared to them to be in the plain text of Scripture, and therefore rejected this or that article of the Creed, it did not follow that they were right or that we need concern ourselves about them. What evidence could they adduce from Scripture that this was the way in which Almighty God intended us to learn His truth?

I could not then tell Milly all that I have since learnt about the Holy Sacrament of the Altar—all that she was herself to learn in the long years during which she would struggle to church in the dark winter mornings, ill and suffering as she was. " If one can do nothing else in the day, it seems to me one ought to hear Mass. That is so much the most important thing we have to do," Milly used to say. " If it tires us, it is quite worth while to be tired. I am told I ought to keep my strength for other duties, as if I had any duty that could compare with this ! "

Archdeacon Wilberforce's book was almost exclusively on dogma. In after years Milly gave me a book to read which I had not seen before. It was a book that was not merely theological and philosophical, but pre-eminently devotional, that *On the Holy Communion,* by Father Dalgairns. Here we found an answer to the questions which we used to discuss while we were as yet outside the Church. Two passages I will cite. One passage describes how God has in this Blessed Sacrament vouchsafed to satisfy the intense desire of the soul for union with Him. The other passage notes the dissimilarity between the saints of the Old Testament and those of the New Testament, and it attributes this dissimilarity to Holy Communion.

Father Dalgairns had been speaking of the natural yearning which there is in the human heart for union with God, and how Christianity has increased that yearning by showing the possibility of satisfying it. He goes on to say: "The knowledge of the existence of such a being as Man-God has created a change in us down to our very heart's core. All the full, vehement tide of our affections has set towards Jesus. All the trembling awe-struck love which we felt for God is fixed on Jesus, without a transfer, since He is God. The craving void remains, but it has lost its despair, for Jesus exists. There is a new feeling upon earth in our inmost soul, which we cannot describe; we can only feel it. It is made up of awe-struck adoration, and of a deep tenderness, in which all earth's affections are centred and outdone. Strange mysterious feeling! He died near two thousand years ago, yet we love Him like those who 'saw with their eyes, who looked upon and handled with their hands' the Word of Life. Childhood lisps His name, youth fixes its fiery affections upon Him; our manly love only adds fresh fuel to the flame, and it burns unquenched beneath the snows of age. The wife loves Him better than her husband, and the mother than her children. Hearts throb with gushing love at the very mention of His name; tears of joy spring to the eyes at the thought that Jesus lives. He is our life, and without Him we are spiritually dead. The thirst of man for God has not changed in kind by being fixed on Him, since our love for Him has for its first element our love for God. It has only acquired a tenderness which it had not before, while it has gained strength a thousand-fold. A new want has arisen in our hearts, and we thirst for union with Jesus. This is the want which God has satisfied in giving us the Blessed Sacrament."

Contrasting the Jewish saints with the Christian saints, Father Dalgairns says, "The pardon of sin and the sanctification of the soul have been the elements of justification ever since the Fall. Six thousand years have made no difference in that. The grace of our first mother after God had pardoned her, does not differ in kind from that of the infant baptized to-day, or of the sinner over whom absolution has just been pronounced. In that respect the Passion of Christ was to the Jews as though it had been already past. The Cross of Christ was the meritorious cause of the justification of Eve as it is of our own. But there was one thing that could not be then, and that was the Blessed Sacrament. God could justify David on the prospective merits of David's unborn Son; but not God Himself could cause the real Body and Blood of Jesus to exist before they were conceived in Mary's womb, that is, to be and not to be at the same time. It is this which makes the difference between the old dispensation and the new; Jesus was future then, and He is present now. Theirs was the time of hope; and ours the time of union with Him. They looked across the lapse of centuries waiting for Him Whom we possess. Clear as is the vision which the Prophet saw of the wondrous Child Whom the Virgin should conceive, and of Him Who came with dyed garments from Bosra; yet, what is the vision of Jesus to the reality? The meanest Christian who makes his Easter receives a greater gift than did the kings and prophets who longed to see His day, and saw it not. For this reason it is that the saints of the Christian Church so far outnumbered the saints of the old dispensation. For this reason it is that, while the Jewish maiden mourned her solitude upon the mountains of Judæa, countless virgins, without thinking themselves saints, abandon all to win the title of spouses of Christ. Trace all these wonders of the Christian Church to their source, you will find it in the Holy Communion. It is the Blessed Sacrament which makes the real difference between the Christian and the Jew."

To those who do not believe in the Real Presence of Jesus Christ in the Blessed Eucharist, I would say, read the sixth chapter of St. John, and judge for yourself whether it is not the teaching of our Lord. "Nowhere does He awaken the least suspicion that He is speaking figuratively when He says, 'Except you eat the Flesh of the Son of Man, and drink His Blood, you shall not have life in you.' The multitude understood Him to be speaking, not of a figurative, but of a real eating; the disciples who went back and walked no more with Him, understood Him in the same way; St. Peter and the twelve who persevered with Jesus also understood Him in the same way; all the explanations given by our Lord confirmed them in their interpretation, . . . and, as if to seal our persuasion that Christ was promising to give His Body and Blood in some true and real manner at the Last Supper, with every circumstance of solemnity, our Lord took bread, and blessed, and brake it, and gave it to His disciples, saying, Take ye and *eat*, for this is My Body."

It cannot be a matter that does not concern you. "What a privation, what a misfortune yours will be, if when it is too late, when you appear before your Judge, you discover that the Eternal Word Incarnate, Jesus Christ, was really and truly present in the world, and you knew it not. Think what a source of grace lies within your reach, if the teaching of the Catholic Church in this point be true. We should pity one born to wealth and honour, who, unconscious of his rights, should pass his days in poverty and toil. More to be pitied are those who pass through life ignorant of the Real Bodily Presence of Christ in the world."[1]

[1] Archbishop Porter.

CHAPTER VIII.

Difficulties in the way of conversion. Reasons why it was delayed. The Crimean War. A first great sorrow. The state of the soul after death. Tennyson's *In Memoriam*. Letters from sympathizing friends. Prayers for the dead. Notes of a High Church sermon on the Communion of Saints. The necessity for penance taught in Scripture. The consolations of Purgatory.

Bournemouth. St. Peter's Church. Spiritual helps in the English Church. The Definition of the doctrine of the Immaculate Conception. Mr. Dean's secession. Extracts from Diary. Thoughts suggested by Mr. Woodford. Extracts from Mr. Woodford's published sermons.. The punishment that rejection of any article of faith entails. The mystery of the Gospel. Lectures on the latter part of the Creed. The Holy Catholic Church. The Alliance of Church and State.

Courbon on *Mental Prayer*. Spiritual consolation. A foreign tour projected.

I HAVE tried, in the preceding chapters, to give an account of the religious impressions of my early years. It may seem that one whose convictions were so decided as were mine had no excuse for remaining in the Church of England. Now I must relate how it came to pass that I went on for some years trying to work out my salvation in that communion. These were, perhaps, years of more seriousness and thoughtfulness than those which had gone before, even if they were also years of greater danger, lest through procrastination or delay in corresponding to God's grace, that grace—the inestimable gift of faith—should have been withdrawn.

God is very merciful. He alone knows how far we have been faithful to His inspirations, or how sadly we have marred His gracious designs towards us, or how negligently we have responded to His call; He knows our weakness and our difficulties as none other can know them. In my case there were tremendous difficulties to be overcome. If I decided that these difficulties should be met by patience and perseverance in the use of such means of grace as were within my reach, until a brighter day should dawn and the shadows should flee away, I would fain have hoped it was not altogether cowardice and human respect that influenced me.

It is very difficult for those who are outside the Church to realize the right that God has to demand their submission in order to acceptance of truths which He has revealed. They think it cannot signify much whether they hold this doctrine or that doctrine. They consider that they are large-minded in being indifferent with regard to what others believe. They forget that it is God's truth which they are dealing with —the revelation which He has chosen to make. It is His revelation, and it cannot be a matter of small importance whether men believe it or not. I do not think that I recognized the supreme claim of God to the obedience of His creatures, and how subordinate to His claim is every human claim, till after I became a Catholic.

Meanwhile, Robert Isaac Wilberforce, whose influence was so great, and whose sincerity could not be doubted, was still exercising his office as Archdeacon of the East Riding. He had not yet proclaimed to the world that he had found his position to be untenable. In 1854 he published his *Sermons on the Holy Eucharist*. It was a supplement to his *Treatise on the doctrine of the Holy Eucharist*, as the *Sermons on the New Birth* had been a supplement to his book *On the Incarnation*. In the autumn of the same year, Archdeacon Wilberforce resigned his preferment in the Established Church, and he became a Catholic.

That year was a year of sorrow. How many homes were rendered desolate by the Crimean War! Two of my brothers (I had three), the eldest only twenty-one, had gone to take part in it, and were destined never to return. They were amongst the first of the victims. Before the end of October both of my brothers were numbered with the dead. It was not a time when I could think as I ought to think with regard to doctrinal questions. A change came over me, and such a change as perhaps a first great bereavement alone can bring. Keen have been the sorrows of after-life. Again and again those whom I most loved have been taken away. Often has the chalice of suffering been drained to the very dregs, but hardly ever again have I experienced the intensity of anguish which was mine when I gazed on the list of the killed at the Battle of the Alma. I felt that if *all* whom I loved were then and there lying dead at my feet, I could not have suffered more. I should even have rejoiced to think that they could not have to endure that which I was enduring then.

This first great sorrow came to me in my early youth. Would it have had the same effect, I wonder, had I been older? The whole world for a time seemed changed; its pleasures were no longer attractive, its annoyances of no importance. What had hitherto appeared so all-engrossing was now so trivial. Death became a reality. My own death, which had formerly seemed but a possibility, suddenly came before me as a certainty. It is not often that death so comes before me now, even when I most try to realize it. As the years go on we find that we have many more friends, many more of those whom we have loved and cherished, in the other world, than remain to us here. But when we are very young, it is a strange and an altogether novel experience to feel that one whom we have known all our lives, one who has been associated with all our fun and merriment, has been taken away from us for ever. He was full of life and gaiety; never again will he talk and laugh with us. Awe and reverence mingle with our thoughts of him. He has knowledge now of the mysteries of the spiritual existence. He has felt

> The new immortal throb of soul from body parted.

That first moment after death! I thought in those days that this must be a grand experience, although I had not been taught then that the soul passes instantly into the presence of its Judge, that it beholds the Sacred Face of Him Who died to save it, and that from His lips it *at once* has knowledge of its doom, for, as St. Paul says, "After death the Judgment." I had not been taught that if the soul was not as yet fit for the bright home for which it is one day destined, there is a prison beyond the grave, a place of purification where it is detained. There it is cleansed from those sins which, although forgiven, have not been expiated. There it is prepared for the Heaven where nothing defiled can enter.

I think that the idea of many Protestants is that the soul's fate is left undecided till the Last Judgment. Meanwhile, the soul is in a place of repose and will not wake up till the last trumpet sounds, and the sign of the Son of Man is seen in the sky. It is urged against the practice of praying for the dead that, "as the tree falls, so it lies," that prayers cannot avail to save a soul that dies in enmity with its Creator. Herein Protestants ignore the Particular Judgment. They suppose that the departed are still waiting to hear their sentence, and that, till that sentence is pronounced, they are at rest. Ages may pass before punishment or reward will be allotted to them. Protestants tell us that we may think of them meanwhile as sleeping.

Sleeping! that idea did not commend itself to me. Yearning for communion with those whom we no longer see on earth could not thus be satisfied. This yearning found expression in the words of Tennyson:

> Be near me when my light is low,
>   When the blood creeps, and the nerves prick
>   And tingle; and the heart is sick,
> And all the wheels of Being slow.
>
> .   .   .   .
>
> Be near me when I fade away,
>   To point the term of human strife,
>   And on the low dark verge of life
> The twilight of eternal day.

Then he asks:

> Do we indeed desire the dead
>   Should still be near us at our side?
>   Is there no baseness we would hide?
> No inner vileness that we dread?
>
> Shall he for whose applause I strove,
>   I had such reverence for his blame,
>   See with clear eye some hidden shame
> And I be lessen'd in his love?

But he puts aside the thought as wronging those who are free from the narrowness and the want of charity of which we ourselves are conscious.

> I wrong the grave with fears untrue:
>   Shall love be blamed for want of faith?
>   There must be wisdom with great Death:
> The dead shall look me thro' and thro'.
>
> Be near us when we climb or fall;
>   Ye watch, like God, the rolling hours
>   With larger, other eyes than ours,
> To make allowance for us all.

The *In Memoriam* is a genuine record, in somewhat obscure language, of the experience of a soul which has truly mourned. Sorrow has taught the soul to avail itself of the consolations which faith can give to it, and to believe in the immortality that faith has promised. I remember that *In Memoriam* was a real solace to me in that sorrow.

I wondered then how any one who has suffered can doubt God's love. It seemed to me that it is never so brought home to those that trust in Him, as it is in a great sorrow. How often we are told of one who is in severe affliction, "She is wonderfully supported." It is a commonplace phrase, but it contains a great truth. God does give a special help to His children, when He asks from them a great sacrifice which they try to give Him willingly, begging Him to

> Forgive [their] grief for one removed
> [His] creature whom they found so fair.

Letters in my possession bring this time vividly before me. Our kind friend, Mr. Somers, wrote:

"October 15, 1854.

"Your sweet letter has been a great comfort to me. I had become intensely anxious to hear about you all, but especially about your mama. She had often shadowed to herself the contingency of this affliction as one of the very possible results of actual service, but when such a calamity comes in all its deadly truth and reality, the heart and mind stagger under it as if the blow were altogether unexpected. And I know how the loss of her brave boy—her first-born—will bring freshly before her, sorrows which time had somewhat benumbed. Love *will* clasp grief.

"In after-times this sorrow will be brightened by the thought of the glorious manner of his death—rushing into destruction at the command of duty. It must be a great support and solace to you now to know that he had well contemplated the possibility of the end which did indeed befall him.

"After all, looking at your loved brother's fate, as compared with that of many, it has been an enviable one. A bright joyous life, a time for reflection, and then a noble, heroic end. From what anxieties and heart-aches he has been saved! 'He has passed into that still country where the hail-storm and the fire-shower may not reach, and where the heaviest-laden wayfarer at length lays down his load.'

"At first in these trials it is as much as we can do to gasp out the words, 'God's will be done.'

Time passes by, and the sad event is viewed under different angles of vision and it presents new aspects, and we are able to say, Blessed be God! Even in His sharpest stroke love and mercy were dealt with it."

The words that follow, I read many a time. They were written by a true Catholic friend.

"God only, Who inflicts these terrible bereavements, can cure the wound they leave behind. We *know* that He is all-wise and all-good, and that He does all things well both for us and for those we love. He is nearest to us, when He seems most to afflict us, and He will ever give us grace and consolation proportioned to our need. Compared with such consolations all human ones are trifling—even the thought of that death in the discharge of duty and on the field of honour, which has been said to come next after the Martyr's fate."

Milly wrote me on the day in which she heard of our loss:

"How I do think of you and of all you have to bear now. I only want to say a few words to tell you how I share in your sorrow, as if I had been your sister, and how I pray for you all. *You* can pray for *him* too, and very great must be the comfort of that. I long to do it, and why should I not?

"Death is not to you what it would be to many, I know, not utter separation. I wish I had your faith, my dear one, I feel to need it greatly at times, and now it would be an unspeakable comfort. I have so little of it, yet *some* I have, and it helps me very much, small and miserably weak as it is, faith in that Perfect Love, which we are so apt to measure by our own imperfection, and so utterly fail to conceive of. Yet I know it *is*, and that it is over you and him now, and must you not all be safe in that Love? It is such unutterable comfort to be able to trust you all to it, even poor and ignorant as that trust is in *me*."

A few days later Milly wrote again:

"October 16, 1854.

"You can hardly know the comfort and happiness your precious note gave me. I did not expect to hear from you so soon. It is very good for me to see how you bear this sorrow, and in some faint degree to take a part in it, for indeed I do this by such true sympathy, which, though I cannot express it, I know you will believe I feel. Your letter made me feel almost happy amid all the grief. I had prayed that you might be comforted, and you have that highest of all comfort, the blessed faith that he is safe, and that it was well for him to go. I am so thankful that you feel this. It does indeed seem to calm and *almost* prevent all earthly regrets and longings for him. Life might have been so full of dangers and temptations to him had he lived. I shall indeed think of you and him in the *Te Deum*. I *do* think nearly all day when I am alone and quiet. It seems so very wonderful to think of him as he is, little as we can conceive of that mysterious world where he is gone, to think of him as perhaps knowing all those things which we so long to know and cannot know. Again I feel a longing for your trusting faith.

"Dear child! if it were not wicked, I could envy you, even your sorrow, borne as it is. And then the glory (for there is a great glory, and though earthly, I hope not wrong) of thinking of his noble death and his bright memory. I feel— is it only fancy?—I could bear to have lost him to have *that* memory left to me for ever."

Another friend wrote the same day:

"October 16, 1854.

" . . . I am sure there is great comfort for you all even in this dispensation, not only in the self-devotion and glory of his death, but in the still more glorious faith and hope of a joyful resurrection. It is very, very sad even to us to feel that his bright smile is lost to us for ever on this side the grave, but these heavy afflictions seem sent to teach us holy lessons and to rend in part the veil that separates us from the unseen world; to take away the fear of Death for ourselves, while we feel that the fears of *life* (and they are many) can never more exist for the departed. And sorrow draws nearer together the hearts of the living. We can never again be *quite* the same as you were before this event, or as I was before last year. We can never feel that great sorrow is unknown by us, but, dearest, let it not weaken our love. I am feeling so deeply with you. Let us never forget that though the sunny years of our childhood have flown, the love of those old days must remain for ever, deeper and deeper, I trust, as time rolls on. How blessed it is to think that even death cannot end it! how earnest the prayer that when the few years of this weary life are ended we may all rest in peace with 'those who have departed this life in the faith and fear of the Lord,' never to be parted again. I am so thankful that you are able to think of all this even now. I have wept many tears for you all."

The following letter is from Milly:

"October 25, 1854.

"I must begin writing to you at once, having received your dear long letter this morning. You say you do like having a letter from me, or I don't think I should dare to send you one again so soon. . . . Perhaps I too need some great trial to teach me by sorrow what it seems I cannot learn by joy, the littleness of outward things, the realities of the spiritual world. Sometimes I think the trial *is* coming, and how weakly I shrink from the very thought of it! Yet there are moments when I almost envy you your sorrow and have a longing to *have suffered*, to have no more to dread, but to have passed the great ordeal, and to be calmed and stilled from all earthly cravings, fears, and ardent wishes; to have been forced, as it were, from making my home and rest on earth, and to have nothing more to long for but to do God's will and prepare for His coming. I don't think these thoughts have a good foundation. I believe they are partly selfish, and less from the desire to be very good, than to be free from care and the anxious weariness of human love. Oh me! thoughts, thoughts —how foolish and useless they are! Your letters always make me feel how little I *do*, especially this last one. It has made me sad: I hope it will do more. It *ought*.

"Yes, I do feel very much that difficulty of repenting definitely and earnestly, of which you speak. For a long time and very painfully I have felt it, and it makes me unhappy and frightened. At moments I feel very penitent, when for an instant it flashes on my mind how awful it is to sin, and then I cannot express how grieved and ashamed I feel, but these repentings are soon over. I can't think why they go away so quickly. Sin is really just as bad the next day as in the moment in which it has been committed. Yet how differently I feel about it even a few minutes after, when something puts out of my head the keen sense of my badness. Will this ever be otherwise? How I long to feel such repentance as some good books express! Don't you know Faber says we ought to look upon ourselves as the greatest sinners upon earth? Is this possible? Ought we to do it? I should like to be able to do it, for I should *like* to be humble, being not as yet at all really as I ought to be.

"Self-examination is difficult. I get so used to doing just the same wrong things, day after day, and so tired of having done them that I don't think my penitence increases every day, as it certainly should, because every repetition of sin aggravates its sinfulness. I feel quite stupid, so dull and unconcerned, as if it were no more than some mistakes I had made in a sum or in writing an exercise. No, I don't at all want to die now, for I want to be very much better first, if only I can hope by living on to grow better. 'Death, and after death the Judgment!' Do you remember the extract you once sent me about that text? I feel its truth more than ever—not enough, though, or it would make me live differently. Sometimes I am quite frightened at myself. I seem to be living in a sort of foolish vain dream, unreal and external, and then, to think of the sudden and fearful waking which *may* come at any moment! Then so often unbelieving thoughts present themselves, such as I fancy you never have, happy thing! and these are the very worst of all. I won't tell them to you. Why should I? It would only be selfish, I fear. . . .

"I did think of you on Sunday so much when we said the *Te Deum*, and I love to think of the Communion of Saints. May we really be so near to the departed? I should so like to believe this, especially now. I don't know whether to believe it or not. I think more of it now than I ever did before. How *I* have longed, too, to know what that first moment after death is like; what *he* felt and thought after that instantaneous change from strife and excitement and bodily activity, to the calm spirit world. Did thought continue without intermission, or was there a pause, a moment of stillness and of rest like sleep before he could realize the change which a moment had made? Then I wonder so what he is doing, in what state he is, whether disembodied or gifted with a spiritual body at once. Every night, just when I lie down quietly, before I go to sleep, I stay awake a little while to think of him. I like that time. It is the only time when I can really think at all. Often I have longed to see him, to have one moment's actual intercourse with him, to be able to imagine him rightly afterwards. I long to know if I may pray for him, and if so, for what? I do pray, but ever with a fear it may be in vain or worse. I don't think it can be wrong, though, to ask only what I ask, and it is a very great comfort. How it changes the view of death and one's feelings about it, to believe we *are* near to those who are gone, and parts still of the same body. Death becomes far less dreadful, and it seems to be such a help to oneself to believe we are so close to the holy invisible world, whither those we have loved are gone.

> One army of the living God,
> To His command we bow.
> Part of the host have crossed the flood,
> And part are crossing now.

"We have been singing that hymn to-night, and practising it, and despite of Samuel's screaming, I am very fond of that hymn. Oh! how one longs to pierce the veil, whatever it be, which hides from us the world of spirits, to see its secrets for one moment, to know what it is we shall be when we die, whether we shall care at all for the things we have left, or know what happens here.

"Your very loving
"MILLY."

Milly in this letter wonders whether praying for the dead can be wrong or useless. It is a natural instinct of the heart that can hardly be disregarded. It is the practice of the Universal Church, as it had been of the Jewish. How, then, could it be wrong? Useless, indeed, it would be were there no intermediate place between Heaven and Hell. Why pray for those who have already entered into the enjoyment of the Vision of God, or for lost souls who by their own deliberate choice have rejected God's love for ever? The Anglicans of that day had decided that there existed an intermediate place, the Limbus which existed before the Death of Jesus, and in which they fancied that the souls of the faithful departed are now in peace. Some notes I made of a sermon on this subject, which interested me, give the then current High Church doctrine. This sermon was on the text, "If we walk in the Light, as He is in the Light, we have fellowship one with another."

The Communion of Saints, it was remarked, was a doctrine on which our ideas might have been vague and indefinite. As forming part of our baptismal faith, it could hardly be unimportant. That it was not so considered in ancient days was proved by the fact that the Creed was not considered complete without it. What, then, was this Communion of Saints in which we professed our belief?

I. Between the individuals of the same family, between the children of the same father, between the members of the same body, there must necessarily exist some sympathy, and some relation. All the baptized, therefore, were outwardly partakers of that fellowship of which the Evangelist spoke.

II. But there was a deeper bond than any bond which could be formed by outward relationship, and which bound in one the hearts of the faithful. If two children were filled with intense love and devotion to the same father, must not a closer sympathy exist between them and draw them to each other, than there would be if mere outward relationship was their sole bond of union? This was the true Communion of God's Saints. The most solitary, the most unfriended, could then never be alone. From many an unknown altar would prayers and supplications be really made for him, and these like ministering angels would guide his steps in life and support him on his journey through the valley of death. He might have been a partaker of the fellowship of those who walked in the Light.

III. If then this fellowship was so real—so spiritual, a supernatural, not a natural work, the result of the Indwelling of God the Holy Ghost, forming of many members but one Body—was there any power which could destroy it? Could Death destroy it? Surely not. The utmost that Death could do was to destroy the body. The soul still lived. Neither Revelation nor Reason could lead us to conclude that such a change could pass over the soul as to cause the whole of its past existence to be obliterated from its remembrance. Could the soul be conceived of as retaining its identity, if at the moment in which it quitted its body, it ceased to have any interest in those who one instant before had been the supreme objects of its affections? Perhaps

with his last breath the dying man had invoked
a blessing on those who were his dearest. Would
their salvation become to him in that instant a
matter of indifference? It was impossible that
it could be so. The nature of the case was in
accordance with the instinct of our hearts. Revelation furnished positive proof that it was not so.
In the vision of St. John the souls of the martyrs
were represented as crying to God for vengeance.
This was enough, if we appealed to no other
passages of Holy Scripture, to prove that prayers
were offered to God by departed spirits, and that
earthly events were the subjects of their prayers.
If they cried for retribution on the depraved, oh!
how much more would they implore grace for all
men of good-will.

Such then was their remembrance of *us*. Did
we forget *them*? No. We had thought of their
interceding for us. Could they need our supplications? It was certain that man's everlasting
doom was determined at the moment of death.
No prayers could bring an impenitent sinner to
salvation, and could our prayers add aught to
the happiness of Paradise? It might be so. The
end was not yet consummated. The Judgment
was still to come. Who, even of the holiest,
could look forward to that searching Judgment
and not tremble? Might not a shadow of its
approaching awfulness be even at times cast over
the peace of the souls in Paradise? Our prayers,
therefore, might constantly be offered for their

perfection, their comfort, and their refreshment. We would, therefore, remember them before the throne of Jesus. We prayed for them; they prayed for us. Such was the Communion of Saints.

"The Prophets, do they live for ever? Your fathers, where are they?" Ah, who could tell? They might be hovering round our path. They might be watching us from their place of repose, and ever from the other side of the dark waters that flowed between us and them there might be ascending a wailing cry of supplication to Heaven, and this for us. We were not left to our own poor prayers. The souls in the Valley of the Shadow prayed for us also. Dark and deep indeed as might be the gulf that separated us from those holy souls, there was at least one act in which we could not be divided—and this was our mutual unceasing prayer.

These thoughts comforted me greatly. They encouraged me to pray as the Church prays in Holy Mass: "To all who rest in Christ, grant, we beseech Thee, a place of refreshment, light, and peace."

Protestants have somehow persuaded themselves that the Death of Jesus has not only made atonement for the guilt of their sins, but that it has done away with all necessity on their part of doing penance, and of making acts of contrition. The Scriptures teach us in the histories of Moses, of David, and of others, that even forgiven sins entail severe temporal punishment. What a chastisement was that which followed a seemingly venial sin—the numbering of the people! Sufferings come to the holiest of men on earth. Even those who are not saints can rejoice in these sufferings. They know that they are proofs of God's Love, and of God's desire to have them all the sooner with Him in Heaven. Some men have their purgatory in this present life. But the majority of ordinary Christians die—in the grace of God indeed and with real sorrow for their sins, and yet—without having done very much of penance, and still attached to the world and to the pleasures of the world. They have not made an act of contrition so perfect as to at once admit them to the presence of their God. He is a God not only of infinite Mercy and Love, but a God also of infinite Purity and Justice. Heaven would not be Heaven to them so long as any stain remained on their souls. The penance which they neglected on this earth must be performed in that prison-house beyond the grave of which our Lord said: "Thou shalt not depart thence till thou hast paid the last farthing." This debt may be lessened and it may be cancelled by the prayers and by the sacrifices which are offered in their behalf on earth. Thus it is our blessed part to hasten the moment when they shall be summoned to the Beatific Vision.

In order to esteem rightly the consolations of

Purgatory a man must be a Catholic and he must believe in God as a Catholic believes. He must believe every article of the Creed in that sense in which the Church teaches it. He must not, I saw, attach his own meaning to the words, "The Communion of Saints, the forgiveness of sins."

.   .   .   .   .

We were away from home when that great sorrow came to us. We did not feel equal to returning at once to Clifton. We went for two months to Bournemouth. There we lived in one of those little thatched cottages of which the place at that time was mainly composed. This cottage was close to St. Peter's Church. That church was not then so grand as it is at present. There was as yet no large town to shut out the lovely view of the sea and to mar the peacefulness of the pretty churchyard. There were services twice every day, and these we never failed to attend. I found comfort in having fixed times for public prayer. The church, being open morning and evening, afforded opportunities for solitude which I could seldom obtain elsewhere. In my mother's deep affliction I could not possibly add to her grief by any display of Roman tendencies. I tried to think that perhaps some satisfactory way of getting on in the English Church might open out, and that I might lead a useful life, and might get a great deal of good where I was. At any rate, I was determined in real earnest to make the best of whatever helps the English Church afforded to the spiritual life.

As a guide to the profitable spending of Advent, I had Avrillon's Meditations, the translation edited by Dr. Pusey. To the meditation for the 8th of December Dr. Pusey appended a note in which he adduced St. Augustine's authority for the Immaculate Conception. This note I found it useful to quote whenever that doctrine was disputed. The definition had just been published and there was much discussion on the subject. The newspapers were uttering blasphemies. Bishop Wilberforce, I think it was, who affirmed that unless Mary had been born in original sin our Lord could not have really taken our human nature, and that the dogma of the Immaculate Conception did away with the Incarnation. What he said sounded deep. Some unreflecting people thought that it was true. I was glad to observe that St. Augustine and Dr. Pusey did not agree with Dr. Wilberforce. Dr. Pusey indeed did not commit himself very decidedly. The feast of the Conception of the Blessed Virgin Mary is retained in the English Calendar, and this no doubt encouraged him to agree with St. Augustine, that the Blessed Mother of God should be excepted where there was question of sin.

It was from Mr. Upton Richards, who paid us a visit at Bournemouth, that we first heard that

Mr. Dean had given up his much-loved living of Lewknor and his fellowship at All Souls', and that he had followed his friends, Mr. Wynne and Archdeacon Wilberforce, into the Church of Rome. It was, indeed, a tremendous sacrifice for Mr. Dean to make. Lewknor was within easy reach of Oxford and London, and it suited him so perfectly. To him, in his infirm state of health, the homelessness and the poverty which he had now to face must have been no slight trial. I spoke before of his wit and his unconventionality. It must not be supposed that these qualities prevented him from gaining the hearts of his parishioners. Years afterwards, one of these, whose life had been a life of sickness and suffering, spoke with the greatest gratitude of his having taught her the practice of spiritual communion. A paralytic stroke which he had when quite a young man prevented Mr. Dean from taking Holy Orders in the Catholic Church. It used to vex me to know how he and such as he were misjudged, and how the noble surrender for conscience' sake of all that had made this world bright to them, was ignored. Because they were debarred from ministry in the Roman Catholic Church they were spoken of as men who had gone back after having put their hands to the plough.

During this winter I kept a sort of spiritual diary. The better thoughts in this diary were suggested by either books or sermons. Thus having been favoured with a glimpse at such a work as Rodriguez' *On Christian Perfection*, I remark that "the saints looked upon the Christian life as a trade that had to be learnt, and learnt as other trades are, with much diligence, with great watchfulness, with many failures, little by little. They have written books on the art of holy living containing the most minute directions how to acquire each virtue—humility, charity, purity of intention, confidence in God, &c. To them the spiritual life was a reality, not a vague idea, as it is alas! with the generality of men. Perhaps this is what strikes us most in reading the Lives of the Saints—that we had no idea before to what our baptismal vows pledge us. Spirituality had seemed an abstraction, not a reality. We had not thought of it as a science; a science that must be gradually learnt as other sciences are, with labour and study, and a science too which it is necessary that all should learn. The impression I often get from sermons is that a religious life consists in pious feelings and aspirations—a vague something—not a system with rules by which a man may test himself and 'prove' his own heart. To say at the end of the day that we are miserable sinners is one thing: to name the specific acts by which we know ourselves to be miserable sinners is another."

January 21, 1855.—"There is no truth that Archer Butler in his sermons insists on more frequently, and with greater earnestness, than the extreme value of every moment. This follows from the fact that what we make ourselves here, that we must be for ever; that the characters we bear with us out of this world will continue in their ultimate tendency to all eternity. The habits we shall need in the other world must be formed here, habits of union with God, of conformity to His will, of charity to our fellows. We could not enjoy Heaven unless we first loved holiness here. The happiness of Heaven would not be happiness to us, unless in the praise and service of God on earth we found our greatest joy. And this thought may lead us to know our own selves better; for we may deceive ourselves in many points, but we can hardly delude ourselves into believing that we find happiness in an employment which is in reality wearisome and distasteful to us."

March 24, 1855.—"One of my favourite prayers is the prayer that asks for 'a right judgment in all things.' I suppose that the difficulties which arise from conflicting duties are part of our probation here, and that we ought not to complain because the right path seems at times so doubtful and obscured as to make it almost impossible for us to determine which it is. It seems that the more anxious we are to do what is right, the more perplexities we prepare for ourselves. And then complications arise which require an immediate solution. I have no time to reflect on what is best to be done and I find I have done what I had better not have done. I don't know which makes me most uncomfortable, being undecided, or feeling that I have decided hastily and perhaps wrongly. Oh! for a right judgment."

The following thoughts were suggested by a sermon which I heard Mr. Woodford preach:

"It is strange how little some parts of the Bible are studied by many who profess the greatest reverence for the Bible, and who claim to derive their system of religious belief exclusively from the Bible. This may go far to account for the differences of religious opinion which are met with amongst those who all agree in appealing to the inspired Word of God as their authority. The Prophecy of Zechariah may be cited as a portion comparatively very little studied. Yet this Book is found to contain very important evidence for the truth of doctrines often denied in the present day. It shows that God carries on His government of the world through the ministrations of angels, and that the angels intercede with God for men. It teaches the personality of the evil spirit, &c. The vision recorded in the third chapter is applicable, not only to the Jewish nation as it then was, but, in a wider sense, to the Church Catholic. Take the first verse: 'The High Priest standing before the Angel of the Lord and Satan standing at his right hand.' Have we not here an explanation of all the striving and counter-striving, all the efforts for the spread of Christianity, and the reason why those efforts should have been so often frustrated; why, in spite of the internal evidences for the truth of the doctrine of Christ, in spite of its adaptation to the wants of mankind, it should at the end of eighteen hundred years not be professed even outwardly by half of the human race?

"In its immediate adaptation, the vision of Zechariah represented the Jewish Church as personified by Joshua the High Priest. The position of the adversary must not pass unnoticed. Not in direct antagonism, not face to face as it were, did the author of evil carry on his work. Satan standing *at his right hand* is not an unapt description of the position the fallen spirit usually assumes in his conflict with the powers of Heaven. It was so in the rebuilding of the Jewish Temple, when, not open enemies, but false friends hindered the work of God. Internal, rather than external, causes—faithlessness within, rather than the pressure of force from without—the craft of Satan prompting the growth of self-deceit, blinding the reason and the conscience, subtly sowing the seeds of disunion, persecuting and outwardly opposing the truth only so long as his suggestions seemed to meet with no answer from within,—has not this been the history of his working in the Church of

Christ? Is it not so now? When through faith we behold Jesus, the Great High Priest, still interceding, still offering Himself before the throne of the Father, is there not one always at work, plotting continually how he may frustrate every scheme, how he may ruin every soul for which that sacrifice is offered, how he may make every prayer fruitless, every grace but an occasion for deeper condemnation? Is not Satan still standing at his right hand?"

Among the sermons that we heard Mr. Woodford preach, was one (afterwards published in his volume entitled, *Occasional Sermons*) on the misery of being forsaken by God. "Ephraim is joined unto idols; let him alone." Mr. Woodford maintained that the idolatry of the Israelites of old found its counterpart in the heresy, the schism, and the false doctrine of our own day. "What," he said, "are the diverse creeds shouted on every side, the diverse doctrines taught in every street, but the groves of men's planting, to the neglect of the temple of the Lord,—the idols of men's own hearts, in place of God's truth once for all delivered to the saints? Wilfulness and impatience of old took the shape of idolatry; they now wear the form of heresy and separation and divisions. It was a zeal for religion which prostrated Israel at the footstool of idols; it is zeal without knowledge which makes men forsake the Catholic faith for crude theories of their own." He went on to speak of the punishment. "Indeed,

indeed, all vengeance is concentrated in the few words, 'let him alone!' 'Let him alone!' it is as if it was proclaimed that idolatry would prove its own punishment; that so sure, so inevitable would be the miserable consequences of forsaking the true God, or corrupting His worship, that it needed no further outbreak of wrath to vindicate the honour of the Almighty."

This lesson was a lesson of very wide application. It did not only concern those who had forsaken God altogether and ceased to fear and obey Him. It implied " more, much more than this. We argue," Mr. Woodford said, "that you cannot drop a single doctrine of the Catholic faith without that doctrine, sooner or later, avenging itself. Let the truth of God be marred in ever so slight a degree, and vast injury must follow. For a long time matters will go on as usual, but eventually evil will result. A Church may, for the sake of peace, compromise some principle, state ambiguously some point of faith. For a while no harm will ensue. By-and-bye, however, even man's eye will be able to detect the pernicious consequences. Take an instance. A large portion of Germany, at the period of the Reformation, rejected Episcopal government, and allowed men to touch the sacraments who had not received the imposition of hands from Bishops of the Apostolical Succession. To many good men at the time it seemed a matter of little moment, a mere point of discipline. Episcopacy was, however, an ordinance of God; and mark the consequences of rejecting it. The reformed congregations of Germany have declined more and more from what is called the orthodox faith. The country is over-run with a wretched intellectualism. The inspiration of the Bible begins to be questioned; the Deity of Christ to be denied; the miracles of the Holy Ghost to be explained away. Apostolical order was repudiated three centuries ago, and it has terribly avenged itself. And this is an exact illustration of the text. It needs not that the Almighty should perpetually step in by visible judgments to uphold His cause; any more than in the physical world it is requisite for Him to interfere again and again in the production of different events. He has implanted in matter certain properties—certain laws of motion. These properties and laws do His pleasure and accomplish unerringly His will. It is so with religion. To every doctrine He has given its own power: if used aright, for salvation; if neglected, for destruction. Let a man or a nation cast scorn upon that doctrine, or refuse to receive it, and it shall not need that the thunder should roll to speak God's wrath, or the windows of Heaven be open as when the flood of waters rushed down. Truth neglected will make itself felt. There will ensue to the negligent, a slow but sure decline in all holiness and knowledge and consolation. Eager spirits may thirst for speedy retribution, and marvel at what appears the delay of judgment. But equally certain will be the penalty; and more terrible, if in place of at once stretching out His arm, God lets matters take their course, saying in His place of judgment to those who follow their own devices, as to Ephraim of old: 'He is joined unto idols, let alone!'"

It was a frightening thought and a true one, fearfully true. This was what gave power to Mr. Woodford's preaching—that he often inculcated Catholic truth with such force that it sank deep into hearts prepared to receive it. The weak point was that he did not see how that truth might be turned against himself. He spoke as a Catholic priest might have spoken about keeping the faith whole and entire, and he overlooked the fact that in order to keep the faith whole and entire, there must be a living, infallible voice to declare what that faith was. All that he said about the rejection of Episcopacy in Germany applied equally to the rejection of the authority of the Apostolic See in England. And must not the judgment which he denounced on any religious body which for the sake of peace consented to an ambiguous statement of an article of faith, descend on that Church which permitted the doctrine of Baptismal Regeneration to be regarded as an open question?

Again, on another occasion,[1] Mr. Woodford

[1] *Occasional Sermons*, "Dimensions and Proportions of the Church," p. 120.

argued that to believe comprehended a vast deal. "If I am exhorted to believe, I ask, In what am I to believe? If the reply is, Believe in Christ, I inquire further, What is it to believe in Christ? and then the right answer must be, that to believe in Christ is to hold fast all those multiplied doctrines and principles which constitute the system of the Christian Church. . . . Oh!" he continued, "you cannot shave and pare away God's revelation. The man who upholds dependence upon Christ, but denies the necessity of good works, does he believe the Gospel? The man who maintains the Personality and efficacy of the Holy Ghost, but denies or scorns the ministrations of angels, does he believe the Gospel? The man who clings to the idea of personal sanctification, but ignores the necessity of Church communion, does he believe the Gospel?"

Then referring to those who urged that to insist on dogma was to do away with the simplicity of the Gospel of Christ, he asked, What was the profit of simplicity if it were got by taking a part and not the whole? "The simplicity of the Christian religion is not, we are bold to say, deducible from the New Testament. I find there a great deal about the 'mystery of godliness,' but nothing about this simplicity. I read of the 'mysteries of the Kingdom of Heaven,' 'the mystery of His will,' 'the mystery of Christ,' 'the mystery of the Gospel, the mystery of faith.' I find an Apostle declaring that he spoke 'the wisdom of God in a mystery.' The whole tenor of the Epistles and discourses of all the Apostles, is what might be expected from men who felt themselves charged with a burden of dread tidings, proclaimers of unfathomable depths, entrusted with 'the secret of the Lord.' There is nothing off-hand in their delineations of their Master's Faith, nothing short and summary in their manner of instructing their converts into His communion. Rather we should say, did they feel themselves wanderers within the walls of a fabric whose grandeur baffled all their faculties, whose foundations were laid too deep for them to discover, whose battlements were lost in clouds which their eyes could not pierce. Rather in receiving proselytes do they seem to have acted as though admitting them to stand where shadows and darkness would ever roll around them, the necessary accompaniments of the Divine Presence; where their ears should be filled with unspeakable words, and their thoughts wafted to wondrous visions, ever on the stretch to 'comprehend,' if possible, 'with all saints the breadth, and length, and depth, and height.'"

These extracts from Mr. Woodford's published sermons give an idea of the force of his language and of how bold he was in his enunciation of dogma. During the Holy Week of 1855, he gave six lectures on the latter part of the Creed. Of these

I wrote my recollections. In the second lecture, speaking of the words, "the Holy Catholic Church," following immediately on our declaration of belief in the Holy Ghost, he showed how the connection between these two articles of faith was not an arbitrary connection, but a result of the truth that to the Holy Spirit the Church owed its beginning, as it still owes its continued existence. No one who had read the Gospels and the Acts, could help acknowledging the difference between the two in this one respect, that whilst in the one, believers were spoken of *individually*, as it were, in the other they were regarded *collectively*, as forming one body, one society. Up to the Day of Pentecost, the Apostles waited as their Lord had commanded. They made no effort to propagate their faith; but no sooner had the promised Spirit come, than Peter lifted up his voice and three thousand souls were added to the Church.

The fact that belief in the Holy Catholic Church is declared in the same formulary in which we profess our belief in the Father, the Son, and the Holy Ghost, proved that it could be no mere human society for the existence of which our faith was demanded. If we asked our fellow-countrymen what they meant when they declared their belief in the Holy Catholic Church, the answer of the majority would be that they meant by the Church the whole congregation of believers in Christ dispersed throughout the world.

In other words, they believe that there are Christians in the world, for this is what their idea comes to, a fact which no man could possibly doubt, and to recognize which, therefore, needs no faith.

There was a deep mystery evidently involved in the being of the Church. It was no work of earth, no kingdom of this world. Prophecy spoke not falsely when it foretold the glory of the Church of Christ. The vision which was vouchsafed to the Beloved Disciple was no unreal vision of the splendour of the New Jerusalem. It might be that in future ages it was reserved for us to see that which now could hardly be discerned through a glass darkly: that sight should take the place of faith, and we should then indeed behold the Church as faith was now teaching us to believe it. One Body, because there is only one Head and one Spirit; Holy, because it is sanctified by that Spirit, and not marred by the imperfection of its members; Unerring, because it is His voice Who is the Truth; Imperishable, because it is sustained by Him Who is the Life. Individually its members might err, individually they might fall away, but error should never prevail against the Church of Christ as a body, nor could any efforts of man or of the evil one efface it from the earth.

That this description of the Church could hardly be made to apply to the "branch" under whose shadow we were at that time recumbent, I tried just then to forget. My wish was to put aside controversial thoughts and to feel thankful at being encouraged and strengthened in Catholic principles. Mr. Woodford's sermons helped me a good deal.

He was nevertheless a thorough Anglican, and was destined in after-years to sit on the Episcopal Bench. Only one more sermon of his will I quote—a sermon very consoling to the English Churchman—preached at the consecration of St. Michael's Church, Bristol. It was on the *Alliance of Church and State*.[1] The text was, "Kings with their armies did flee and were discomfited, and they of the household divided the spoil."

It was Mr. Woodford's plan, in most of his sermons, to start with touching on some topic irrelevant to the subject on which he intended mainly to speak. In this one he begins with an eloquent passage on the influence that our ancient ecclesiastical edifices possess of awakening deep emotions and solemn thoughts. But, he maintained, a building newly dedicated to God has a power no less impressive. Instead of looking back to the past, we look onward to the future, to the many souls who shall there be regenerated in the waters of Baptism and be strengthened to the end of time by the Bread which cometh down from Heaven.

He then passes on to the expediency of the connection of national Churches with the civil

[1] *Occasional Sermons*, xiv.

power, and urges that this connection is not only lawful and expedient, but was the method which was contemplated by God for the spread of Christianity after its first promulgation by the Apostles and their immediate successors. He considers that the need for miracles ceased when the civil power lent its aid to the Church. "The alliance of the Church with the civil power is to us now in lieu of supernatural gifts. This is the vantage-ground vouchsafed unto us to occupy. The miracles which the Founders of the Faith were enabled to achieve, were the instruments we consider of hastening this result. The general and ultimate instrumentality was to be another gift of God, even that of legal and national institutions."[1] It follows that, "hastily to get rid of all alliance with earthly rule, is to cast to the winds the spoil we have won; to abandon the position to which God has led us."[2]

Considerations such as these, may have reconciled even such a valiant defender of the Church's prerogatives as was Dr. Woodford, to the Royal Supremacy, and to the necessity of kneeling before his Sovereign and repeating that act of homage wherein the Bishops of the Established Church acknowledge that they receive their episcopal power spiritual as well as temporal from Queen Victoria.[3]

---

[1] P. 219.   [2] P. 222.
[3] Dr. Tait, after being consecrated Bishop of London, thus describes this ceremony: "I was conducted by Sir George Grey

Such an acknowledgment renders unto Cæsar much more than the things that are Cæsar's. An alliance between the Ecclesiastical and the Civil Powers as ordained by God is one thing: the entire subserviency of the National Church to Crown and Parliament, such as is the case in England, is another.

Was the text a happy one as applied to the Church in question? "Kings with their armies did flee and were discomfited, and they of the household divided the spoil!" We have read of Attila and his savage hordes quailing before Leo, and of that German Emperor who knelt in penance at Canossa. We know the fate that in more recent times has befallen other Emperors who have dared to lift their hands against the Vicar of Christ, but, however much spoil may have been given her to divide, is there any record

---

into the Queen's closet, a very small room, where I found the Queen and Prince Albert. Having been presented by Sir George, I kneeled down on both knees before the Queen, just like a little boy at his mother's knee. I placed my joined hands between hers, while she stooped her head so as almost to bend over mine, and I repeated slowly and solemnly the very impressive words of the oath which constitutes the Act of Homage. Longley, the new Bishop of Durham, who had accompanied me, then went through the same ceremony. He had not escaped so quietly from the ceremonial when he was consecrated Bishop of Ripon. His oath was then taken to William IV., and no sooner had he risen from his knees, than the King suddenly addressed him in a loud voice thus: 'Bishop of Ripon, I charge you, as you shall answer before Almighty God, that you never by word or deed give encouragement to those d——d Whigs who would upset the Church of England.'" (*Life of Archbishop Tait*, vol. i. p. 206.)

of the Established Church of England having put to flight discomfited kings with their armies?

· · · · ·

I must not forget to mention a little book which was given me by Mrs. Cleveland. It helped me very much—an *Instruction on Mental Prayer* by Courbon, in the form of questions and answers. The translation of this book for members of the English Church bore the *Imprimatur* of the Rev. Upton Richards. It first taught me to meditate in accordance with a fixed method. Rules not too elaborate were given for the three parts of prayer: the preparation—the body of the prayer—and the conclusion.

Each part consisted of three things. In the preparation we (1) placed ourselves in the presence of God; (2) acknowledged our unworthiness; (3) asked the help of the Holy Spirit.

The body of the prayer was composed of (1) Adoration, (2) Communion, and (3) Co-operation.

1. Adoration. We considered the subject, as for instance one of the Divine attributes, or some portion of the Life of Jesus Christ, or some virtue, humility, charity, obedience, &c., as manifested in our Lord, dwelling on what He said, did, and thought, with regard to it, making acts of adoration, love, praise, thanksgiving, joy, &c.

2. Communion. We saw how deficient we were in the virtue on which we had been medi-

tating, and in our imitation of our Lord. We made acts of humility. We considered what we ought to avoid and what we ought to do in order to be more like Him, most earnestly asking for the grace we so much needed.

3. Co-operation. In this point we were to make resolutions in order that we might co-operate in securing the grace for which we had been asking—resolutions to be carried into effect at once, having seen what we had to avoid, what obstacles to overcome, our own utter helplessness and entire dependence on the mercy of God.

In conclusion we (1) thanked God for the graces given us in our prayer; (2) asked pardon for any faults we had committed during the time of prayer, and (3) begged that God would bless our resolutions.

This and other methods of mental prayer taught us to study very deeply and lovingly the Life of Jesus Christ from its beginning as an Infant in Mary's arms to its close when He hung for three hours on the Cross with Mary standing by. A new world of contemplation was opened up to me. To spend a certain portion of every day with our Lord, His Mother, the Holy Apostles, and other Saints, made life much more interesting. I found that by degrees we learn to take their view, to listen to their words, and to be ashamed of having thoughts and desires so very different from theirs. We would fain become a little less unlike them.

By dwelling on the mysteries of our Lord's Life with a resolute will to imitate Him in their measure, many who are outside the pale of the Visible Church find themselves almost unconsciously brought into harmony with her ascetical spirit and system of devotion. These devotions become, therefore, a source of uneasiness to the sound Anglican, who regards them as dangerous, and not in accordance with the sobriety and moderation of " our " Church.

That Easter-tide of 1855 was a time of much quiet happiness to me—shall I rather call it spiritual consolation? I thus write of this time in my journal:

"As there are certain days whose influence may be traced through large portions of after-life, so also are there weeks when the whole inner life receives as it were the impress of some one idea or train of ideas, which when first grasped seems to open a new world for meditation and contemplation, to shed new light upon the past, to remove former difficulties, to put life and our own position in it before us in a totally different point of view from that in which we have hitherto regarded it. Such have been the last few weeks, when the great realities of the Gospel, the wonderful facts of Christianity, have presented themselves before me and claimed my love and adoration in a way that they have hardly ever done before. God does not often reveal Himself and His truths so clearly. That He has done so now is, I know, not from any merit of mine. I have done nothing to deserve such a grace. It frightens me to think that it is one responsibility the more, that I have now to manifest in my daily life these truths. I have to guard the faith, that most precious treasure, against the chilling atmosphere of the world of sense, I have to act on my convictions and thus deepen them and plant them so firmly in my heart that they may never be uprooted. 'Whilst we have light, let us walk in the light.' 'The night cometh.' Such is the warning which holy seasons—seasons holy to us—should ever bring."

. . . . .

Our life at Clifton was now drawing to a close, and we were beginning to look forward to new scenes. My brother's health was not strong. It was thought advisable that he should be removed from school for a year, at all events. We had, therefore, no ties to England, and thus a good opportunity for foreign travel presented itself. Of this it was decided that we should take advantage. We were to go first to Switzerland. We hoped to spend the winter in Rome.

CHAPTER IX.

A Foreign Tour. Morning at Bruges. High Mass in the Cathedral. Rubens' pictures at Antwerp and Malines. Church of St. Appolinaris at Remagen. Arrival in Switzerland. Thun. An earthquake.

Mr. Barker. His ideas and conduct. My brother's letters from Kandersteg and Weggis. Grindelwald. The churchyard at Weggis.

Arrival in Italy. Journey from Cività Vecchia. First impressions of Rome.

I MUST say a little about our first few months in foreign lands, as they have some reference to the subject of my book. Our stay at Rome was the most important part of this time abroad, not only in duration, but in its subsequent influence. A few words, however, on our experiences in Belgium and Switzerland may not be out of place.

I shall always be grateful for having crossed the Channel, and for having spent more than two full years on the Continent whilst I was yet in my teens. Since then whenever I have found myself on foreign soil it has been with a feeling of ever-renewed delight. The first impression perhaps was one more of bewilderment than of delight. One requires to get a little accustomed to travelling and to the novelty of the life altogether, before one can thoroughly enjoy it. I found, nevertheless, something to enjoy even in our tea at the Lord Warden, and in our five or six hours in the steamer from Dover to Ostend, in a very early landing at the latter place, and in the railway journey to Bruges which followed. At this quaint old city, our first morning abroad was spent. They are an early folk in Belgium. They were up and doing long before we generally think of rising. On this occasion we had nothing more comfortable than a cabin's berth to rise from. We had time to see a good deal before eleven o'clock. At that hour I returned to the Cathedral. There was to be a grand function there. This of course I was anxious not to miss.

The Catholic's Vade Mecum had been recommended by Mrs. Cleveland as a convenient little book to take abroad to enable us to follow the services. I had this book with me that day at Bruges, when for the first time I found myself present at High Mass. I had studied the service before and I was a little disappointed at not being able to make out what was going on. Had I been present at the beginning of Mass I might have found it easier to follow. After a time, however, I happily caught the words, *Orate fratres.* This enabled me to find my place and to join in the more solemn part. I put down in my diary that evening: "Much as I liked it, I shall like it better another time. Some would call it a very formal service. To me it suggests the immense importance of Divine worship."

Next morning I spent some time in the Cathedral at Antwerp, and I wrote it down that I assisted at a Low Mass and felt much happier than I had done the day before, as I could follow it better. On St. Peter's day, when we heard High Mass in the Cathedral at Aix-la-Chapelle, I began to feel a great deal more at home.

Besides my brother and his tutor, Mr. Barker, Oswald and his wife were with us on our leaving England. We were a merry party. Even Oswald had to unbend at times and to join in the general hilarity. But, as usual, the improvement of his own mind and of our minds was his first object. He was intent on our seeing everything that there was to be seen. We lionized more of these Belgian towns than could be done quite conveniently in the time, making little journeys by railway, alighting with our guide-books, visiting the churches and other buildings of interest, seeing all that we should see, and then going on to another place to begin again. This way of proceeding was more pleasing to me than to Olivia, who easily got fatigued.

Of my first experiences abroad I gave an account in this letter to my aunt.

"I have so enjoyed these few days. I wish I could tell you all about them. I have felt so *up to* all the sight-seeing and never too much tired. Getting a good sleep in the steamer was a great advantage. It enabled me to enjoy Bruges, 'the belfry brown and old,' the quaint buildings and Memling's pictures so much more than the others could.

"We spent two nights at Antwerp, and I should have been glad of a longer time there. Rubens' pictures are magnificent. I care for them much more than I expected to do. The specimens of his paintings one sometimes sees are often so coarse. But in these there is such real deep feeling, and wonderful imagination combined with the most glorious colouring, that I think I hardly ever enjoyed any pictures so much."

"I am writing in the station at Aix-la-Chapelle, waiting for the train to Cologne. We spent two hours yesterday morning at Malines, a most picturesque town. In the Church of St. John is a magnificent altar-piece by Rubens—'The Adoration of the Magi'"—with scenes from the lives of St. John the Baptist and St. John the Evangelist on each side. I particularly liked the painting of St. John writing his Gospel. He is represented gazing upwards whilst he writes. In the Cathedral is Vandyke's celebrated picture of the Crucifixion. The interior of the Cathedral was too white for my taste. The music in the Church of Notre Dame was beautiful. A Requiem was being sung. I find that visiting these churches is very conducive to a *good* state of mind. One sees so many worshippers in every church. The poor and the old are thoroughly at home there. They go in to pray when no service is going on. Religion seems to be mixed up with everything. I have not yet seen anything to shock me, which you prophesied would be the case in a Popish country.

· · · · · ·

"I could say much about the Cathedral at Cologne, but as you have seen it I need not expatiate on its beauty. We were glad not to sleep in that city. A short railway journey took us to Bonn for the night.

"The next morning, after an expedition up the Drachenfels on donkeys, we drove along the banks of the Rhine to Remagen. Here is the Church of St. Appolinaris. This we had been recommended to see—a new church, small, and built in the shape of a cross. It contains frescoes by Deger, the Müllers, and Ittenbach. Those representing the Crucifixion, the Resurrection, and the Ascension, are very beautiful. There are scenes also from the life of St. Appolinaris. We were told that St. Appolinaris was one of the very early saints. He was ordained by St. Peter, and there are many legends about him.

· · · · · ·

"I am writing now from Frankfort. Our plan is to go on to Heidelberg to-morrow, to stay there a day or two, and then to proceed to Basle and Thun.

"Our journey up the Rhine was very pleasant. We employed ourselves on the boat in reading legends of all the places that we passed. These legends were in German poetry. They were mostly about beautiful maidens and disconsolate knights. Mr. Barker is very anxious to acquire the German language. These poems will hardly help him to converse with the natives.

Pray impress upon Mr. Cleveland that we thoroughly appreciate all the beautiful things that we see. He need not have distressed himself with the idea that we were missing all the Belgian towns. We saw Bruges, Antwerp, Malines, and Liège.

"Malleray, July 12, 1855.

"Now we are in Switzerland. For the first time since we left England we are passing a night in the country at a little village half way between Basle and Berne. . . . . Yesterday we left Heidelberg. The railroad to Basle passed through very beautiful scenery. For a while we could see in the distance the long line of the Vosges Mountains, and on the left the mountains of the Black Forest. The lights were so lovely. The evening was most delicious. We stayed out till ten on the balcony overhanging the Rhine in the hotel at Basle, and at nine this morning we set off. 'A rainy cloud possessed the earth,' so we had reluctantly to close our carriages. Fortunately in the afternoon when we came to the most beautiful part of the Val Moutiers, there was a temporary cessation. The coverings of the carriages were removed and oh! the scenery was so splendid—the high

T

rocks and the stream (the course of which we followed all the way) rushing through the narrow valley, with delicious waterfalls every now and then, and the foliage so bright and varied. I don't think it lost anything by the gloominess of the weather. I hope it will be fine to-morrow, as if it is clear we expect to see snow mountains. Olivia is much delighted at the prospect of being settled and getting into a fresh dress. She does not like the limpness and the dustiness which journeys, especially railroad journeys, involve. Yesterday our appearance in the train struck her as an illustration of the hymn,

> Where every prospect pleases
> And only man is vile.

The *voiture* method of journeying is much more attractive, and Olive is much pleased to have left the old towns behind her—those dear old towns which I enjoyed so immensely. However, they are very small in comparison with these grand passes through which we passed to-day. These seem to me a revelation of the power and grandeur and beauty of God such as ought to make us much better. I do feel thankful for to-day and yesterday.

"This is a dear little inn, and we have settled ourselves very comfortably. Now I ought to be going to bed, as we got up at six this morning and do so again to-morrow, but I am not a bit tired."

"Berne, Friday evening.

"We have had a most exquisite day for our journey, the sun so ardently hot. We went through such splendid passes, hardly more beautiful than those we saw yesterday, but the sunshine made them bear a different aspect. And then as we approached Berne the line of the Bernese Alps broke upon us. It was not a clear day, but we could see their white tops more like clouds than mountains. Then we watched the rosy tints which the setting sun cast on them till they faded away, and only a white streak could faintly be traced. We came in to tea at nine. I like the Swiss breakfasts and teas, and we all have good appetites. How scornful Oswald would look at my mentioning this!

"You cannot think how indefatigable Mr. Barker is in learning German. This occupation engrosses him all day. His dictionary is hardly ever out of his hand. When we were going through that magnificent scenery he was actually studying Ollendorff! Now I must conclude. Mother would be grieved if she knew that I had been sitting up finishing my letter. It is a great delight to get up at six o'clock. This is the Swiss habit."

"Thun, July 18, 1855.

"We are much enjoying our time here; it is such a lovely place, and it is pleasant to be *settled* for a little while. To-day the snow mountains are wonderfully clear and bright. Yesterday they were enveloped with clouds, but the nearer mountains were of an intense blue. The sunsets have been so glorious. I hope you often think of us. I expect the time will go very quickly, and that it will not seem long before we are again walking together at Lystone.

"I am writing out of doors. Charlie and Mr. Barker are in a neighbouring summer-house 'studying,' Charlie looking very resigned. I don't think that he objects to his lessons, and it is a comfort that he and Mr. Barker get on so well. The latter is much amused at his jokes. We had a German lesson this morning. This entertainment is to be repeated every day whilst we are here.

"You have not mentioned how you like *Westward Ho!* I wish you would do so. Say, too, whether it would be a nice book for your nieces, and quite as suited to them as *Hypatia*. We may be able to procure a foreign edition of it for a very small sum. Olivia has met with a copy of *Yeast*, and has been perusing it again. She is fonder of Kingsley than ever. Mr. Barker has not read Kingsley's works, but he made the remark that if what he had heard was true, Kingsley was not at all a *sound* man. Whoever would think of accusing Kingsley of being *sound*?

"Olivia is gone to sketch in the churchyard, from whence there is a beautiful view. I enjoy the repose of our life here. We breakfast at eight.

This gives us a good long day, which we spend for the most part out of doors, well occupied I hope. We are studying languages. I want to get up as much as I can about Italy before we go there. I am trying to sketch. Sketching is unsatisfactory, inasmuch as it is so impossible to do any sort of justice to what one tries to represent, especially when the subjects are so good as they are here. However, sketching does one good, not only as an exercise in humility, but in impressing these beautiful scenes on the memory, and making one *observe* a great deal more than one would otherwise do."

"Thun, July 27, 1855.

"Olivia will have thanked you for your 'injudicious' epistle, which however was very pleasant. There will be nothing very special in my letter to-day. It will be merely a talk such as we used to have when walking through the woods at Lystone, or when going to St. John the Baptist's at Bristol. I like to look back on that fortnight when you were at Clifton. We had so many nice talks. There are certain times which leave—one can't exactly tell why—a soothing and pleasant recollection. That is one of those times!

"You would have been in a great fright if you had been here the last two days. It was on Wednesday morning about one o'clock (a very rainy day, so every one was indoors, and Olivia and I were sitting upstairs on our respective beds), that a slight trembling in the room took place, suggesting the cabin of a steamboat. It however increased, and the whole house seemed to be tottering. I can't describe the sensation. The idea of an earthquake instantly came into my mind. We immediately flew to the door, as did simultaneously all the inhabitants of the house. Simultaneously also we all rushed downstairs. The shaking was over, however, by the time we got to the bottom. You can hardly imagine what a strange sight it was. Every one had instinctively made his or her exit from the house. I never before witnessed such a collection of deadly pale faces, bereft of every atom of colour. It really was a very awful sensation, and one which I think no one could imagine who had not experienced it. Our rooms were at the top, so that it was the more unpleasant to feel the whole house rocking about, and that there might at any moment be a repetition of the shock, which would occasion the walls to give way. We dreaded this more at night. Some one propounded a theory that the earthquake would probably be repeated in twelve hours, *i.e.*, at one o'clock in the night. Many of us therefore did not go entirely to bed until after that hour. That was Wednesday night, but no fright happened till the next morning about ten o'clock, when we were having our German lesson, and again upstairs. The shock was much less severe, and people did not seem nearly so alarmed. However, we spent the day out of doors as much as possible, and there was another still slighter shock about two in the afternoon. These upheavings of the earth produce the uncomfortable sensation that one has after being on a steamer, as though everything were moving. I slept very well; many people were in a highly nervous state, and remained awake. But as there are, I believe, no *rules* for earthquakes, if one sat up one night one might as well do so for the rest of one's life. There is no getting out of the reach of their influence, for in removing from one place you may but get nearer the centre of the agitation. The shock was very severely felt at Interlachen. The side of one of the hotels cracked, and some chimneys fell down. I am very glad we were not there.

"It strikes me that I need not have said I had *nothing special* to tell you. That observation referred to travels and to sight-seeing. We have not been moving about at all during the past fortnight. Our stay here has been very quiet, but very enjoyable. We all feel rather sorry to be leaving Thun to-morrow. We are to go to Kandersteg till Monday, and see some unspellable places near the Ghemmi. We propose going to Interlachen on Tuesday for a week, and from thence to the Lake of Lucerne.

"Dr. Pusey's son is here with Mr. and Mrs. Donkin. Mr. Donkin is Professor of Astronomy at Oxford. Both are very pleasant. Poor Mr. Pusey is quite a cripple and deaf, but he has wonderful spirits. I am glad we have met them, and they are coming to Kandersteg to-morrow. Mr. Donkin says that an earthquake was felt in Wales last year, something of this sort, and that nothing came of it. I believe that an eruption of Hecla has been going on. Not long ago there was a dreadful earthquake in Turkey. The earth seems in a very disquieted state.

"Did you get to church on St. James's day. That festival recalls a beautiful sermon I heard Mr. Woodford preach on the text, 'We are able.' The impression that it left still remains. The last words of it especially I have always remembered: 'A strong will and a sure confidence—these will lead you through the dark waters to the haven where you would be.' Do you know how sometimes a sentence that one hears by chance seems to convey a special message to oneself? It is the same, too, with beautiful pictures or scenery. The other evening when it was getting quite dark I sat down on a little hill which overlooked the quiet lake and the mountains beyond, and the far-away white peaks—such a perfect picture of stillness it was, almost awful in the depth of its repose. And then I turned to look in the opposite direction. There below me lay the little town with the surrounding landscape, and mountains also, but smaller mountains. The last tints of the sunset were still lingering in the sky, and there came up the sound of distant voices, the hum of busy life—a great contrast to the other scene, although it, too, was beautiful. It suggested how from the noise and weariness, and also from the attractions of this life, we may turn to those Divine truths, dim and shadowy to us here, but real and enduring as are the everlasting hills, and find in them the true rest, the only real repose for our souls. With these pious thoughts, I conclude."

Mr. Barker, mentioned in the preceding letters, came abroad with us as tutor to my brother. He had been recommended by Oswald. We were, therefore, disposed to like him. In the event he proved very tiresome. Even before we left Clifton, a letter that mother received from him showed that he was a good deal wanting in sense. He was engaged to instruct a youth of sixteen in Latin and Greek, and in other branches of knowledge. As he was a clergyman, he chose to consider himself bound in addition to exercise supervision over that youth's mother and sisters, and to preserve them from Romish error. He wrote to mother, that he thought it would be well that we should have some rules to limit our intercourse with any Roman Catholics whom we might meet with abroad, and that certain principles should be laid down with regard to our frequentation of foreign churches. The letter perturbed mother. She consulted Mr. Woodford. He made the sensible remark that he did not see how we could limit our intercourse with

Roman Catholics. How could we say that we might know ten, but that we must not know twenty, or that we might see one church in a city, but not another, or that we might be present once a day at a service but not twice? Anxious to have the authority of Mr. Woodford to quote, and knowing what was the practice of that eminent divine himself when he was abroad, I asked him whether he did not think that it was quite right to attend Roman Catholic churches on the Continent. After a moment's hesitation, he replied by another question: "What do you mean by *quite right?*" "I mean," I said, "exactly what the words imply. I mean, for instance, that in Belgium and in Italy, where we are going, it would be the right thing to attend Mass." "You would certainly not *hear* anything you could disapprove," was the rejoinder. Perhaps nothing less evasive was to be expected from an Anglican clergyman. Mr. Woodford deprecated Mr. Barker's idea that we were to be in alarm with regard to the influence which Rome would have on us. He thought it absurd to make any such rules as fussy little Mr. Barker was so anxious should be adopted.

Mr. Barker appeared just as anxious to make acquaintance with Catholic churches as we did. After those first few days in Belgium there was, however, no opportunity of doing so for some time. We were destined on several Sundays to enjoy to the full the privilege of Mr. Barker's ministrations. He would have wished always to have officiated himself, and not to have attended the English services, which even then were held in most places of popular resort in Switzerland. In this we did not encourage him. When we were at some place out of the reach even of the ubiquitous British chaplain, he used to engage the public *salon*, and put up a notice that service would be conducted by the Rev. T. Barker. This made us feel very British, a quality which we were most anxious should not be ours. He was bent on acquiring the German tongue. In season and out of season he would pursue his studies. He purchased a set of small dictionaries. These he always carried about, and brought even to meals. At the *table d'hôte* we used to watch him looking out a word. Then he would reflect, and after a few minutes he would venture on a sentence to some native of Germany who might happen to be within reach. We could always tell the word that had been looked out! We were much affronted at his habit of carrying on his studies while taking his breakfast. This was no less aggravating than was his engrossing himself with Ollendorff's grammar when we were passing through the most magnificent scenery. I described him to my aunt as "one of those men who provoke one to say rather wicked things."

We spent the remainder of the summer in Switzerland. After our visit to Interlachen, we stayed for some time on the grand Lake of

Lucerne. When it became rather chilly there, we moved to the Lake of Geneva on our way to Italy. My brother Charlie's predilection was for large hotels like those at Interlachen, or the Hotel Byron, near Villeneuve. He did not so much enjoy the retired places, which were more suitable for his studies. He got on, however, very well with Mr. Barker; it would have been difficult to find any one that Charlie did not get on with. He was very easy-going, and he took people as he found them. He made acquaintance with every one, and he was supremely happy. He wrote from Kandersteg, July 30th:

"I enjoyed myself at Thun thoroughly! I made acquaintance with all the people in the Pension, and a nice time we had of it for the last week. One party I determined to make friends with as soon as I saw them, and I did! Mrs. G—— and her two daughters. The eldest daughter was most handsome; I have hardly ever seen so sweet an expression of face before. Her sister was not so pretty, but I liked her extremely also. There were other people, and we all amalgamated and had great fun. I was rather astonished to find that I was known very well to the G——s by name. Such things do startle one sometimes, but I am beginning to get used to them. We used to sit up till twelve o'clock every night nearly, and play at Consequences, and have music and singing, &c. Now don't think that I was always very late in the morning, for we had breakfast at eight, or a quarter past, and I was always down in time. I hope to meet my friends again at Interlachen, where we go to-morrow.... Of course mama has told you all about the earthquakes. We felt four shocks. I never experienced such a strange sensation before, and I can assure you that it was anything but pleasant. Try and imagine yourself sitting at a table quietly writing. Suddenly you hear the doors and windows shaking violently, and you think that it is the wind. But as soon as the table rises, and the chairs too, and the whole room moves just like a steamboat, a warm sort of shiver creeping up your legs, you will then have some idea of what I felt when the first shock came.

"We have been to the top of the Gemmi to-day, and the view was more magnificent than anything I had yet seen. Of course we passed over lots of snow. It is about ten miles to the top. Mr. Barker walked both ways. I rode up the very steep parts, but walked a good deal. We were all of us agitating at four o'clock this morning, but we did not start till nearly six. This house is wooden, and consequently creaks horribly, and at first I used to imagine everything an incipient earthquake."

A little later Charlie wrote from Weggis: "We are at present in a very beautiful—though very *slow*—spot, and you may imagine how sorry I was to part with all my Interlachen friends. My stock of poetry is rapidly increasing: ideas flow more quickly than they did at first. I have also begun to write a novel, and am by degrees compiling a book called 'Odds and ends.'"

This "slow" spot had sufficiently compensating charms to make us tarry in it for three or four weeks. It was indeed beautiful, especially at sunset, or when the moon rose over the mountains and cast a long stream of light on the still waters. We rowed on the lake every evening, landing at a different place every time, and carrying away some hasty sketch as a memento. To me this was more enjoyable than were those long excursions in which people so often spend their days in Switzerland. I could not thoroughly participate in the delights of a mountain expedition. The exhilarating air, delicious as it was, did not make up for the extreme fatigue. I have mournful remembrances of being ignominiously carried in a *chaise à porteurs* over the passes of the Scheideck and Brunig, and by the glacier of Rosenlani, whilst the others were walking or riding.

But one little expedition—a very valorous one—that Olivia and I made on our own account to a glacier at Grindelwald, I like to remember. It was an unique experience. After walking for more than two hours up the hill by the side of the glacier, we arrived at the place where we got on to it, the path looking somewhat dangerous. However, we had strong nerves, and alpenstocks, and a sure-footed guide, and we met with another man who cut steps for us on the ice, and gave his assistance when there were narrow ledges to go over with precipices on each side. It was a wonderful sight, those sheets of ice, with the bright sun shining on them and the very blue sky above. At last we came to our goal—a cavern down which our guide threw large stones. These stones seemed to be falling down tremendous depths, "deep calling unto deep." They made a sound as of loud thunder inside the earth, which never seemed to stop, but went on interminably. It was as though a way had been opened into another world, below the surface of this earth on which our daily commonplace life is spent. Where should we get to, could we follow those stones?

The effect which the sublimity and grandeur of such scenes should make on the mind was not here marred by the presence of the tourist. A night on the Rigi to see the sunset and the sunrise was a less edifying and a very doubtful pleasure. It had to be done under the usual adverse circumstances. Having passed some chilly hours in rather damp sheets, we had to hurry out in the morning, only half awake and very cold, to find some hundred co-tourists gathered together, looking business-like and unromantic, to see the sun rise. Directly they had "done" it, they hurried into breakfast, well pleased that it was over. Having duly performed this duty we were free to remain quietly in our little house at the foot of the Rigi, unenvious of the parties that were daily brought by the steamers to accomplish the ascent.

The people here were Catholics, and I watched them coming down in crowds to the little church, which stood in a beautiful situation. I used to like to sit quite alone in the churchyard and think. The news of the fall of Sebastopol had just reached us. I wrote to my aunt:

"September 13.

"I am feeling very sad, knowing how miserable many must be in their anxiety for definite news from the East. This time last year comes vividly before me. Yesterday was the anniversary of the day we left home. I remember wondering what would have happened before our return. That time of trial made me realize the uncertainty of everything, and how there is one thing only of real importance. It also awakened in me an interest in others and a power of sympathy that I had not had before. I fancy I can always see now whether people have met with any great sorrow. Some, indeed, do not seem to have sufficient depth of feeling to be capable of great suffering, but one can't tell whether this is the case. Perhaps their feelings have never been called forth.

"Mr. Barker has lent me Isaac Williams' *On the Study of the Gospels*. Williams quotes the Fathers, and he suggests a good many thoughts. His style is not attractive. It is often obscure, and perhaps there is too much repetition. We must try to get that humble and child-like spirit which he observes was characteristic of all to whom our Lord was pleased to reveal His doctrine. I suppose that Williams would be thought fanciful by our friends of the Broad Church party. They would not admit the idea of there being a mystical meaning in every word and action, and even in every look of our Blessed Lord's.

"Mama read me a sermon on 'Things Temporal and Eternal' to-day, while I was sketching in the churchyard. The sermon was much in harmony with the scene. If only we could look forward to death, as those saints did who longed for the hour when they would be free from the possibility of sinning, when they would no longer be separated from Him 'Whom having not seen, they loved.' Such a longing comes, I suppose, to those who do spend their whole lives in preparing for His Presence in Heaven by constantly living in His Presence on earth. I wish I thought more about these things. Grammars and dictionaries take up a good deal of my time. How I wish you were here, sitting with me by the lake, the only sound being

> The water lapping on the crag,
> And the long ripple rushing 'mid the reeds.

"I had a very amusing letter from Mrs. Cleveland, detailing the little tour that they have been making through many old towns. They think of starting for Rome about the middle of October, and going straight to Marseilles, and thence *by sea*. This part of the journey Mrs. Cleveland does not *envisage* with delight, but she will endure it. She knows that Mr. Cleveland will be happier for the rest of his life when he has visited the tombs of St. Peter and St. Paul! I am afraid we shall miss them, unless the cholera subsides and we are able to go into Italy sooner than we at present expect to do.

"Your affectionate
"Minima."

The journey to Rome caused us some anxiety. It was very different then from what it is in these days of railroads, and we heard much about dangers from brigands! Eventually we decided on crossing the Alps by the Simplon Pass. Well do I remember the delight of descending into Italy. From Domo d'Ossola, our first night's halting-place, Charlie wrote:

"And now we are really and truly in Italy! The drive over the Simplon was most delightful. Would that I could describe its beauties to you adequately. It *is* certainly finer than the St. Gothard, and I have said this about it in my journal: 'But it would be impossible to describe the wonders of the Simplon—the magnificent

Gorge of Gondo is past all description. How we went along a road from above which everlasting glaciers were looking down upon us, how we passed through great cuttings in the mountain-side, and tunnels in the solid rock, over which waterfalls were gliding; how we saw lofty mountains of eternal snow and glaciers stealing down upon the road; how all the while a roaring torrent was gushing and foaming far away beneath us, and how above us was an ethereal sky of the deepest blue; all these, I say, it is needless to relate. Are they not all written in Murray's Handbook, and may they not there be read?'"

"Rome, November 10, 1855.

"Dearest Aunt,—It is rather long since our last despatch from Spezia, and there ought to be a great deal to say. First, we are really in Rome —that seems strange. We were told that we should be disappointed at first, but I was not at all. It looked very like what I had imagined, and very different from any other place. And then the delight of being at our journey's *end* was great, for Rome had begun to seem such an unapproachable place. We wondered how we should ever get here, and at the last it seemed to happen so *suddenly*, the cause of this being that the weather permitted us to take the boat at Leghorn, and we had a beautifully calm passage. Very fortunate we were, for lately the sea had been something tremendous, and the night before we arrived at

Leghorn was the worst of all. We had to wait a day or two for the French steamer. We made use of the time to visit Pisa, where there is much to see—too much to make a very brief visit anything but unsatisfactory.

"We had but a short land journey when once we arrived at Cività Vecchia. It seems that people are always anxious to get over their land journeys through the Papal States as quickly as possible, and especially to get to their journey's end before dark. Whether there is any real cause to fear brigands one can't make out exactly. We were kept several hours at Cività Vecchia over custom houses and passports. Although the boat was in at six, we did not get off before eleven. We were glad to find that two other carriages were to accompany us on the road. One contained three Americans, and the other was full of Germans. The Americans were very civil on the boat, and offered mother the vacant place in their carriage, which she did not accept. Their vicinity, however, made the road more cheerful and more safe. We were always glad when we saw any French *gens d'armes* about. It was such a lovely day, and the hills looked so beautiful. These two days have been occupied in looking for houses, and settling prosaic matters. We have not even been to St. Peter's. We have a very sunny apartment, the view from which is its great attraction. It looks all over Rome, and the situation is much nicer than any other that we saw.

"I must not forget to tell you that we had a glimpse of the Pope to-day. Our carriage suddenly stopped, and, to our great happiness, the Pope passed close by in his carriage, drawn by four beautiful black horses, and surrounded by military. I hope we shared in the blessings which he was distributing around. I felt so very glad to see him."

"Rome, November 19, 1855.

"This will not be at all an interesting letter— I mean not interesting as a letter coming from Rome should be—because we have hardly been to see anything yet, or had time to realize the romance with which we are surrounded. The many English who are to be seen about, and the multiplicity of English advertisements stuck up in the streets, rather tend indeed to obscure the romance. I expect that mother has been writing a very dolorous letter, as she has been very 'lone and lorn' of late, and discovering that 'everything goes *contrairy*.' This state of things will not last long however, I hope, as Charlie is getting better rapidly. Soon we shall get settled and be able to go and see things, and then we shall all recover our spirits and our good-humour! For myself, I am inclined to be cheerful, though this week has been somewhat tantalizing. Mama has not been able to get as much fresh air as she ought to have, and has been standing about so much in Charlie's room that she has got tired and worn. *He* is really much better, and goes out driving now regularly, and though much weakened will, we hope, soon recover his strength.

"I am thinking what I shall tell you about, and now I remember that I have not written since we went to St. Peter's. It was some days before we could go there, but when at last we went my expectations were fully realized. I cannot imagine that any other building could give the same impression. I don't think that I could quite describe what that impression is. It is one which must be felt to be understood. Apart from higher thoughts, there is something very wonderful in feeling oneself in the largest and most magnificent building in the world. At first one does not realize its *vastness*, for the proportions are so exquisite. It is when it is nearly empty, and when one's eyes rest upon some solitary wanderer, that one feels 'how small man is in the presence of religion, even when you are but considering its material fabric.' And then imagine what it is to stand near the great altar, with its hundred and twelve lights, and to gaze up into the dome, and then down again to the crypt beneath, where is the tomb of the great Apostle! I feel thankful that I have been there, and I always have a longing to go again and again, only I have a dread lest the feeling that I now have should wear off. But this I am told will not be the case, and, in fact, that it is not till after repeated visits that one can at all take in the grandeur of St. Peter's. I should like to go there every day. We have seen very little besides, except the Church of St. John Lateran, and that only superficially. Churches in Rome are very different from any churches that we have been accustomed to see. I like them very much. Mr. Barker cannot tolerate any style but the Gothic. He is unable even to appreciate St. Peter's! His remarks make us somewhat indignant. Don't you know how aggravating it is to hear any thing or any person that you reverence very much spoken of in a commonplace, and matter-of-fact manner? I think there is hardly anything more trying. I hope that it is not very wrong to be so provoked with people who say provoking things.

"We saw the Pope again the other day. He was just leaving the Vatican, and as he passed he looked into our carriage and gave us his blessing, which we had all to ourselves! I was so pleased, but I should like to see him more satisfactorily.

"It is such an exquisite day, so mild. The dome of St. Peter's is standing out so beautifully against the bright blue sky. Such intense clearness and brightness of atmosphere one has never seen in England. I am longing to go to the Vatican and to the Capitol. We feel in want of some one very superior, who would come with us and tell us about everything. I hope some such person will turn up.

"Your most faithful
"MINIMA."

CHAPTER X.

The varied attractions of Rome. Its highest interests appreciable only by the children of the Church. Aggravating Protestants. Mr. Barker's remarks on St. Peter's. Visits to various churches. Benediction at the Trinità dei Monti. Evening parties. The Sistine chapel. Impressions in Santa Maria Maggiore. Olivia's lines on the grave of Keats.

Visits to the Catacombs. Description of the chapels and their paintings. Altercation with Mr. Barker. Christmas Eve. Midnight Mass at the Trinità. Matins and Lauds, and the Aurora Mass at St. Peter's. The Pope's Mass. Pius IX.

Mr. William Palmer. His early partiality for the Russian Church. His visit to Russia. Conversation with him about his submission to Rome. His method of controversy. His devotion to his friends. Mr. Palmer's discussion with the Archimandrite Philaret on the Invocation of Saints.

Mr. Robert Isaac Wilberforce. Visits to the Mamertine Prison and to the Palace of the Cæsars. The Convent of the Trinità dei Monti. Church of St. Cecilia. Crypt of St. Peter's. The Christian Museum in the Lateran. A letter from my mother.

Uneasiness of Mr. Barker. His behaviour. A general upset. An episcopal warning. My reflections. Some remarks from Olivia. Mr. Barker's pupil. The last days of the Carnival. Studios. Di Rossi, Tenerani, Overbeck. Dome of St. Peter's. Holy Week. Easter Sunday. Illumination of St. Peter's. Depression at the thought of leaving Italy. Audience of His Holiness Pius IX.

IN one of his beautiful sonnets Mr. Aubrey de Vere writes of his first coming to Rome, and of how he stood before St. Peter's by moonlight. He says:

> That hour fulfilled the dream of many a year.

We were not poets, and our entrance into the Eternal City was effected in the commonplace way which has been described in the preceding chapter. We were, however, very far from being insensible to the fascination which Rome must ever possess, even for those who are incapable of appreciating its best and highest attractions.

I pity those to whom Rome is simply on the level with any other historical city. I pity those who are too æsthetic to allow themselves to be overpowered by the grandeur of St. Peter's. Still more do I pity those who go to Rome as they might go to Paris or to London, to lead a life of amusement and of fashion, and to pass the time in a genial climate amongst pleasant companions. Yet these and various other classes of minds were gratified in their own way in the Rome that I remember. The lovers of antiquity had their Forums and their Colosseum, their Temple of Vesta, their Baths of Caracalla, and many other immortal ruins. The lovers of art could rejoice in the *stanze* of Raphael, and in Fra Angelico's frescoes in the Cappella di San Lorenzo. They had Masaccio's history of St. Catherine in San Clemente, and the works of Pinturicchio in Sta. Maria del Popolo, and in the Ara Cœli. They had those countless treasures of ancient Grecian and Roman art, which during so many centuries have adorned the galleries of the Capitol and of the Vatican and the palaces of the Roman nobles.

For the lovers of pleasure there were blue skies, and a balmy air, and some mild hunting. There were promenades on the Pincio and in the gardens of the Villa Borghese. There were balls and a society which was then extremely pleasant. It was not too large. The same people met continually. They got to know each other well. The evening parties began early and ended early. Night was not turned into day. Society was recreative without being fatiguing. It was part of one's daily life. It was so simply managed that it entailed no great expense. It did not demand its members to do violence to their consciences in any way. Their days might be spent in a rational manner, for society in Rome was no tyrant. Its claims could be satisfied, and its pleasures enjoyed without sacrifice of one's liberty of action. And then the palaces were so beautiful and so full of inspiration. How different from the drawing-rooms of Belgrave Square! People were also more interesting. The very fact of being in Rome seemed to remove barriers in the way of making friends. A topic of conversation was always forthcoming. The sights which had been seen during the day suggested one at once. We soon found out whether new acquaintances were likely to prove sympathetic or not. The cosmopolitan element in the society added to its interest. Thus it was that we very much enjoyed the gaieties in which for the first time in our lives we had our share. Perhaps we became a little too much engrossed in these worldly pursuits.

Those alone can really appreciate Rome to whom its spiritual treasures are its chief attraction. Although these treasures cannot be enjoyed in their fulness by one who has the misfortune of being outside the Roman Church, such an one may still share in some of the blessings of the place, and be thus brought nearer to the blessed hour when he will be no longer an alien, but a fellow-citizen with the saints of the household of God.

> Cive
> di quella Roma onde Christo e Romano.

I used to feel that the thoroughly self-satisfied matter-of-fact Protestant had no business to be in Rome. He was quite incapable of entering into the spirit of the place. Talk to him of the delight of kneeling in the church which stands on the site of St. Paul's hired house, or of the joy which fills the soul when it worships in the glorious Basilicas where rest the remains of the great Apostles, and the reply will be: "I don't know what you mean. Rome looked quite different in the Apostle's time from what it does now. You can think of the Apostles and of the early martyrs just as well in our own highly-favoured land as you can on the spot where they suffered." It is sadly material, and altogether unworthy of an intelligent being to suppose that one gets any advantage by praying in the churches built over their remains."

How aggravating such people are! They cast a leaden cloud of commonplaceness over everything. One cannot argue with them, and it is better to avoid their society as much as possible. I could not, however, persuade dear mother to do this, although she was particularly liable to be aggravated. Mr. Barker was no slight trial!

My mother narrated her first impressions of Rome in a letter to her sister:

"I never came to a place of which I had thought much, and which I had pictured to myself, that proves to be so like what I had imagined as is Rome. To-day when from a hill we looked down upon the Campagna, and had a beautiful view of the city, it was quite odd how like it was to what I had for so many years imagined it. I wonder whether it would strike you in the same way. I don't like to think that you will never pass the Simplon and go through the Gorge of Gondo, and all the lovely country between that and Domo d'Ossola, and at last *see Rome*. In after-years if I live it will be nice to *think* over all this. In the second lesson yesterday afternoon the verse was read, 'When he was in Rome he sought me out very diligently.' It seemed strange to think that I was really in the city where St. Paul had been sought for.

"I am rather disappointed in the service at the English chapel. I fancied it was something exceedingly nice, and that Mr. Woodward was quite a first-rate High Churchman. However, he preached an excellent sermon yesterday."

The following is my *addendum* to the above letter:

"Rome, November 27, 1885.

"I am afraid you will expect a great deal more from a correspondent in the Eternal City than I am likely to give. I think in my last letter I told you about St. Peter's, as well as I could, that is, for words cannot describe the impression it made on me. It seems indeed the Temple of the World. Do you remember what Lord Byron says of it in *Childe Harold*? If you have time to be poetical, and to think about what we are seeing, a re-reading of those verses will amply repay you. We were at a very pleasant party last night. I talked a great deal to Mr. M——, the great sculptor, and I am glad to find that he thinks it quite allowable for any one to be entirely carried away with admiration for St. Peter's. He says that whatever may be its defects as a work of art, it is certain that no other building of equal grandeur and sublimity ever existed, even amongst the ruins of ancient Greece. This unique position of St. Peter's is due to its moral power. However men may deny it, it *has* a moral power which is felt in all quarters of the world. It is difficult to imagine how any one can fail to recognize this power when standing beneath that wonderful dome. But there are such beings, and Mr. M—— said it was owing to a defect in their organization. I must therefore be patient rather than be angry with people who can't appreciate St. Peter's. Mr. Barker is amongst this number. Mama and Olivia are much enraged when he enunciates his opinions on the subject. The one is very *provoking* and the other is very *snubby* in her answers, so that I hope he won't again have sufficient pluck and effrontery to broach these opinions. I believe it is rather the fashion amongst a certain set of people to fancy that there is not much that is worthy of admiration in St. Peter's. According to the principles of art there may be a good deal to find fault with. As yet, however, I have not cared to criticize details. I am so entirely satisfied with the effect which St. Peter's produces as a whole.

"We have been to several most interesting churches, chiefly of the Basilica style. This style was the earliest that was adapted to Christian worship. Some of the best specimens of it are, I believe, in Rome. One or two retain the ancient arrangements almost entire. They are rich in mosaics. It is curious to observe the difference in successive centuries with regard both to the subjects of the mosaics and to the treatment of them. We went this afternoon to the Church of St. Paul, some little way outside the walls. There

St. Paul is buried. Twenty years ago the original church, which was very ancient and beautiful, was almost entirely burnt down, the tribune and the mosaics alone remaining. It has been rebuilt, and it is now nearly finished. The interior is splendid, with double rows of marble columns and with altars of malachite and of coloured marbles. The very ancient Roman churches are wonderfully interesting. There are quantities of churches, ancient and modern, decorated with pictures and gilding and marbles. No doubt the style of architecture that prevails here is more adapted to the character of the country than would be the Gothic of our cold northern climes. It is very unlike the style to which we are accustomed. Some English people find difficulty in reconciling themselves to the difference. I am told that the Italian Gothic, of which there are no specimens in Rome, is really the highest and purest form of Christian architecture.

"We are close to the Church of Trinità dei Monti. On Sunday afternoons we go there for Benediction. It is a lovely service, so solemn and devotional. The nuns, to whose convent the church belongs, sing very beautifully. As yet we have not been to many services. On Sunday we shall perhaps go to the Sistine chapel. I have met with a great deal that edifies me. People say that one does not see the Roman Church to such advantage abroad as in England. With this I cannot agree. Mr. Barker objects to the way in which the Italians decorate their churches on feast-days, with hangings of red and gold. He says that it is theatrical; I think that it gives a nice festive feeling!

"I suppose I ought to tell you about something else beside churches. We have been to some very pleasant evening-parties, but we have not yet seen any one whom we care for super-eminently. Olivia was introduced to a good-looking Marchese, and had a long conversation with him. He is said to be superior in mental cultivation to most of the young Romans. These have not the reputation of being particularly well educated. Whether this is true I don't know, time perhaps will show. I had much fun with a youth who seems to think himself very clever on account of his knowing as little as possible about the antiquities and the other wonders of his native city. He told me that he should never have *thought* of going up to the dome of St. Peter's if an Englishman had not taken him.

"Mr. and Mrs. Scott-Murray arrived last week, and are living very near us. Lady Grey lives nearly opposite, and we are going to a party at her house to-morrow. I am afraid that mama does not at all like going out of an evening. She thinks it her duty to go because of her daughters, and they are, indeed, very grateful.

"The English chapel is within a pleasant walk from our house. It is nicer than any that we have met with on our travels. Perhaps this is no great praise! Mr. Woodward preaches very good sermons.

"Olivia advises you to read *Corinne* again, particularly the description of St. Peter's."

A few days later my mother wrote:

"We went yesterday to the service in the Sistine chapel. The singing was very fine and impressive, but we could not see well, on account of the screen, which much impedes the view. The Pope and a grand procession passed through the chapel, the Pope carrying the Blessed Sacrament from the Sistine to the Pauline chapel. The Pauline chapel was most brilliantly lighted. The light however was subdued, and the effect was wonderfully fine. A beautiful hymn was sung while the procession moved along.

"The part of the Sistine where people sit, outside the screen, is very badly arranged. The benches are so high and are so close together that it is next to impossible to kneel for any length of time. Altogether the service was not as imposing as I had expected it to be, but then I was not able to follow well, so I did not know what was being done, nor what the choir was singing. At the commencement of the service the Pope sits on his throne on the south side of the altar, and the Cardinals do homage, kissing his hand and bowing. I like the Pope's countenance very much indeed. I could not see his face well during the service, but I was close to him when he walked in procession.

"We had a charming evening at Mrs. Scott-Murray's, no party, only Mr. Morris a priest, and Lady FitzGerald, who is a sister of Sir Thomas Fremantle. It was very pleasant meeting her and talking about the Fremantles, &c. She has a daughter in a convent here, and another who is in the Novitiate, meaning to be a nun. A third is married to the Marchese Serlupi, and Lady FitzGerald has apartments in their palazzo. We had a long talk together and to-day she called, but I was out. I hope I shall see a good deal of her.

"This afternoon we had a delightful drive into the Campagna, seeing two churches on our way—Sta. Agnese, which was founded by Constantine on the spot where the body of St. Agnes was discovered. There is a curious old mosaic of the seventh century. Sta. Costanza is close by, built by Constantine; it is a round building, also very interesting. The Alban and Sabine hills and mountains beyond looked very beautiful, for it was so bright and sunny. I wonder whether you have often pictured the Campagna to yourself. I always imagined it so lovely, and it is in its way very lovely, but very peculiar.

"There is a decided change in the weather. It is a good deal colder, and they say the cold will last for about six weeks. But walking on the Pincio between twelve and one, in the sun, and sheltered from the wind, I was quite hot. The Italians, I am told, like to have this sort of weather in winter. The delicious mildness which there was when we first came, suited me much better."

In my diary of Saturday, December 1, I wrote of a visit to Santa Maria Maggiore that afternoon:

"The sun shone into the tribune and lighted up the grand mosaics. At four o'clock there was a service in the chapel of the Blessed Sacrament, the Litany of Loretto and Benediction. This was indeed *common worship*. All, men, women, and children, were absorbed in devotion. They made their petitions with an energy and strength of purpose which seemed *meant* to reach to Heaven. What sublime and thrilling beauty there is in that Litany! Then came the Benediction. All were bowed in silent adoration.

"In the actual presence of the Blessed Sacrament I feel an awe which silences questionings and doubts. Even when my soul seems too cold to elicit one act of love there is something which forces me to confess, 'I believe, Lord, I believe. I believe Thy Word.'

"'Lord, I believe, help Thou mine unbelief.' 'Lord, *increase our faith*.' Even those who lived in the visible presence of the Son of God could find no better prayer."

·   ·   ·   ·   ·

"Dear Aunt,—We have at last been to the Vatican. We went with the determination of seeing Raphael's frescoes, which Mr. Somers thinks would amply repay the journey here if there were nothing else to be seen. We wandered through galleries filled with sculpture, &c., before we arrived at the pictures. I am very glad to have known them so well beforehand from engravings. The frescoes are unfortunately very much spoilt, and the day was not bright enough to see them to the best advantage. There was just sufficient light to enable us to get some idea of the grandeur of the compositions. Mama and I mean to spend much time examining them with the help of Kügler and other books.

"Do you remember that evening when M—— read us Shelley's lines, written in dejection near Naples, and you said how morbid and unhealthy they were? Beautiful as his poetry is, there did seem an unreality in it when we had been listening to Mr. Woodford's sermons on the Creed. Well! I must tell you how we visited the English cemetery, which is in a most lovely situation. We wanted to find Keats' and Shelley's graves. You will recall the description Shelley gives of the spot in the lines he wrote to the memory of his friend. I found Keats' grave. The sun was shining upon it and we made out the inscription:

This grave contains all that was mortal of a young English poet, who, on his death-bed, in the bitterness of his heart at the malicious power of his enemies, desired these words to be engraven on his tombstone: 'Here lies one whose name was writ in water.' February 24, 1821.

"Olivia wrote some verses suggested by our visit to this cemetery. Of these I will insert the following :

> Here where wild weeds are clambering, slumbers one
>   Not unforgotten, not unknown to fame.
> Guard well, O Earth! thy brightly gifted son,
>   Tho' the pale tombstone may not tell his name.
>
> A few short words is all we there may read,
>   Telling how sadly passed thine earthly life.
> Oh, wherefore mourn that Death with timely speed
>   Bore thy tired spirit from its weary strife!
>
> ' My name I wrote in water,' this is all!
>   Some bitter words besides are added there,
> Which tell how envy changed his hopes to gall
>   And taught a gay young spirit to despair.
>
> ' My name I wrote in water.' To the sea
>   Of endless years flows on Life's downward stream:
> Not unforgotten then the name shall be
>   Which dwells enshrined in Memory's fairest dream.
>
> ' My name I wrote in water.' After-time
>   To prove thee true may yet this record give:
> ' The name of him who penned the matchless rhyme
>   Can dare the stream and daring still may live!'
>
> Still dwells thy memory in the undying song
>   Of him whose heart alone near thine may rest :
> Has *he* not told the story of thy wrong
>   And shamed the hand which pierced thy gentle breast?
>
> Was not the verse which told a poet's grief
>   The proudest monument thy soul might crave ?
> Then of his lays reigns *that* henceforth the chief
>   Which wove the crown that Love to Genius gave.

His life methinks was not so sad as thine :
   More gay, more hopeful moved he 'mid his peers.
His glorious name thro' future years will shine,
   His glorious verse yet waken smiles and tears.

Too bold alas ! he loved to play with Truth
   And question things beyond a mortal's ken.
Bright genius thus misused from earliest youth
   Failed from the earth to raise his fellow-men.

Oh ! had he lived the king of purest thought
   Nor written for Life's book so drear a page,
His strains to man some brighter hopes had brought,
   His matchless verse had taught a recreant age.

God's peace be with him now !—for here alone
   Rests the tired heart which once throbbed high with pride.
And violets I have gathered near the stone
   When wandering thoughtful there at eventide.

God's peace be with him now ! Death closed his eyes
   To ope we trust upon a brighter shore,
Where his freed spirit saw with glad surprise
   How false and cold the creed he owned before.

God's peace be with him now ! The funeral sod
   Is bright with flowers which tell that strife is past.
Leave then the Poet's heart to rest with God,
   Whom now he learns to love and bless at last."

From my Mother.

"December 12, 1855.

". . . I must tell you about our doings, and I can't make up my mind what subject to handle, because the girls will tell you everything and they will be much more entertaining than I can be. But I know you never object to have different versions of the same thing in our letters. First,

I want to tell you how very kind your friends, Mr. and Mrs. Scott-Murray, are to us: it is quite a comfort their being here. On Sunday afternoon we went with them, Mr. Northcote, and Mr. Morris, to the Catacombs of Sta. Agnese. Sunday was the only afternoon Mr. Northcote could come with us, and he is learned on the subject. I can't give you any idea how deeply interested we all were. A feeling of melancholy fastened upon me as we walked through the narrow dark passages, with the spaces on each side in which the dead of those long past ages were laid. Many of the graves have never been opened. Mr. Northcote read and explained to us some of the inscriptions. We all carried lights. Every now and then we came upon little chapels, and these with their quaint frescoes were most interesting. But Minima intends to write about them, so I will say no more.

"To-morrow we are going to Mrs. A——'s, and we shall meet Robert Isaac Wilberforce. I wonder whether he is quite satisfied with the step he has taken, and is happy in his mind.

"The girls will tell you about our evening at the Palazzo Doria, which I liked better than any evening that we have had. The palazzo is magnificent, and the Princess is very pleasing and graceful. There is an elderly Prince Massimo, whom I like very much. He speaks English, which is a comfort. His wife hardly ever goes out, but we are to make acquaintance with his sisters, who have receptions once a week. The French Ambassadress has three receptions next week. To one (when there is some ceremony about the Cardinals) I hear one cannot go in a black dress, so Mrs. Scott-Murray kindly offered to take the girls, and I shall be very glad *not* to go."

My "version" of our visits to the Catacombs shall follow. I quite shared in that feeling of melancholy of which my mother spoke. Whence did it come? Did it come from the fact that the Catacombs brought the early Church before us with such distinctness that we were made to realize so vividly the days of persecution, and therefore the question could not but arise in our minds whether we should be as willing and ready to suffer for our faith as were the Christians who used to assemble here for worship? And did it come also from a suspicion that if those martyred Bishops of Rome were to re-visit their Episcopal See, they would not recognize in the services conducted by Mr. Woodward, the counterpart of the ritual, simple as it necessarily was, which they had been accustomed to in these subterranean oratories?

We wandered through long narrow passages on each side of which, one above another, were graves, some marked with inscriptions, some with the palm-branch rudely traced in the mortar, which denoted that there a martyr had been laid. Or if he had won the crown of martyrdom by a bloody death, it was usually the custom to place a vial with his blood near the grave. The traces of where these vials were placed are to be seen. Very often several are to be found together as we should expect to find them in times of persecution.

The chapels are of two kinds, those for instructing the catechumens (which are without any painting whatever), and those for the celebration of the Holy Eucharist. The arrangement is very simple. A martyr's tomb always formed the altar. It was perhaps in allusion to this custom of the early Christians that in the Apocalypse the souls of the martyrs are represented as crying to God from under the altar. The paintings are very rude. Subjects from the Old Testament are the most frequent, with the exception perhaps of three from the New Testament, viz., the Good Shepherd, the Raising of Lazarus, and the Cure of the Paralytic. These three subjects are very often repeated. The history of Jonah, the Ark of Noah, and the life of Moses, are very favourite subjects. It has been remarked that the symbolism of the Catacombs never speaks of the sufferings of Christ and of His Church, but always of His Resurrection and of His victory over death. The thought of His Passion seems to have been submerged in the joy of the contemplation of His glory.

The paintings in Sta. Agnese have been so injured that very often it is difficult to decipher them. We went to the Catacombs with our old Clifton friend, Mr. Northcote (now a priest). I wish I could remember all that he told us. He explained everything most satisfactorily. He has spent much time in these underground regions studying their history.

"The following Sunday we visited San Callisto, which in some respects is even more interesting. Here St. Cecilia was originally buried. Close to her tomb is a chapel where lie the bodies of several of the early Popes who were martyred. The paintings too were better preserved, and very quaint. I remember a representation of the Good Shepherd. On one side of Him was a goat, on the other side a sheep. Contrary to custom, the goat was placed on His right hand. An explanation of this might be found in the supposition that it was the wish of the artist to bear witness against a heresy which arose in very early days. This heresy denied that the Church had power to forgive certain sins, such as apostasy, &c. Two figures, one on each side of the Good Shepherd, were represented as running away from Him. These no doubt denoted the Apostles whom He sent to preach to all nations, probably St. Peter and St. Paul, the one the Apostle of the Jews, the other the Apostle of the Gentiles. Before each of these Apostles stood sheep in different attitudes. The attitudes of the sheep very emphatically expressed the different degrees of attention which they were paying to the message which was being delivered to them. One had altogether turned away. Another was giving a half attention. A third was listening most earnestly. Some perpendicular strokes above these sheep were supposed to symbolize the grace which is given from Heaven to all. It might be mere fancy, but certainly the thickest rain was that which was falling on the best sheep. In the same chapel there are pictures of the seven loaves, and of Moses bringing water out of the rock. Moses, Mr. Northcote says, is sometimes certainly meant to be a type of St. Peter. In one instance the word *Petrus* is actually written over the figure of a man who is striking the rock with a rod. The rod, he says, is never found except in the hands of our Lord, of Moses, or of Peter.

"Mr. Northcote said that if the Catacombs were not originally the work of the Christians (which, it appears, some deny), it would be quite impossible to account for their origin, as the soil in which they are dug could not have been worth excavating. It can hardly be imagined, moreover, that excavators would have preserved such narrow intricate passages, or that they should have carried on their work in a way that could have been adapted by the Christians for such burying-places as have come down to us. The Christians got the idea from the Jews. A sand-pit was generally chosen for the *entrance* into the

Catacombs. The entrance could thus be better concealed.

"The Catacombs fell into oblivion when the bodies of the martyrs were removed. There was then no longer the same inducement for the faithful to go there to pray. Probably about the eighth or ninth centuries pilgrimages to the Catacombs were discontinued. Subsequently nothing was known of them till the fifteenth century, when they were accidentally discovered by Bosio. He devoted many long years to the study of their history. Many very interesting discoveries have been made lately."

At the period when the foregoing letter was written, there was no good English book on the Catacombs. We therefore appreciated very highly the privilege of being shown some portions of them by one of the authors of the famous work, *Roma Sotteranea*, which has since been published.

From Olivia.

"Rome, December 18, 1855.

"Minima and I had meant to have written one of our joint chatty letters, but this we cannot do, because Mr. Barker is in the room, and he is, as usual, intent on his Italian exercises. To-morrow we shall have no time to write, so I am constrained to try and do my best alone.

"Yesterday evening we went to three receptions, but hours here are fortunately very early and sensible, and we were in bed by one o'clock. We first went to the house of some princess whose name I can't spell. She received for the new Italian Cardinal. We then proceeded to the Colonna Palace, where Madame de Raynevale received for the French Cardinal. We did not stay long at either place, as there was a tremendous crush. Mrs. Scott-Murray very kindly took us. It is not etiquette for people to go in mourning, so mama could not accompany us. We met her afterwards, however, at the Princess Doria's. The Roman ladies were magnificently dressed, and wore splendid diamonds. The gentlemen were mostly in uniform. The Cardinal stood at the entrance of the room, receiving bows and curtseys from all who passed. The Italian Cardinal looked extremely pleased and cheerful, and said something pleasant to every one. The poor little Frenchman, who is quite old, seemed to be rather bored, and very tired, and as if he only half liked it. There is another reception at the French Embassy on Thursday, the day that the Cardinal's hat is given, and to this I suppose we shall go. We found mama awaiting us at the Doria's, where there was a great crowd, but not nearly such a crush as at the other receptions. We were dressed all in white, with violet flowers in our hair. I mention this, as I know you like to hear little details.

"Last Saturday we went to the Vespers at St. John Lateran. The music was quite heavenly.

Only four or five Psalms were sung, the *Magnificat*, and the *Te Deum*, but it lasted about three hours. The *Te Deum* was magnificent.

"We hope to go to St. Peter's on Christmas night. All through that night there are services at different churches, but I think we shall content ourselves with St. Peter's.

"The preaching in the Coliseum is a very picturesque sight. We were there for a short time on Friday afternoon, in spite of its being somewhat cold. A Franciscan discoursed with much emphasis and eloquence. I do like the Italian style of preaching. The sermon was so very simple that we could follow it entirely, and Italian is such a beautiful language to listen to.

"Yours affectionately,
"OLIVIA."

I noted in my diary the interest that I felt in witnessing an ordination in St. John Lateran, the last Saturday in Advent. "The service began at a very early hour. We came in time for the ordination of the priests. It is the custom for the newly-made priests to repeat the words of the Mass with the celebrant, and so Mass was said much more slowly than usual, and I could follow it entirely." Mr. Barker took a prominent position amongst the spectators at this function. He had with him a folio copy of the Roman Pontifical. This he had borrowed for the purpose of assisting at the rite. About this time he thought it well to give me an admonition. One afternoon when I had returned from Benediction, he cleared his voice, and stated that he did not think it was the wish of our mother the Church of England that we should attend these services. Promptly did I reply, "Then, Mr. Barker, I wonder that you do attend them. For myself I don't care what the Church of England wishes, or what she does not wish. But you do. I dare say, therefore, you won't go again, or at all events you will not take that gigantic *Pontificale Romanum*." As I took this line, he did not pursue the subject with me. Naturally enough, my response to his suggestion did not tend to allay the growing fear that he had about our steadfastness in Anglicanism. Among the number of people with whom we had made acquaintance, there were a good many converts. On hearing a report (which proved to be false) that Mr. Manning was expected in Rome, Mr. Barker tried to exact a promise from my mother that she would not see him. This promise, it is needless to say, she entirely declined to make.

From my Mother.

"Rome, St. Stephen's day.

"I fear my letter will be extra stupid to-day. I have a bad cold, and I am only just up, though it is nearly luncheon-time. I must offer you my best and my most affectionate wishes for the New Year. Tell the children that I hope they are having a *merry* Christmas. It is only in quite one's young days that that can be, for anniversaries so soon bring nothing but melancholy feelings and recollections, and the days that are seem so different to the days that have been. If it were not for the hope that all things are working together for our eternal welfare, the contrast of the present would be dark and sorrowful beyond measure, set beside the fond hopes and bright visions of years gone by.

"I must tell you about Christmas Eve. I should have felt thoroughly up to it in inclination had it not been for my cold. We went to bed directly after dinner, to ensure a little rest. At eleven, Minima and I were to have got up for the midnight service at the Trinità dei Monti. Olivia had made up her mind to forego that. Minima slept soundly till the appointed hour, but I could not get any sleep, and my cold was so bad, that I thought it was not prudent to go out. While Minima was making ready, we had a comfortable tea. Then, at one o'clock, Olive and I got up. Minima came back, and we set off at two for St. Peter's. It was such lovely moonlight, and St. Peter's looked so very grand, and there was something more solemn than I can tell when we entered that immense sanctuary. The chapel in which the service was to be was brilliantly lighted; in the rest of the church were only lights here and there. St. Peter's is always deliciously warm. We found ourselves too early for the service, so I went apart to say my prayers, and wished much for you. The music was very fine. We were there about three hours. Then we went home to tidy ourselves and to have breakfast, and at a quarter-past eight we drove off again to St. Peter's, to hear the Pope say High Mass. Of this I can only give an imperfect sketch, I felt so knocked up with my cold, and from want of sleep. First came in the Noble Guard, and ranged themselves in order. Then came a grand procession, and the Pope arrived under a canopy, with Cardinals, &c., before and behind. The Pope has a very sweet countenance. He looks so *humble*. When he elevated the Host, trumpets from the dome sounded. This had a very fine effect. The music was very beautiful and very solemn. The service was long, and I was too tired to enjoy it thoroughly, or to enter into it as I should otherwise have done. After it was over we drove to the English Church, which we reached in time for Holy Communion. I remained at home the rest of the day, and by half-past seven I was in bed! We all slept so soundly after the fatigues of the previous night and day. Mr. Palmer called just before dinner. He is extremely clever. He has travelled a great deal, and he talks in a most interesting manner. He said that he had called with the intention of offering to come in the evening, and to talk to us about Egyptian hieroglyphics. I told him how fast asleep my mind was, and how tired and stupid

w

we all were. He had been up all the preceding night also, so finally we settled he should come another evening instead.

"Robert Isaac Wilberforce called one afternoon. How delightfully he talks! the tone of his voice is so soothing. Every topic he handles becomes interesting. He speaks like a thorough Christian. I am so glad that I am to meet him this evening at dinner.

"On Sunday evening Prince Massimo called, and stayed till ten. Mr. Barker had gone out to tea, so we had him to ourselves. I believe that many people think him prosy, but I like him very much. I always contrive to get him to talk on something interesting. He speaks English well.

"The sun was exquisitely warm this morning, so warm it was quite odd to think that it is Christmas. Last week it was very, very cold. There was even a little snow, and my bed-room is so cold.

"I am quite thankful for the change, and if we have no more wintry weather, we shall have nothing to complain of. They say that it is unusually cold for Rome this year. I ventured on a little drive into the Campagna, but the sun went in, and I am none the better for it. Lady Lothian and her two daughters called just after we came in, and they sat with us for some time. She is so pleasant, and so friendly. I feel that I should soon get to know her well."

I very much enjoyed the Christmas which my mother described in the preceding letter. Some Catholic friends took me to the Masses at the Convent of the Trinità. The first Mass began a little before midnight. I did not then know anything about the Nuns of the Sacred Heart, who live in this convent. The Society of the Sacred Heart has since become very dear to me. Even then I felt that it was a great privilege to be in the holy and elevating atmosphere of this convent on such a night. It helped me to realize the wonderful mystery which was being commemorated. When others received Holy Communion, the sense of being an alien came upon me very painfully. I prayed that I might not always be an alien.

After the Masses at Trinità dei Monti, I went home to rest, and then we drove to St. Peter's. The night was exquisite, the moon was very bright, and there was something quite indescribable in the grandeur of St. Peter's by this light. We went in. It still wanted some time to Matins. I remained in the Blessed Sacrament chapel. It was dimly lighted and perfectly quiet. I thought of the shepherds keeping watch over their flocks *by night*, and of how the Angel looked when he brought them the tidings of great joy. Those were happy moments that I spent in the stillness of that chapel. The words came into my mind, "Ye that *by night* stand in the House of the Lord, in the courts of the House of our God." I thought what a special blessing must be given to those who are bound by religious rule to rise every night and to sing the praises of God, at an hour when so few are awake to think of Him, and when those who are not asleep are but too often offending Him.

Afterwards we went to the *Cappella del Coro*, where were sung Matins and Lauds. At five o'clock the Aurora Mass began, the second of the Masses which the Church celebrates at Christmas. Later on we assisted at the grand ceremony of the day—the Pope's Mass in St. Peter's. We had got a glimpse of the Pope as he passed in his carriage. Even that glimpse had rejoiced me. Now, however, we were for some considerable time within a few yards of him, and we could hear his voice and watch his countenance, and it is a singularly beautiful countenance. Once I gazed at Pius IX. at the moment of the Elevation of the Host. I thought that a man who did not believe in the Real Presence could hardly fail to be convinced of the truth of this doctrine could he behold the expression of faith and of trembling adoration that was depicted on the face of Pius IX. Well might my mother say that he looked so humble! Was not a glance at him sufficient to refute Dr. Cumming's interpretations of the prophecy about the man of sin? These interpretations indeed were not confined to Dr. Cumming and to his sect, but were preached from many pulpits of the Established Church in England.

Very soon after we arrived in Rome, we made acquaintance with Mr. William Palmer, of whom we saw a great deal this winter. He was unlike any other man I ever met. It would have been difficult to guess what was his nationality, so essentially cosmopolitan was he. It had been his dream to make the Eastern Church recognize the Catholicity of the Anglican Church. His expedition to Russia for that purpose in 1840, his discussions with Russian ecclesiastical authorities — Monks and Archimandrites, and the Metropolitan of Moscow—the impressions he received from their religious ceremonies and customs, are very quaintly described in the diary that was published after his death and edited by Cardinal Newman. This diary is thoroughly characteristic of its writer. I can hear Mr. Palmer taking part in the discussions, so vividly does it bring him before me. He looked at things from a point of view which was all his own. In truth, he did not belong to his century, so little was he influenced by its manners and customs. I used to think that he would not have felt out of place in any century of the Christian era, had the world suddenly rolled backwards. He would perhaps have been most at home in the early ages of the Church. I thought that he might just have been visiting St. John Chrysostom in his troubles, or have been discussing with St. Jerome the interpretation of some passages of Scripture.

Mr. Palmer had made his submission to the Roman Catholic Church only a few months before we first knew him. Although his cast of mind was directly antagonistic to modern Protestantism, it must have cost him not a little to make this submission. He told me how he found himself in Rome on his way from the East, and how his friends urged him to make a retreat. "It was a good thing to do, so I could not refuse," he said. At the end of the retreat he had no doubt with regard to his duty of placing himself in communion with the See of Peter. Two years earlier he had published at Athens in modern Greek a volume of *Dissertations on the Orthodox Communion.* An English version of these dissertations he also published in London. His attraction to the Eastern Church probably arose from a desire of finding a form of Christianity which was more identical with that of the early ages than was to be found in the West. The Greek Church, seen in its most favourable aspect in Russia, seemed to him to be such a form. It retained the Catholic doctrines that England had rejected, and at first sight it appeared to represent unimpaired the religion of antiquity, so stationary had it remained. Too stationary, indeed! It has not grown and developed as a living body must grow and develope. It is local and national. It lacks the note of Catholicity. It is forced against its will to bear testimony to the absolute necessity of union with the Apostolic See.

Mr. Palmer displayed great fairness and impartiality in discussing questions of controversy. He said that it was a good plan for opponents to change sides. If you find your adversary can state fairly and accurately the arguments for your opinions, you are then disposed to hear what he can urge against them. If he is in total ignorance of your position, how can he assail it? Much time and trouble would be spared were this suggestion adopted. Mr. Palmer would himself offer to give the arguments for Protestantism in the strongest possible form.

His devotion to his friends was unbounded. He possessed that power of self-sacrifice without which real friendship is impossible. There was no trouble he would not take, no inconvenience to which he would not submit, if he could be of use to a friend. Some unappreciative people found him wearisome. Mr. Dean, whose opinion on men and things was generally worth having, said he would rather be bored by William Palmer than be amused by most people.

Mr. Palmer in his later years interested himself very much in the Book of Daniel. On this book he wrote a treatise in Latin. The last time I saw him he said he should like to live to see if Bismarck was a certain little horn that is spoken of by the Prophet Daniel!

In his diary Mr. Palmer relates a conversation that he had as an Anglican in 1841 with the Archimandrite Philaret on the Invocation of Saints. In this conversation Mr. Palmer tried to show that invocation of saints and prayers for the departed were not matters of express revelation or commandment. They were rather acts of natural piety, and the practical result of faith in the Communion of Saints.

Philaret refers to the Lutherans and points out how "having misunderstood the matter from the first they have brought things to this pass, that now every invocation is for them an impiety, and the consequence is that those habits of mind, of affection, of humility, of faith in the Communion of Saints, are no longer formed in them, which the frequent use of invocation is intended to develope. Especially," he says, "there seems to me to be a strong bearing of pride in the tone and manner in which Protestants will have none but our Lord to do anything for them. All work surely is in Christ, and apart from Him nothing can be good or profitable either in ourselves or in others; but yet surely in the unity of His Spiritual Body it is a good and salutary thing to find we can be aided, and to be disposed and look to be aided one by another. It is good, and greatly tending to humility, and really to Christ's glory, to submit ourselves one to another, to reverence, honour, and esteem the holiness and spiritual rank of others, higher than our own, all in the spirit of love, in the unity of Christ, and the true faith and fear of God. Now, I repeat, I think there is something very like pride in the way in which Lutherans refuse help from any created being, but only directly from Christ, and cannot bring themselves to the humility of saying, 'O Most Holy Mother of God, save us.'"

The Archimandrite spoke more to the same effect, and his Anglican guest replied in his own line of argument, as I have stated it. The Anglican drew from this conversation the following conclusion: "I fear, in reflecting upon what passed between us, that the Protestant assertion—I mean that prayers to the saints are derogatory to the glory of the One Mediator and lower the religious temper—is not quite borne out by our experience. That is, the rejection of the prayers of departed saints, and of the habit of expressing the wish of being benefited by them, has not increased in us a disposition to think much of the prayers of the living, or of prayer itself, or that humility, which thinks of others as better and nearer to God than ourselves. I will add that I was much struck when I first came into Russia, how much more the national character seemed to be tinctured with humility, brotherly kindness, and warm feeling, as well as reverence for holy things and religious faith, than our own is. I knew of course before I came here, that we could be accused of pride and *egoism*, but I had no idea of the extent of the evil till I was here, and saw the contrast."

This passage shows the impartiality of Mr. Palmer's mind, and the power which he possessed while yet an Anglican of throwing himself into the habits of thought and feeling which are prevalent in foreign countries. At that time he regarded the English Church as part of the Church Catholic, and he was most anxious that her claims should be recognized. He did not, however, set out with the assumption that every practice which she did not inculcate must necessarily be wrong. He was quite ready to give consideration to the idea which was suggested by his opponent, that the spirit which refused to have recourse to those effectual, fervent prayers of the saints, which St. James tells us are so availing, was a spirit of pride and impiety rather than of humility and faith.

. . . . . .

From my Mother.

"Rome, January 2, 1856.

"We spent a very pleasant, quiet New Year's Eve. I was so glad we had not been cited to any gay scene, but only to a small party at Lady C———'s. We had been in the afternoon to the Gesù to hear a fine *Te Deum*. The Pope came in procession with the Cardinals, and we had a capital seat in the front.

"On Friday we went to the Mamertine Prison

with Mr. Robert Isaac Wilberforce. It made all the difference going with him. He gave an increased interest even to such a place of intense interest as is the prison where St. Peter and St. Paul were confined. Here is the fountain, or rather well, in which St. Peter is said to have baptized his gaolers.

"After our visit to the Mamertine Prison we went to the Palatine. There stand the ruins, the mighty ruins, of the Palace of the Cæsars. I can't tell you how delightfully Mr. Wilberforce spoke about it all, and explained sites, and quoted poetry. An intelligent companion makes sight-seeing much more instructive. He is going with us, we hope, on Saturday, to the Crypt of St. Peter's. . . .

"To-day we went with Miss Hare over the Convent of the Trinità dei Monti. There is such a beautiful view over Rome from the convent garden. It is a delightful garden, so large and sunny. The nuns have a school for girls, which is, I believe, an excellent one. The few young ladies we saw looked very happy. Most of the pupils were not in the school-room. The nuns have schools also for the poor, and these schools seem to be admirably managed.

"After this, we went to the Church of St. Cecilia. Her body was found in the Catacombs in the ninth century, and was thence removed to this church. The sculptor Maderno made an effigy of her in marble, exactly as he saw her in her tomb when it was opened in the sixteenth century. The position is singular, but it is a most lovely figure. The hands and feet are beautiful."

From Olivia.

"Rome, January 8, 1856.

"My dearest Aunt,—Mama and Minima having gone out to hear a French discourse, and I being left all alone, it seems a fitting opportunity to begin a letter to you. I had intended hearing the sermon also, as I believe the preacher is a famous one, but I was very tired this morning. This afternoon we are going to the Christian Museum at the Lateran. Mr. Northcote is to lionize us. I expect it will be very interesting, especially now that we have seen so much of the Catacombs, for we shall see there many of the inscriptions, lamps, &c., which have been removed from the Catacombs.

"There is a hot sirocco wind blowing to-day which I like very much, so far as the feeling of it goes, only it invariably brings a cloudy sky and rain. I do not know whether mama has written to you since our visit to the subterranean church in St. Peter's. Mr. Wilberforce accompanied us, and we had also a Mr. L——, a clergyman, and two of our Italian friends. We first saw the treasures. These I did not care for much. They are very interesting to people who are learned in such things, and Mr. L—— was delighted. There was a beautiful chalice set with diamonds which was presented by our own Cardinal York, the last of the Stuarts. We saw also the robe, or dalmatic, I think it is called, which was worn by Charlemagne at his coronation. The crypt is most interesting. Should you not like to see the spot where St. Peter was buried?

"Mr. Wilberforce, not being in the least tired, was rather anxious to ascend the dome after we had been wandering for about two hours in the church below. However, fortunately, we had not got our order with us, so that fatiguing ascent was postponed. . . .

"Your affectionate
"OLIVIA."

From my Mother.

"Rome, January 9, 1856.

" . . . Yesterday we went to the Christian Museum in the Lateran. Mr. Northcote was our guide. He read and translated the inscriptions that have come from the Catacombs. Many of them are very pretty and very touching. He and Lord Y—— were talking about books on the Catacombs, and they mentioned Macfarlane, which you wrote about. Mr. Northcote says Macfarlane has fallen head over heels into all sorts of absurdities, and has made every possible mistake he could make. He is not an author to be depended on. How you would enjoy seeing all these things. I should enjoy them doubly in your company. . . . Last week we went to the Ludovisi Villa to see some celebrated frescoes by

Guercino and Domenichino. There are very large gardens, which in summer must be charming, and from the roof such a magnificent view over Rome and the Campagna. It must be a sort of Paradise in a Roman summer. The villa contains some fine sculpture. A Mars in repose particularly pleased me, and a colossal head of Juno. I don't in general like colossal things. We had a pleasant evening at the Palazzo Serlupi yesterday. . . . Many amongst the highest class of Italians seem to be very religious, and to devote themselves to visiting the poor and the hospitals. Some of the men whom we meet at balls belong to confraternities, and after they leave the parties they often go to visit the sick. I don't think the English people here in general have any idea how self-denying and how charitable their Italian friends are. These good people do everything so secretly without making any talk about it. I was so very glad to find out this.

"I was introduced a few evenings ago to Mgr. Chigi. He belongs to one of the oldest and greatest families in Rome, and used to be very fond of the gaieties of the world. Now he is a priest and near the Pope. He talked of the change that had passed upon him, and altogether was so interesting and *edifying*, as Minima would say.

"And so William Wheeler is gone over, and he and Mrs. Wheeler are expected in Rome some time in Lent. I was introduced yesterday evening to Lady E——, who is a great friend of his, and she is very unhappy about him. She seems to think that no one was ever as good as he is, and now, although grieving over his secession, she believes his motives to have been good and pure. I said what I could to calm the kind old lady.

"People told me that in Rome such efforts were made to convert every one, but I really have seen nothing of it. I think that if any one was supposed to be unhappy in his mind or wavering, *then* many would be ready to lend a helping hand, but certainly there is no *set* made upon people, and henceforth from my own observation I should contradict such an assertion.

"The only way of calmly enjoying Rome would be to be living here for several winters. This week we have engagements every evening. When I go to dress, I invariably long to be going to bed, but I like to see the girls and Charlie enjoying themselves. In Lent there is no dancing in Rome, only quiet receptions. The evening is the best time for seeing one's friends, because there are galleries, museums, churches, ruins in such abundance to be visited, that unless one seizes on almost every afternoon, one would leave Rome without having gone over a tenth of these things.

"I went to hear the Bishop of Poitiers preach in French. It was an admirable sermon, and till quite the last part a sermon that any Protestant might have listened to with edification."

When dear mother wrote this letter she had no suspicion of what the next post from England would bring, and the extreme annoyance that it would cause her. The intercourse with Mr. Wilberforce, which we enjoyed so much, Dr. Northcote's kindness in explaining the Christian antiquities of Rome, together with remarks that my mother had made to the effect that as yet no one had attempted to convert her, had greatly alarmed Mr. Barker. He thought that she was standing unawares on the brink of a precipice. He had always intended to *be* alarmed when he got to Rome. He had hoped that we should all be likewise alarmed. He had made up his mind that there was only one proper line of conduct for us to pursue. This was that we should constantly apply to him for guidance, that we should not receive any Roman Catholic visitors unless he were present, and that his consent should be obtained before we attended any services, &c. In direct contradiction to these ideas of his, we were going on in the pleasant way described in our letters, making acquaintance with all the people worth knowing who came in our way, totally regardless as to whether they were "members of our Church" or not, receiving visitors at hours when he was engaged in directing his pupil's studies: how could he tell what efforts were not being made to weaken our allegiance to our own Church? When he expressed an opinion, we did not appear to attach the importance to it which he considered it deserved. We were bent on enjoying ourselves, and we were evidently unaware of our dangers.

In his perplexity Mr. Barker conceived the idea of writing for advice to his Diocesan in England. His letter stated the difficulties (as he called them) of his position with regard to us. Possibly he meant his communication to have been confidential. It was not so regarded by the Bishop. His lordship thought fit to send at once for our relatives and to acquaint them with the contents of the letter. He urged them to write serious remonstrances and warnings. He himself wrote to my mother. Owing, however, to his peculiarly illegible handwriting, his letter did not reach her for a long while. This accident was attributed I believe to the espionage which is exercised by the Papal postal authorities, and not to the real cause.

The poor little Barker was rather alarmed when he found what a commotion he had made. He could offer but a lame excuse for his conduct to the three indignant ladies before whom he was arraigned. My mama was really wounded and unhappy. Olivia was wrathful at what she considered the impertinence of his behaviour, I was equally anxious that he should be made to see that it was both meddling and foolish, and that we by no means admitted his right to interfere with our freedom of action in any way. We were both very outspoken on the occasion. A day or

x

two afterwards, when I had been meditating on the forgiveness of injuries, and wished to make up for any unnecessary rudeness, I expressed a hope that he had not thought me unkind or uncivil. This overture was not taken as it was meant. Poor Mr. Barker had a way of always saying the wrong thing. After a long pause, during which he might have hit on something more appropriate, he announced that he *did* feel he was not treated with the respect due to a priest of the Church of England. "But it is such a foolish thing to be," rose to my lips, although politeness prevented the words from being uttered. I felt amazed that Mr. Barker should not know me better than to advance such a claim to my deference.

It was very disagreeable having such a fuss made, because it caused great vexation to my mother. She was very sensitive, and worry made her ill. I must say that the letters she received were highly provoking. My relations' reverence for the Bishop and the earnestness with which he spoke got the better of their judgment. The Bishop felt very strongly on the subject. Like most people who knew her (unless they were Mr. Barkers), he felt a warm affection for and deep interest in my mother. He had the reputation of being a High Churchman. Nevertheless he took it for granted that salvation was not to be found in the Roman Church. This was manifest from his letter when after some weeks it was recovered from the Poste Restante. In very strong language he represented to my mother the sinfulness of exposing herself and her daughters to temptation. He wrote about the Judgment Day, and about the perilous condition in which he considered our souls to be, and urged the necessity of flight. He counselled us to leave Rome at once. As the letter was not addressed to me I had not to answer it. I should not have minded answering it.

To my aunt I wrote what I considered a very sensible letter. I said that we entirely declined to live in the state of perpetual fright recommended by Mr. Barker. He wished us to be continually moaning over the awful perils by which we were surrounded. I was indeed rather ashamed to confess that we had latterly been more taken up with vanities and gaieties and other interests, than with the religious influences of Rome. As to "letting it be understood that we meant to be entirely guided by Mr. Barker," as the Bishop and our worthy relatives suggested, that was an idea which we should not for a moment entertain. When she found it expedient to be guided entirely by Mr. Baker (the semi-fatuous old parson of her parish), then, and not till then would we submit to be controlled by Mr. Barker. "Though as a matter of fact," I wrote in conclusion, "mother has not been talking on controversial points with any one, I must state my opinion that she has a *perfect right* to do so if she chooses. The law of personal responsibility is one from which no one can escape. We have no right to refuse to use that reason which has been given us for the sake of following in place of it a self-appointed guide."

A week later Olivia wrote:

"January 22, 1856.

"I am deputed, being the 'frivolous one,' to write you a gossipy letter. I should like to have kept it till after the Doria ball, which happens to-morrow night, only the letters will have to go next day, and I know I shall be in bed then and much too sleepy to write anything amusing. Charlie's passion for dancing by no means decreases, and I think it will be a good thing for him when the Carnival is over.

"I am very glad, my dear aunt, that your last letter was in rather a more lively strain than the former one. When I think of Mr. Barker's goings on I really feel too cross, and as I desire to be in charity with him I imagine it will be best if I make no comment on his behaviour. It really is too bad of him to worry mama in the way that he has worried her. She is so very little able to bear this sort of annoyance. You know how a small thing will sometimes keep one awake all night, and just at present she is far from strong and is therefore easily fretted. Mr. B——'s denseness and want of tact amaze me. . . . Poor mama does not much envisage the Doria ball. I wish sitting up late did not tire us all so much. We have got some very bonny little dresses for the occasion, trimmed down one side with white roses, and made with three skirts. The Borgheses have a ball next week.

"We had a long drive this afternoon into the Campagna. The air was so balmy and exquisite and it was so perfectly delicious, I fear we are beginning to sing, like the lotus-eaters, ' We will return no more.'

"The days are getting much longer now. They never have been very short. To-morrow we mean to begin dining at six, in order that we may stay out till that hour. We go early to the Dorias to-morrow as there is a sort of evening party first, when the Cardinals and the Monsignori will be there. I believe it is not etiquette to dance in their presence, so I suppose the ball will not begin for some time."

If Mr. Barker wanted a misery, he would have been quite within his rights had he contented himself with bemoaning my brother's predilection for the pleasures of society. This might legitimately have given him cause for complaint, although it could not well be helped. Charlie knew nothing of that which had made us so displeased with his tutor. He had, however, his own little grievance which he details in the following letter:

Rome, February 1, 1856.

"My dearest Aunt,—Many thanks for your letter which I received yesterday morning. Alas! alas! I am in low spirits, for the Carnival is well-nigh over, and dancing is nearly at an end. We have had four balls one after another this week, and they have been so jolly. The festivities of the Carnival also have afforded us great amusement. Everybody becomes a child for eight days, and the air is filled with *confetti*, bouquets, bonbons, hurrahs, shouts and laughter for three hours every day from two to five o'clock: it is the greatest fun imaginable. How I long to give you a good description of it by word of mouth, for I don't think I could do it well in a letter. The Princess Doria gave one splendid ball and the Princess Borghese another, and they were most enjoyable. The latter was composed chiefly of Italians; there were only five dancing Britishers there, of whom I was one. Some of the Italians are rather jolly, though rather slow at the same time. The ladies are scarcely as handsome as I had expected, or the men either.

"Who was it that sent my last letter to F—— to the *Guardian?*

"You say that you think Barker a sound sensible man, &c. So did I till to-day when he propounded a most strange theory to mama in manner following. That is to say, the Rev. T. Barker thinks that I, his charge and pupil, have no right to talk like a man of four-and-twenty, and that it is a great pity that I do so, and that I, a boy of sixteen, should put myself forward in the way I do. The aforesaid reverend gentleman also thinks that I ought not to mingle so much with young ladies, and certainly ought not to go nearly so much into society. To which I, the above-mentioned charge and pupil, beg to make the following remarks: In the first place, if I do talk like a man of four-and-twenty, I am exceedingly glad to hear it, and I don't think he could have done me more good—no, not even if I had worked twelve hours a day and made myself as thin as a walking-stick, and gone to bed and dreamed of him and ancient Greeks and Romans every night. And I consider, moreover, that such a charge is frivolous and vexatious, and that instead of being annoyed, he ought to feel gratified at having the charge of a youth in whom the 'march of intellect' is so agreeably apparent.

"As to the next complaint, I believe it to have arisen from having heard me talk about a bachelors' ball, which we 'bachelors' had been taking into consideration, but which never came off as there was no time. As to my mingling with young ladies, I consider that to be a little bit of pique, because the fair sex show no weakness towards him. And lastly, I fancy that he wishes me only to go to whatever parties *he* goes to, and always to be at home and in bed by half-past ten—a notion which I need scarcely say, never so much as flashed across my brain.

... Now it's all very well for him to kick up a row because I don't do much in the way of studies, but I cannot see how this evil is to be avoided. It is the wildest possible idea to imagine that a man can read at Rome. In general I am in with him all the morning till one o'clock, but really all the afternoon it would be nonsense to expect me to stop in and never see anything while I am here. Who knows whether I shall ever return! After dinner I am much too stupid to do anything as it ought to be done; besides which we are always going out somewhere, and I could never keep myself in a tranquil frame of mind if mama and sisters went out and I was left at home. And, moreover, the large lesson-book of *the world* is one in which a man may learn very many more practical advantages for his future life and welfare, than from deep researches among fusty old Greek and Latin authors. Not that I would in the least cry down the use of these latter, for they form and tutor the mind well, but I feel sure that a mind ought not to be crammed merely with what *was*, leaving out the knowledge of what *is* and *will be*. There is where we differ. He thinks that a boy's mind ought to be strictly conformable to his years. I maintain that a boy cannot be too far advanced. If I had remained at Cheltenham, doubtless I should have been considerably fuller of dead languages, . . . but no amount of these would have opened my mind so much as the six or seven months we have spent abroad. One thing some time ago aggravated him rather, namely, that I began a novel, and I do not think he quite approves of my writing poetry. I have been agitating about private theatricals lately, and what *will* he say if the 'boy of sixteen' is loudly applauded as a capital actor?

. . . . . .

"I watched the sunset to-day from the top of the Coliseum, and anything more beautiful can scarcely be imagined. Oh! the sweet blue mountains that bound the wide Campagna. What is so exquisite as the colouring and distinctness of them? And the setting sun threw its rosy tints over the snowy peaks so far away, and mingled with the purple of the nearer mountains; and the whole sky, unblemished by a single cloud, was of the deepest blue, except at the horizon, where the rose, orange, and blue all blended wonderfully. Such a sky is never seen in England, nor is such a sunset. Oh! how much I wish that I may spend many winters in glorious Rome, and if I should not, this one, at least, will never be forgotten. I don't think I ever enjoyed myself so much or felt so strong and well as I do now.

"Mr. Dean (late of Lewknor) is here now. I saw him for a few moments the other day.

"Give my love to all the children, and tell

them I hope they will have improved much in *acting* by the time I return.

"Ever your most affectionate nephew."

"Rome, February 1, 1856.

"Dearest Aunt,—This being an 'evening at home' after four nights running of balls, your nieces think they cannot employ it better than in writing a condensed account of Carnival gaieties, which may briefly be summed up under three heads. The nights spent at balls, the mornings in bed, and the afternoons on a balcony in the Corso, where we pelted the friends who were below in carriages with chalk, *confetti*, bouquets, and sugar-plums. This latter amusement was rare fun, and exactly what you would enjoy; indeed your company has been much wished for.

"The last two evenings have been extremely pleasant. We so enjoyed the Borghese ball, as there were hardly any English partners. We considered ourselves very fortunate to get an invitation. The Borgheses do not care much for our compatriots. Last night our neighbours had a little dance. To-day being a strict fast, Olivia and I were in a great fright lest all the Italians should take their departure at midnight, and lo! they all marched away like Cinderellas as the clock struck twelve. We thought it so pious and right-minded of the young nobility tearing themselves away from dancing in which they delight, and of which they have so little this year.

"Lady S—— very kindly asked us to come to her balcony every afternoon during the Carnival, but the fun in the Corso stopped to-day on account of its being a feast; to-morrow it stops on account of its being a fast, and on Sunday because it *is* Sunday. It recommences Monday to end on Tuesday, and then everything will be over, and we shall have nothing in the way of gaieties except little tea-parties and *converzationes*.

"It seems rather peculiar to be having a quiet evening, and much as I have enjoyed these balls, I shall not altogether regret their cessation, as we have been doing very little in the way of seeing things lately. . . .

"Your most affectionate
"MINIMA."

From Olivia.

"Ash Wednesday, 1856.

"The Carvinal has ended, and I have a bad cold which quite prevented me from going to church this morning, and which I did not improve last night at the 'Moccoletti,' which was great fun. After the *pelting* with *confetti* was over, and after the horse-race down the Corso, the people in the carriages and on the balconies had lighted tapers, and the amusement consisted in every one blowing out every one else's taper. Rather a dangerous sport, don't you think? We went to our last ball on Monday night at the French General's, but your gay nieces' spirits are revived by hearing that there is a chance of some more balls after Easter.

"Your friend, Mr. Dean, accompanied by Mr. de Bamville, has arrived in Rome. Yesterday I saw Mr. Dean for one minute on Lady Lothian's stairs as we were coming away from her balcony. He informed us that he was lodging with an eminent ecclesiastic, but who it was I could not discover. He told us also that his 'director' was sitting below in a carriage, and lo! when we descended we perceived a stout old lady in black. He said that he had grown very serious, and that he meant to come and see us when the Carnival was over."

Olivia proceeded to make a few remarks on the barkings of Mr. Barker, but as the subject caused her to feel uncharitable she would not dwell on it. She had always been averse to saying anything unkind of any one. The knowledge that his gossiping stories had suggested the expediency of our being removed from the manifold delights of Rome, did cause some legitimate irritation to which it was hard not to give vent. Moreover, it was a trial that Mr. Barker, instead of accepting his dismissal, would linger on. He put off his departure from week to week, and adduced the most frivolous reasons for doing so. He did go away for ten days, but he came back and remained apparently regardless of the *gêne* and discomfort that he caused both to us and himself. For surely we must have appeared quite as unreasonable and provoking to him as he did to us. His pupil was the only one of us he got on with well; although he did not possess sufficient tact and knowledge of the world to be of the use to such a precocious "boy of sixteen" that he might otherwise have been.

The storm of remonstrance and advice that his behaviour brought upon us from our relatives showed the strength of their Protestant prejudices. I was annoyed that those prejudices should be so plainly brought before my mother at a time when it seemed that she was getting over them. An additional difficulty was put in the way of my embracing Catholicism. I had tried to impress upon Mr. Barker that it was no business of his if I did. My mother had told him that we had no idea of becoming Catholics. Great would have been his triumph had his prediction proved correct with regard to any one of us.

"Rome, February 13, 1856.

"Beloved Aunt,—. . . Mama has a wretched cold which never goes, and which makes her feel very poorly. The constant going out at night does not improve it, but she is so kind to us, and she does not like that we should miss these pleasant parties. Would that you were here to be entertained by the varied specimens of the human race we meet! It is so interesting to see people of all nations and countries. We are much displeased with Uncle P—— for talking of Italians as 'scoundrels.' We consider them the 'salt of the earth.'

"On Monday I went with Mrs. Scott-Murray, Mr. Dean, and several other people, to some Catacombs which have been recently discovered about seven miles distant. After having explored these, we had luncheon on the ground. This, I dare say, sounds to you a cold proceeding, but we in our Roman February did not find it so. You would have been provoked, and you would have made a repartee to which I was not equal, had you been in my place when, on beginning this repast, Mr. Dean glanced round the company, and, fixing his eyes on me, remarked 'there was *one* pagan present.' Mr. Dean was in his most amusing mood, and in first-rate spirits. He told me to tell you that that *is* coming to pass which you did not anticipate could ever happen— namely, that he is making great progress in the government of his tongue, and is becoming very serious. The proofs of this reformation were manifested in occasional pauses when he was about to say things, in order that he might consider whether, *if* he said them, he should be misunderstood. He says that he is always being misunderstood, even by his co-religionists, who suppose him to be wanting in fervour. He told me that I could not imagine how often he nearly choked in the effort to govern his tongue! He does not like having nothing to do here: otherwise he enjoys Rome much. The Pope, I am told, is interested in him, and he is to have a private audience soon. Mr. Dean says that he hopes the Pope does not contemplate asking him to stay always *near his person*.

"We went the other day to Di Rossi's studio. He has just painted a large picture of the Resurrection, in which the figure of the Angel who has rolled away the stone is much talked about. I cannot say that I altogether liked it. The expression is contrary to my idea of the angelic—so much of wonder and merely human emotion in it. Lord S—— has bought two pictures of this artist—one of Judas casting down the money, clever and original, although a very painful composition; the other is a mythological subject, to which I much preferred one by the same artist in the Raphaelesque style. This really was very beautiful.

"We went on to Tenerani's studio, the Italian sculptor. His principal work is an Angel who is represented as awaiting the moment when he shall blow the trumpet of the resurrection. There is wonderful calmness and sublimity in the face, and indeed in the whole figure. It is to be placed at the entrance of a mortuary chapel somewhere in Hungary.

"Overbeck's studio is only to be seen on Sunday. He is a most picturesque-looking old man. There is a sketch here of his celebrated picture at Frankfort, 'The Triumph of Christianity over the Arts.' In the centre of the upper part of the picture is the Blessed Virgin with her Divine Child. She represents Poetry as being the foundation of all the arts, and holds a pen. On the left are the Saints of the Old Testament, with David, as Music, in the foreground, and Solomon, and others. On the right are the Saints of the New Testament—St. Luke in his character of painter, St. John, as architect, from his description of the New Jerusalem, being the most prominent. A fountain is in the centre of the picture, the water of which reaches to the clouds beneath the Virgin's throne. This may represent the aspiration of earthly art after the heavenly ideal. There are two mirrors also. Are they intended, I wonder, to symbolize the reflection of Divine truths in earthly images, as in the efforts of art? On the left side of the fountain is Raphael, in a white garment. Dante is reading. Michael Angelo is seated, and in the act of enjoining one of his scholars to listen to Dante. On the right are some of the earlier painters—Fra Angelico, Perugino, and Bartolommeo; and beneath, both on the left and right side, the development of secular and ecclesiastical art. An Emperor is the principal figure in the one group, and a Pope in the other group. The architect of Strasbourg Cathedral is presenting his plan to the Pope. Overbeck's outlines are beautiful, but his colouring is weak. There were many sketches that interested me exceedingly. His designs for the Seven Sacraments, five of which are completed, I thought very beautiful.

"Now I must leave off, as we are going to the Vatican. We hope that Mr. Palmer will accompany us to expound the Egyptian Museum. We had a very nice afternoon with Mr. Wilberforce at the Baths of Caracalla and the Palace of Nero. Idle Olive does not like these afternoons on which mama and I insist on *seeing a good deal*. We don't think that we mean to return to the quiet life at Clifton of which you remind us!

"Your affectionate
"MINIMA."

Mother writes about our expedition to the dome of St. Peter's: "How wonderful it is looking down into the church from the galleries of the cupola, and fearful also, for the height is stupendous. Upon the roof of the church there is quite a village, where the workmen live who are always employed about the building. It was so sunny, hot, and exquisite—and we looked over the Campagna to the mountains and hills that bound it, and on one side the sea, then on Rome lying at our feet, the ruins in the distance; and such an interest shed over all! I almost dread the thoughts of leaving Rome. I have a feeling about it which no other place with the exception of Jerusalem could inspire, and there the feeling would be still deeper and more reverent. It is a great privilege to be in a place where the Apostles were—where they laboured and suffered."

The *Diario Romano* is a useful little publication. It tells, amongst other things, in what churches are "the Stations" each day. During Lent we used to visit these churches. Thus we saw many of the very oldest, and some which are not open at other times.

In Holy Week we took part for the first time in the beautiful Offices with which the Church celebrates that solemn season. Of late years the Ritualist party have, I believe, succeeded in their efforts to introduce some of these touching services into the Anglican churches, as they have also the triumphant Alleluias of Easter. But in my youth nothing of the sort had been attempted. My mother used to lament that, with the exception of the Psalms and Lessons, there was nothing to distinguish Good Friday from Easter Day. The latter was not more festive than was the former. Good Friday was indeed the day that Evangelicals mostly selected on which to partake of the Lord's Supper. What day, they asked, could be better fitted for that commemorative rite? To them it was a rite merely—not a feast.

It was, then, in Rome that I first learnt to

understand the beauty and the pathos of the Lamentations of the Prophet, though each succeeding year has added something to my realization of their depth and tenderness. But my first associations with them were in Rome; the associations, that is, which connect the Lamentations with the mourning of the Church over the Death of her Spouse, and over the transgressions of the Divine Law which caused that death, Lamentations which suggest the unfathomable evil of sin, the desolation, the ruin, and the misery that it causes.

"How doth the city sit solitary that was full of people! how is the mistress of nations become as a widow. . .

"Weeping she hath wept in the night, and her tears are on her cheek: there is none to comfort her among all that were dear to her. . .

"And from the beauty of Sion all her beauty is departed.". .

Sin—the havoc wrought by sin—how is it told in the wailing of this solemn Office, and how also the tenderness of Divine mercy in the oft-repeated pleading:

"Jerusalem, Jerusalem, be converted to the Lord thy God."

"O My chosen vineyard, it is I that have planted thee: How art thou become so bitter that thou shouldst crucify Me and release Barabbas?"

From my Mother.

"Rome, Easter Monday, 1856.

"It was really impossible to write last week; what with our own church and with attending the services and ceremonies at St. Peter's, we really had not a spare moment. Each day we came home so knocked up that we could do no more than have tea and go to bed, and get as much rest as we could before beginning again the next day.

"The crowd in the Sistine chapel was so dense that we could not manage to hear the *Miserere* there. We stood at the door on Friday for some time, but people would talk; this prevented us from hearing well, so we went to the chapel in St. Peter's, where the *Miserere* was most beautifully sung. A good many Psalms were sung first. As each Psalm is finished a candle is put out, so when the *Miserere* begins there are no lights, and the church is almost in darkness. On Good Friday the one hundred and twelve lamps which usually burn round the high altar in St. Peter's are extinguished. You can't think how strangely quiet Rome seemed that evening. No bells ring, nor do the clocks strike. There was complete and unwonted stillness, for ordinarily so many bells are to be heard.

"Certainly it was a very fine sight yesterday to see the Pope give his blessing to the thousands who were kneeling in the Piazza of St. Peter's. We saw it from a balcony on the Colonnade. I cannot describe the effect of that immense multitude of soldiers and people on their knees, and of the Pope's clear, beautiful voice pronouncing the words of benediction.

"In the evening there was the illumination of St. Peter's, which was unlike anything one had ever seen before. We could have seen it very well from our windows. We went, however, to a friend's house where there is a balcony overhanging the Tiber. There I sat in the dark, looking down on the river and on St. Peter's opposite. The moon threw a light over different parts of Rome, and it was very beautiful.

"We could not contrive to see the Pope wash the feet of the pilgrims, but we went to the other ceremony of The Supper. It was a terrible crush to get in. Fortunately we were befriended by a French officer, who took us straight through ranks of soldiers, and though we had not tickets, he got us capitally placed in the Sala Regia. The Pope, Cardinals, &c., came in, and we saw the Pope wait on the pilgrims, and Monsignori bring in the dishes.

"This is such a summer's day; a cloudless sky, the birds singing, and all so lovely. I cannot bear to think of leaving Italy!"

From Olivia.
"Easter Monday, 1856.
"... I believe mama has told you nearly all that is to be told about our goings on, but

perhaps she has not mentioned the washing of the pilgrims' feet by the ladies, which we went to see on Friday evening. I thought that this was just the sort of thing a High Church friend of yours would like to get up in his parish. We went with an Italian lady, who was one of the washers, a very nice person. By going with her we escaped the crush and crowd. The Princess Lancilotti is at the head of this congregation of ladies; they wore a very pretty costume. They first washed the pilgrims' feet, which were not over clean, and which they had to rub with their hands, not with soap or sponges! Then they gave the pilgrims a supper and put them to bed. We only remained to see the first operation performed, for it was past eight, and we were getting tired. Indeed I am glad that *at last* there is nothing more to see, and that we may have a little rest."

By this time we had so many friends in Rome that our letters are mostly filled with anecdotes of them, accounts of a few more balls which took place after Easter, horse-races in the Campagna, expeditions to Tivoli and Albano, afternoons in the villas—those lovely villas, many of which have now been destroyed to make room for the straight rows of vulgar houses that modern Italy delights in—and increasing lamentations at the prospect of our approaching departure from Rome.

"How low we feel! I am soon going to set myself to make out a route, as Mr. Cleveland would say; but alas! we can get up no enthusiasm for the dear old German towns about which he used to go into such ecstasies. Augsburg, Nuremburg, Bamburg, Würtzburg—all the Burgs—what attractions can they offer after Italy? Olivia hates the very sound of them.

"Mama and I were saying yesterday that we were falling, or had fallen, into a state of 'dreamful ease,' from which we try in vain to rouse ourselves. We hope it is merely a passing state, the effect of the climate, and that if it is our fate to return to our 'island home,' we shall be as inclined for 'the trivial round and common task' as you seem to be. Mr. Dean, who has just been here, declares that he longs to find himself under the tree in Lystone Garden, and that he prefers the common there to the Campagna, and its climate to that of Rome. So do *not* your nieces.

"There is a great decrease in the gaieties now. This makes us feel rather dissatisfied, for we have sociable dispositions and we like to see our friends.

"We spent a profitable time in the library of the Vatican, with a friend who knew what to ask for. We began with looking at the rooms and the frescoes, and devoted the time that remained to the manuscripts. This valuable collection is not generally visible. The manuscripts are locked up in cupboards, so that, as 'Murray' says, you may walk through the whole gallery without knowing that you are surrounded by the richest literary treasures in the world. You have to name the MS. that you wish to see, and then it is brought out.

"*April* 23.—This morning, as we were having an Italian lesson, we were told that two gentlemen wished to see the frescoes in our apartment, for which we obligingly gave permission. They proved to be the son of Prince Albert of Prussia and an uninteresting companion, who paid more attention to the frescoes and less to the young ladies than did the former. The Prince is a very nice-looking youth: he professed himself much shocked at intruding on us."

Olivia described our interview with His Holiness Pius IX.: "There were so many people to be presented that we had to wait a full hour, if not more, before our turn came. When it did come the interview only lasted about five minutes. We had to make a very low curtsey at the door as we went into the room where the Pope received us all alone, another curtsey when we had got half-way up the room, and yet another when we approached him. He was quite charming, and has such a very benevolent smile. Although he only said a few commonplace things, he said them so kindly and so prettily. He is not at all a person to be afraid of, and yet, I did feel a little bit nervous at the time. Prince Massimo told us last night that if he had known we were going, he would have arranged for Princess Massimo to have accompanied us. Then they would have told the Pope about us, and we should have had a longer audience."

Thus wrote Olivia.

I do not think that under the circumstances I myself should have cared for a longer audience, for I was obliged to approach the Holy Father as an alien and a foreigner, and not as his dutiful, devoted child. I felt guilty and insincere. There was a pain at my heart. Would not this pain have been increased had the interview been longer? It was possible indeed that it might have been otherwise. I might have been impelled to give utterance to the desire of my heart, ' Holy Father! let me become your child.' Oh, that my good Angel could have prevailed, and have delivered me from the fetters of British reserve and correct demeanour, which have withheld so many from obeying the best impulses of their souls!

Dear Angel! you did what you could, but my folly was great. What must you have thought of me? Why did I not kneel? Why did I only curtsey, as I should have done to a mere temporal Sovereign? Might not the Bishops of the Established Church of England rise up and condemn me? Do they not kneel to do homage to their supreme Head?[1]   And was there not here one greater than Queen Victoria—the lineal successor of him who derived his right to rule the Flock from the sacred lips of the Divine Shepherd Himself?

[1] See note, p. 279.

CHAPTER XI.

Regret at leaving Rome. Assisi. Dante's description of St. Francis and his Bride. Florence in 1856. Thoughts suggested by the old painters.

The Baths of Lucca. A summer in Tuscany. Extracts from books. The *Divina Commedia*.

A second winter in Rome. Drive in the Campagna. Children's First Communion in a convent. Monsignor George Talbot. The Aurora Mass in St. Peter's on Christmas morning. Miss Congleton. New Year's Eve at the Gesù.

San Lorenzo. Queen Christina. Lady Lothian. Dr. Manning.

Candlemas day. Illness and death of Robert Isaac Wilberforce. Consecration of the Bishop of Clifton in the Sistine chapel. Dr. Manning's sermons. The different impressions which these sermons produced. Devotion to the Blessed Virgin. Sermon on poverty of spirit. Reflections. Holy Week services. Easter Sunday.

Visits to sites connected with the holy Apostles. St. Philip Neri's delight in making the pilgrimage to the Seven Churches.

IT was with very great regret that we said goodbye to Rome. Even had there been a prospect of our returning (as in fact we did return the following winter), we should still have been sad enough. We had come abroad only for a year. Nearly eleven months had passed. We were now to pay a visit in Germany. After that should be finished it seemed but too likely that we should resume the country life in England which we had formerly led. And so the farewell to Rome was heartbreaking. During the first few hours of our journey, although the city was entirely hidden from view, we were consoled by the sight of the mighty dome of St. Peter's. At last that too vanished from our gaze, and we were disconsolate indeed.

Our journey to Florence by *vetturino* occupied six days. We took the longer route by Narni, Spoleto, Perugia, and Arezzo. We spent two nights at Perugia in order that we might see that city and visit Assisi. How lovely Assisi was both in itself and in its associations! The spirit of St. Francis seemed to linger amid the scenes of his earthly life, and to impart to them a sacred charm. It was here that Francis had wooed and won that bride for the love of whom he did not shrink from encountering the wrath and ill-treatment of his father. Dante has told us how the bride of Francis had, during more than a thousand and one years, remained a widow, unsought, unknown, and uncared for, although she could bring a dowry to him who should wed her—a rich dowry such as no other had to give—the possession of peace and security in a world of sorrow and of strife. So beautiful was she that Christ her Lord would not be parted from her in His Death; He invited her to ascend the Cross with Him when He left His Mother at its foot.

Holy poverty was the name of her whom Francis made his companion for life. Dante has recorded moreover how the sweetness, and peace, and joy which illumined the face of Francis when this loving union had been consummated, filled the minds of others with holy thoughts, and how first one and then another would bare his feet and eagerly follow the happy pair; and how for all their eagerness and all their haste, it seemed to themselves that they were but slow and slothful in their progress towards their longed-for goal, the goal of peace which Francis and holy poverty bequeathed as an inheritance to their children.[1]

In his magnificent "Canticle of the Sun," Francis prays that the Most High may be praised and glorified by every creature, by the sun, the moon, and the stars, by wind and cloud, by water and fire, by our mother earth, and lastly by those who pardon injuries for love of their Lord, and who toil and suffer with patience, and who bear their infirmities with a joyful spirit. He concludes: *Beati sono quei che in pace vivono perché saranno in*

[1] La lor concordia e i lor lieti sembianti
   Amore e maraviglia e dolce sguardo
   Facean esser cagion de' pensier santi;

   Tanto che 'l venerabile Bernardo
   Si scalzò prima, e dietro a tanta pace
   Corse, e correndo gli parv' esser tardo.

   O ignota ricchezza, o ben verace!
   Scalzasi Egidio, e scalzasi Silvestro,
   Dietro allo spose, sì la sposa piace.

   (*Paradiso*, canto xi.)

cielo coronati!—"Blessed are they who live in peace, for they shall be crowned in Heaven!"

. . . . .

If the interest of Florence was of a different character from that of Rome, the two cities had this at least in common, that the longer we stayed in either city the less inclined did we feel to tear ourselves away from it.

It is a cause for thankfulness to have visited both cities before the "modern improvements." San Miniato was yet unspoiled, the interior of Santa Maria Novella had not been restored, nor bereft of its fine *Cantoria*, and the picturesque old walls that surrounded the city with their characteristic gateways remained in their integrity. True, the lovers of art find some compensation for much that has been taken away, in the free access now allowed them to the deserted Convent of San Marco, decorated with the frescoes of Fra Angelico. The whitewash has been in later years removed from the walls of some chapels in the Church of Santa Croce; and now are disclosed to view those scenes from the life of St. Francis of Assisi, and the two St. Johns which were portrayed by Giotto, and which have been so greatly praised by that ardent admirer of Giotto, Mr. Ruskin.

On this occasion we were living in the Piazza of Santa Maria Novella. The frescoes in that church, and in the Cappella degli Spagnuoli of the adjoining Chiostro Verde, afforded us much enjoyment. *Mornings in Florence* had not then been written, and so we contemplated the frescoes in this *cappella* without the aid of Mr. Ruskin's original interpretations!

Florence no doubt is the place in which to begin the study of painting, and Venice in which to complete it. One should go to Venice last. No other school, as a whole, can compare with the Venetian for gorgeousness of colour, and for fertility of imagination, although the works of individual painters, such as Raffaelle or Leonardo, may surpass those of the Venetian school.

It was an idea of mine that it is only the second-rate men who have succeeded in doing their very best. It seemed to me that the greatest men have never done quite as much as they might have done. Their actual work always fell short of their capabilities. Entranced as we might be with their masterpieces, there remained the secret feeling that they might nevertheless have done better. When a man's work impressed me with the conviction that he had done his best I felt as if that man was not of the *first* order of genius. The paintings of Perugino, and Titian, and Andrea del Sarto, satisfied me. Could these painters have produced anything greater than their greatest work? I thought not. Of course Titian must be seen at Venice, and Andrea del Sarto at Florence, and the master of Raffaelle in his own native city of

Perugia. Thus seen, it appears to me that there was a sense of completeness and finish in the works of these masters that left nothing to be desired. But it was different with Raffaelle and Tintoretto and Leonardo. Of a higher order of genius to my mind than the three former, the very greatness of their genius impressed me with a sense of incompleteness, and made me long for something greater. Surely men who had done so much might have done something more. Or was it that the very greatness of these men consisted in suggesting to us the idea of a beauty and perfection which could never be realized on earth?

And yet how very much they had done. How vividly had they shown in their paintings that spirit of faith which was in them! What had they not told us about the Infancy of our Lord! How lovingly had Fra Angelico traced for us the history of His Life on earth, and set Him before us in each mystery of the Passion, never losing sight in the midst of His deepest humiliations that He was in very truth the Son of God! How had these Christian painters familiarized us with the stories of the saints! what distinctness they gave to our conceptions of the saints! To their pictures might we go to be taught lessons from these heroes of our race, and to increase our love and devotion. Often did I regret that St. Ignatius Loyola and St. Philip Neri lived when art was in its decline, and that no painter had arisen to tell us about these saints secrets such as Fra Angelico has told us about St. Dominic, and Giotto about St. Francis of Assisi.

We could not see half that there was to be seen during this first visit to Florence. The heat of an Italian summer was beginning, and before June was ended the pavements were quite scorching. Our reluctance, however, to leave Italy did but increase every day. We betook ourselves, therefore, to the Baths of Lucca, as a refuge from the extreme heat, and as a convenient halting-place till we could resolve on our future plans. That place consisted of three villages. The one that was called the Bagni alla Villa, was considered the most respectable, and in every respect the most desirable, by some English acquaintances of ours who resided there—perhaps because of its vicinity to the English chapel. Our friends secured for us a pleasant little villa in a garden. Here we took up our abode for three or four months with the hope of being able to remain another winter in Italy. That it was dull after Rome is not to be denied. There is always something depressing in a valley. It was to its being in a valley, and the consequently early disappearance of the sun, that this place owed its comparative coolness. We had to get accustomed to there being hardly any twilight. We forgot this at first. We found ourselves benighted in our walks amid the chestnut-woods,

z

darkness coming on suddenly when we were far from home.

If some time of solitude and abstinence from all mundane gaieties were needed as a penance for our dissipation during the winter, we got it here. There were no temptations to worldliness and frivolity, though there might be not a few to indolence. In northern climes I find boredom is the inevitable result of doing nothing. It is not so in Italy, especially in the summer. There is something delightful and satisfying in the mere fact of existence. I never experienced in Italy that feeling of *ennui* which an unoccupied life in less-favoured lands would inevitably cause. However, I got through a fair amount of reading, and I resumed the practice of writing in my notebook remarks that interested me in books, together with thoughts that were suggested by these remarks.

From one of the later volumes of his *History of England* was taken the following passage in which Macaulay accounts for the fact that the Roman Catholic Church numbers amongst her converts so many of the profoundest intellects.

"No powers of mind," he says, "constitute a security against errors in religion. Touching God and His ways with man, the highest human faculties can discover little more than the meanest. In theology the interval is small indeed between Aristotle and a child, between Archimedes and a naked savage. It is not strange, therefore, that wise men, weary of investigation, tormented by uncertainty, longing to believe something, and yet seeing objections to everything, should submit themselves absolutely to teachers, who with firm and undoubting faith, lay claim to a supernatural commission. And thus we frequently see inquisitive and restless spirits take refuge from their own scepticism in the bosom of a Church which pretends to infallibility. . ."

It is not quite easy to determine how far Macaulay approves or disapproves of the conduct of these men whom he designates as *wise*. They are longing for truth and have recognized their own inability to discover it. They see that there is a Church which claims to have a Divine commission to teach. They satisfy themselves with regard to the reality of her claim, and then they submit unquestioningly to the teaching of this divinely appointed messenger. Certainly this seems a wise and a sensible thing to do. The Church which "pretends to infallibility" can make good her pretension, to the satisfaction of the wise, as well as to that of "the inquisitive and restless spirits" who are drawn to "take refuge in her bosom." But Macaulay rather insinuates that these are driven to it in spite of themselves as their only escape from scepticism.

Stanley's *Life of Dr. Arnold*, and Niehbuhr's *History of Rome*, were two books that I borrowed from the library attached to the English church at the Bagni. I found much that described my own perplexities in Dr. Arnold's letters, and much that I liked, although in applying his words to myself, I used them often in a sense which was different to that in which he used them. Thus where he wrote "Christianity," I wrote "Catholicism." "We cannot and do not pretend," he said, "to remove all the intellectual difficulties of religion; we only contend that even intellectually unbelief is the more unreasonable of the two, and that practically unbelief is folly, and faith is wisdom."

In another page he writes: "If I were talking with an atheist, I should lay a great deal of stress on *faith* as a necessary condition of our nature, and as a gift of God to be earnestly sought for in the way which God has appointed, that is, by striving to do His will. For faith does no violence to our understandings; but the intellectual difficulties being balanced, and it being necessary to act on the one side or the other, faith determines a man to embrace that side which leads to moral and practical perfection; and unbelief leads him to embrace the opposite, or what I may call the devil's religion, which is, after all, quite as much beset with intellectual difficulties as God's religion is, and morally is nothing but one mass of difficulties and monstrosities. You may say that the individual in question is a moral man, and you think not unwilling to be convinced of his errors: that is, he sees the moral truth of Christianity, but cannot be persuaded of it intellectually. I should say that such a state of mind is one of very painful trial, and should be treated as such: that it is a state of mental disease, which like many others is aggravated by talking about it, and that he is in great danger of losing his perception of moral truth as well as of intellectual, of wishing Christianity to be false as well as of being unable to be convinced that it is true. There are thousands of Christians who see the difficulties which he sees quite as clearly as he does, and who long as eagerly as he can do for that time when they shall know even as they are known. But then they see clearly the difficulties of unbelief and know that even intellectually they are far greater. And in the meanwhile they are contented to live by faith, and find that in so doing their course practically is one of perfect light: the moral result of the experiment is so abundantly satisfactory that they are sure that they have truth on their side."

"Faith does no violence to our understandings."

"Faith determines a man to embrace that side which leads to moral and practical perfection."

"Practically, unbelief is folly, and faith is wisdom."

This was the conclusion to which Dr. Arnold came with regard to belief in Christianity in the imperfect form in which Christianity came before him. I asked myself, "Might not I also come to the same conclusion with regard to Catholicism?" To my mind Catholicism presented fewer intellectual difficulties than did Protestantism.

In this letter Dr. Arnold goes on to say that he does not believe that conscientious atheism exists. I thought he was right in thus believing. I was not, however, quite satisfied with all that he said on this subject.

He seemed to make too much of intellectual difficulties with regard to the existence of God, and to suggest that the arguments for and against the existence of God were pretty evenly balanced. Therefore perplexity and doubt might be the portion of a good man to the end of his days. "His goodness will save him from unbelief, but not from the misery of scanty faith. . . . The assumption that God is, or is not, depends on the degree of moral pain which a man feels in relinquishing the idea of God. And here," Dr. Arnold thinks, "is the moral fault of unbelief: that a man can bear to make so great a moral sacrifice as is implied in renouncing God. He makes the greatest moral sacrifice to obtain partial satisfaction to his intellect: a believer ensures the greatest moral perfection, with partial satisfaction to his intellect also: entire satisfaction to the intellect is, and can be, attained by neither."

I thought that Dr. Arnold could not mean that which these words implied, namely, that the intellect cannot be entirely satisfied with regard to the existence of God.[1] Perhaps he meant that in the Divine existence there must be mysteries which no human intellect could grasp. But then, why might not man's intellect be entirely satisfied with that which is a necessity of its finite condition?

My principal study at the Baths of Lucca—a study with which the summer days that we spent there will ever be asociated—was the *Divina Commedia*. This I read right through from beginning to end, in Italian. My edition had copious notes which explained the historical allusions and obscure passages. Without such notes it would have been impossible to understand the poem. However thorough might be the reader's knowledge of the Italian language, the mere text would be unintelligible without some insight into contemporary history and ideas. The minor personages who are mentioned inspired me with an interest similar to that which I felt for the donors who are so often introduced into the pictures of the great painters. They played but subordinate parts in a great drama, but they had nevertheless their value and their interest.

[1] The Vatican Council says, "Holy Mother Church holds and teaches that God the beginning and end of all things, may certainly be known by the natural light of human reason through created things: for the invisible things of Him, from the creation of the world, are clearly seen, being understood by the things that are made." (Romans i. 20.)

It was not, however, as a mere work of imagination, or as a contribution to history, that I regarded the *Divina Commedia*. There was a vividness in Dante's descriptions which brought the spiritual world before me in a way that it had never been brought hitherto. Hell and Purgatory and Heaven no longer appeared shadowy and indistinct. They came before me as realities. They were going on now, and our lives, that were seemingly so commonplace, were connected with these realities in wonderful and mysterious ways. I thought that Dante's narrative must be of scenes that he had actually witnessed, and of conversations in which he had taken part, so life-like was his account of his journey to the world of spirits.

. . . . .

Very quiet and uneventful were the three months that we spent at the Baths of Lucca. We had gone there with the hope of returning to Rome. Some time, however, elapsed before this hope seemed likely to be realized. At last, to our great joy, it was decided that we should spend another winter and spring in Italy.

It was when we were once more on our way to Rome that my mother wrote from

"La Scala, November 11, 1856.
"We are now halting for our mid-day meal (which is very long in making its appearance), at a small and dirty inn standing alone on the

roadside. The country all around is bleak and desolate. One can easily understand how landlord and brigands would have it all their own way hereabouts. However, there are now no brigands to be feared in Tuscany. In the Papal States we are told that they are sometimes met with.

"We left Florence yesterday morning at seven o'clock. It was a lovely bright morning, but cold. The girls were very sorry to say farewell to Florence. They have had much enjoyment in seeing the beautiful works of art that it contains, and they have made good use of their time. Most of our way yesterday was through lovely country, highly cultivated and smiling. The environs of Florence are beautiful on all sides. When we arrived at Siena it was dark. We could see nothing of the Cathedral or gallery and other objects of interest there. We were off again at six the next morning. We hope to return at a future period when the days will be longer and the weather more propitious."

This letter was finished by me as follows:

"Mama had only written these few lines ere she was called away to her mid-day meal. This consisted of various species of fowl, and was on the whole more *fanciable* than we had dared to expect. I take up the thread of the narrative from Bolsena, where we are halting in the middle of the day. Ever since we left Siena, the country has been singularly dreary and desolate. So at least it appeared to us. We saw it however under unfavourable circumstances, for rain began yesterday afternoon and has continued ever since. There was a howling wind and a dense fog as we ascended the mountain of Radicofani, on the top of which stood the inn that was to be our resting-place for the night. When we arrived we were informed that there were no rooms to be had. All the rooms that were still unoccupied were being reserved for Lady Lothian and several people who were travelling with her. Our *vetturino* had neglected to take the precaution of securing rooms for us. Mother was in despair. The landlord was most unsympathizing and very unaccommodating, and we were so tired. However, when Lady Lothian did at last arrive, she very kindly gave up to us what must have been the best room, as there was an inscription over the door which recorded that Pius VII. had slept there. Some of Lady Lothian's party were very wet when they arrived, one of their carriages being open. It was such a dreadful night. The wind was tremendous. When at last, however, a room was assigned to us, we managed to make ourselves very comfortable till the early hour for rising arrived.

"We left Florence with regret, having passed a very pleasant time there, and Mr. Aubrey de Vere came the day before we left and paid us a long visit. We were so delighted to see him again. He talks of coming to Rome in about a fortnight. He had spent some days at Spezzia visiting Shelley's haunts."

"Setti Vene, Thursday, November 13.
"We are arrived at our last night's resting-place by broad daylight. It is a solitary inn round which the wind is whistling, situated on the confines of the Campagna, only twenty miles from Rome. At present there are no other travellers here, all the carriages which have accompanied us on our road hitherto, as they were posting, have gone on to Rome. We might also be wending our way thither were it not for some tiresome regulation for which I believe mama's friend Prince Massimo is partly responsible. This regulation forbids *vetturini* to do the whole journey in one day.

"We have not been in as great a fright about brigands as we expected to be, for though the road is extremely desolate and lonely, we constantly met with other travellers. It did, however, give us a shock when an old lady, travelling in her own carriage, swept by, escorted by three *gens d'armes*. Last night we were out rather late, but there was another carriage near us containing two Neapolitans. These 'noblemen' afterwards partook of a collation in the room where we were having tea. They were young and good-looking. As they took it for granted that we did not understand their language, they talked about us in a low voice. This amused us, as fortunately what they said was flattering. They looked at mama and observed, *La madre e ben conservata*. They made a few more remarks in her praise. I think it was Olivia who they thought resembled a *ritratto di Tiziano*. On entering the room they surveyed us, and one said to the other, *Belle femmine!* They breakfasted earlier than we did, and they have already started for Rome, so now we are left alone on the road. May the remainder of the journey be accomplished without an attack from brigands! The *contadini* whom we pass are attired in a somewhat brigandish and very picturesque manner. We often see ominous-looking bands of three or four men who turn out after all to be only peaceable shepherds!

"Can it be true that to-morrow we shall behold the Dome?"

. . . . .

Thus after all our hopes and fears we found ourselves again in our beloved Rome. Very delighted we were. I did not share the predilection that some people have for novelty. I cared much more for places when I knew them well, and when they had gathered round them not only the associations of their own history, but also those of mine. Rome especially requires to be known. Then we had many friends there. We did not feel that we were strangers. There was no Mr. Barker to make tactless and unsympathetic remarks. On the other hand, we had not the beautiful view over Rome that our apartment of the previous winter commanded. We missed Charlie, and my mother's spirits were depressed on account of his absence. She was very unwell this winter. Thus her letters are rather melancholy.

"We have just had a lovely drive with Mr. de Vere," she wrote. "We went to Monte Mario and walked in the grounds of the uninhabited villa, from whence the view over Rome and the Campagna is quite exquisite. It was a little before sunset, and the colouring upon the *now* snowy mountains and on the Sabine Hills was beautiful. And then the purple light at their base, and the Alban Hills which are lower, and have a thinner coating of snow upon them, and St. Peter's standing up so grandly against the sky, I can't tell you how lovely it was! I hope if I live to be old, that the delight I take in nature will never be lessened. It is such a superior pleasure to almost all others.

"We saw Mr. Wilberforce this afternoon. He is going to be a priest after all, and is now at the College studying. He stood by the carriage and had a talk; he mentioned having had a letter from his brother (the Bishop). I should think that they must be very attached brothers.

"There were a good many people at Princess Lancellotti's last night. One never knows beforehand whether there will be many or few at these Italian receptions. I sat by Princess Doria when we first went in. She is in deep mourning for her mother and for Lord Shrewsbury. I had a very nice talk with her, and we are going to her on Friday evening. She will have no grand receptions this year, on account of her mourning. Lady Lothian was there also, and I much enjoyed my little conversation with her. She is one of the most really *holy* people I know. We never discuss doctrine, so pray don't imagine that I am running into danger!

"*December* 12.—I was driving with Mrs. Y—— in the Campagna yesterday afternoon, and as we were coming home we met the Pope. He was walking, and it was a pretty sight to see him coming in his red cloak, attended by Monsignor Talbot and by one or two more. The Noble Guard followed on horseback, and the Pope's carriage. We had to get out of our carriage to make a low reverence as he passed. In return he gave us his blessing. He has such a kind, thoroughly benevolent countenance. There were two or three poor people in the road who knelt as soon as they saw him coming, to receive his blessing, and one of his attendants gave these poor people money. I have often seen the Pope go by in his carriage, but I had not seen him on foot before. It was really an interesting sight, taking place as it did in the Campagna. There was such an exquisite glow over everything.

"Mrs. Y—— was saying that on one's first return to England one misses the colouring of

Italy so very much; that at first the cloudy sky and comparatively small amount of sunshine quite depressed her. She told me a little about her past life. She said that it had been so singularly happy and prosperous that sometimes it almost made her tremble. She had really hardly had a trial of any sort. I suppose that she has not *needed* trial to draw her heart to God. She appears to have a loving, grateful spirit. Cannot we imagine God in His love and mercy delighting to spare all His children sorrow, when His work can be done in their souls without it—when in the midst of happiness and prosperity, a heart can be as devoted to Him as other hearts are only after long years of sorrow and trial? It is not often that one meets a person of our time of life who has had no trials to undergo."

It was a theory of my mother's that it was easier to love God in the midst of worldly prosperity than in adversity. We used to tell her that this was an un-Scriptural theory, and that the Bible said, "Whom the Lord loveth He chasteneth," and "Blessed are they that mourn." She said that to *her* it was easier to realize the love of God when she was happy, and when everything was going smoothly, than in times of sorrow. I cannot say that this is my experience.

The letter continues, "Minima and I went before eight o'clock this morning to a convent in Trastevere to see fifty girls receive their First Communion. It was a sight I wanted to witness, and in some respects it was very interesting, but there were things I did not like. They were poor girls. A number of their friends and relatives were present, who seemed much moved during the service. After the Cardinal Archbishop had gone into the chapel and to the altar, the girls came in, in procession, all dressed in white, with long veils and a little crown of flowers. Each girl carried a lighted candle. They knelt the whole time. They seemed a good deal excited. They came in crying, and cried throughout the service, except while the Archbishop was going round administering Holy Communion, and that was really very impressive—there was such a hush, only sobs occasionally. But what seemed strange was that, while he was saying Mass, a priest was all the time preaching to the girls most energetically, and to my mind this spoilt the service. I longed for him to be quiet. I suppose his sermon, or rather address, was very exciting, for every now and then the girls burst out into a loud cry. He had an immense deal of action."

Well do I remember that very vehement exhortation which I could not enjoy, because I felt it must be shocking my mama. Mgr. Talbot had arranged for us to attend this ceremony. He told me afterwards that he had begged the preacher to be as quiet as he could. This fervent priest certainly was anything but quiet. However, as Lady Lothian said, the great thing was that the girls should be edified, and they were Italian, not English girls, and their ideas were very different from ours!

Mgr. (George) Talbot had been absent from Rome the previous winter, so we had only just made his acquaintance. We saw a good deal of him.

A High Church friend of my mother's, Miss Celia Congleton, arrived in Rome. She was rather a character. She possessed an unfailing fund of good-humour and merriment. Mama enjoyed her society very much, and they had many talks on " Church matters."

Mama writes on December 22nd : " Celia went with us on Saturday to San Giovanni Laterano to see the ordination of priests and deacons. It was an extremely interesting sight, and one I much wished to see. The service was very solemn. I was particularly struck with one of the deacons; he seemed so wrapt in devotion. Celia was exceedingly pleased with the service, and I liked it more almost than any I have seen in the Roman Church. Had I thoroughly understood the meaning of everything, I might have appreciated it yet more. But the Cardinal Vicar of Rome has not the unction that our Samuel has.

"*December* 28.—On Christmas Eve we went to bed soon after seven, to ensure a good rest before going to St. Peter's. I got a good sleep, and did not hear Celia (who was going with us) arrive at ten o'clock to take possession of the sofa in the drawing-room. She came to call us at one, looking so merry. She had kept up such a nice fire. The room was so warm and looked very cosy when we came a little before two o'clock to have coffee. Then the carriage drove up, and we stept out into the night. It was mild, but there were dark clouds about. St. Peter's, as we entered it, looked so solemn and grand. There were lights dim and few, and people already kneeling in different parts. We had soon to take our places in the chapel in which the service was to be. The music was beautiful—finer than last year. We heard Matins. The Aurora Mass followed, and we were nearly five hours in St. Peter's. It was Palestrina's music, and so very exquisite. I quite long to hear it again. The day was dawning when we left, a delicious-feeling morning, but cloudy. It was very different from last Christmas morning, when the moon was nearly at the full, and gloriously bright."

That Aurora Mass in St. Peter's remains in my memory as distinctly as the Midnight Masses in the Trinità the previous year. A conviction came to me that faith in the Blessed Eucharist was a greater gift than anything else, and that whatever sacrifice it might involve I could never give it up. That faith must triumph over everything.

It was about this time that Miss Congleton

observed that kneeling at the Elevation and at Benediction gave offence to weaker brethren, amongst the number of whom I fancy was her papa. This being the case, she suggested that it might be better for us Anglicans to stand instead of to kneel at such times. Standing, after all, was a reverential attitude. I resolved not to adopt this suggestion. Being much smaller than was Miss Congleton, and a less important personage, my proceedings were not likely to cause remark.

To say the truth, I cared very little for the "weaker brethren." I thought that Anglicans were too ready to conceal their principles. They were too much afraid of an outward manifestation of their faith. It was their illogical position, indeed, which led them to act thus. It gave them no choice but to be apparently insincere. Thus if when they were in a Catholic church they showed the reverence which they felt for the Blessed Sacrament, their act was interpreted—and they knew that it was so interpreted—as a sign that they contemplated renouncing Anglicanism, a step which they had no intention of taking. If, on the other hand, they assumed a sort of neutral attitude when present at Catholic worship, they were not asserting that belief in the Real Presence which they knew was the belief of the primitive Church, and which they considered that their Church allowed them to hold.

I quite understood Miss Congleton's motive in

urging us to adopt the course which she deemed advisable. It arose from her loyalty to the Church of England. This loyalty she missed no opportunity of displaying.

Olivia wrote, January 1, 1857:

"Yesterday afternoon we went to the Church of the Gesù. The *Te Deum* was sung there in thanksgiving for the blessings of the past year. The Pope came in after the Vespers, just before the *Te Deum*. He gave Benediction himself. It was very impressive. I could not see well, for the tiresome people in front of me, who were English, would stand up when they ought to have knelt. They talked, and they stared about them. This behaviour quite spoilt the effect, which otherwise would have been very fine, especially at the Benediction, when all the soldiers of the National Guard and the Swiss Guard went down on their knees. Williams (our English servant), who was outside the church, said it was a beautiful sight to see the Pope and his Guard come into the piazza. He had a good view of the Pope alighting from his carriage. He thought the Pope seemed 'a very nice, pleasant sort of a gentleman!'"

From my Mother.

"We went this afternoon to *San Lorenzo fuori le Mura*, to which I had not been this year. It is one of the old Basilicas, and very interesting.

While we were there a funeral procession of brown monks went by to the cemetery, chanting, and looking so picturesque. Minima sketched a little, but it was cold. We are not having nearly such delightful weather this winter as we had last winter.

"On Saturday we went to a ball at the French General's. Queen Christina arrived soon after we did. She is a remarkable-looking woman. I could not discover much remains of the great beauty she used to possess. I do not think she could ever have been as handsome as is her daughter, Princess del Drago. She came in state with her ladies, and was seated between the Austrian and French Ambassadresses at first, with her ladies behind her.

. . . . . .

"Lady Lothian thinks as I do, that Manning is looking very worn and ill. I can't tell you how much I like Lady Lothian. She seems so truly spiritual. She looks upon the things of the world in their true light. It seems grievous that such a woman should have turned from our Church. I think there are few people in the world to be compared to her.

"Mgr. Talbot is a convert. He was telling me about his conversion, which took place many years ago. I told him of my hope, which is also my theory, that there must be some great work in the Roman Church, which is to be done by the great and good men who have joined her from our Church. Good may thus be brought about through the merciful providence of God from that which seems to us but an evil and misfortune.

"(*January* 19.)—Mr. Wilberforce has been ill with gastric fever, and is gone to Albano for change of air. Mr. de Vere was going yesterday to stay a few days with him. He has been really quite ill. Being at the Academia did not agree with him. I always thought it great nonsense that he should go anywhere to *learn*. I told him I was quite sure they would teach him nothing in Rome that he did not already know. If Albano were not so far off I should like to drive over and see him."

In many of my mother's letters she mentions the pleasure and profit she derived from Lady Lothian's society, as also from that of Dr. Manning, who really did arrive in Rome this winter. The worst fears of Mr. Barker would have been realized, for not only was Dr. Manning in Rome, but after a few weeks he took an apartment in the same house as ourselves. He was able, therefore, often to pay us a little visit, which he did mostly of an evening, before we went out. I remember how alarmed Olivia and I were, lest he should come when we were dressed for a certain fancy ball and had our hair arranged with powder. We feared any favourable opinion he might have of us would be gone for ever; for

Dr. Manning was very severe in his views, and did not at all approve of balls. I could not see that they were wrong, as he said they were. I felt sure that people might enjoy them without getting any harm, and I think so still. After I had passed many years without taking part in such active forms of recreation, I went as a spectator to a ball in London. Dancing struck me then as a strange form of amusement. It was difficult to imagine how rational people could derive any enjoyment from it. But my own youthful experience came back to me. I recalled the great delight I had in rapid motion, in even running quickly up and down a staircase or a room. When in addition to this natural love of motion there were suitable companions, exhilarating music, and plenty of space, dancing certainly did afford an intense and a most innocent enjoyment. There seemed to be no reason why one should be debarred from this enjoyment. So I did not feel disposed to agree with Dr. Manning that dancing was altogether wrong. I was ready to admit that it might be harmful to some people.

Dr. Manning often made me uncomfortable, by discoursing on the vanities of the world just as we were about to take part in them. On these occasions my enjoyment of the evening was somewhat spoiled, unless I could get some edifying conversation with one of my more serious friends. Dr. Manning said that our intercourse with the world had deteriorated us, and that we were less good than we were when he saw us at Clifton. One thing that puzzled me was that he would not admit that any one could conscientiously remain an Anglican. I did not ask him to say that *I* could. It was quite possible that I was inexcusable, but surely that could not be said of every one. There was my dear Milly, for instance. There was my mother also. Neither of these could believe in the Church, though they liked it so much. Perhaps Dr. Manning thought that I might make an unwise application of the Church's teaching concerning invincible ignorance if he explained it to me. I did not understand it, and for years the wrong conception which I had of the doctrine *Extra ecclesiam nulla salus* was a great misery and perplexity to me. I thought that if I became a Catholic I should have to pronounce a formal anathema on all who were outside the visible pale of the Church. I found that a similar misconception has kept many at a distance from Catholicism.

I longed for Robert Wilberforce to be a priest. I felt sure that he would understand my perplexities, and that he would tell me what I ought to do. Somehow I could not talk to Dr. Manning freely on the few occasions when I happened to see him alone. He was not the "comfort" to me which it seems he was to my mother. Perhaps he made me unhappy because he helped me to realize how far I was from possessing that spirit of sacrifice and humility, which submission to the Church required. He did not minimize difficulties. To be a Catholic might involve so great an amount of suffering that it did not fall far short of martyrdom. For this I did not feel prepared. He reminded me of how St. Agnes stood alone before the whole of Rome, and of how gloriously she had triumphed. He said that the same grace which had enabled her to overcome was not wanting now to those who had the courage to leave all and to follow Christ. If they had not to encounter the same sharp persecution which dear little St. Agnes encountered, converts to Catholicism often met with unkindness and ill-treatment that almost amounted to persecution. Certainly they needed grace similar to that which was given to martyrs. The persecution to which they were subjected might drag on for years. It might entail a life-long struggle, whereas bodily torture and death were quickly ended.

. . . . . .

On Candlemas day we went to St. Peter's. We had tickets for a balcony. Therefore we looked down on the ceremony from a considerable height, and a grand ceremony it was, and very long. For the Cardinals, Bishops, Generals of the different Orders, members of the *corps diplomatique*, &c., went up to the Pope and each one received a candle from His Holiness. Then the candles were lighted and a magnificent procession took place round the church. This was a very fine sight. Mother got into a comfortable corner from whence she could see well. She thoroughly enjoyed the ceremony, thanks to a kind Irish priest who sat by her. He explained to her all that was going on, and helped her to find the places in the Missal.

My mother wrote to her sister, February 4, 1857:

" . . . Sad news has been brought me this morning. I told you in my last letter that Mr. Wilberforce had been very ill. He died yesterday at sunset, at Albano, whither he had gone some three or four weeks ago for change of air. Mr. de Vere has been with him the last fortnight. Manning and Mr. Wynne were with him the whole time. Yesterday Lady Lothian and Mrs. Leslie went to Albano and did not return. Lord Ralph Kerr called late in the afternoon and told us how *very* ill they feared he was, and how the doctors thought he could not live through the night. But Lord Ralph had hopes; he could not help hoping, he said. From what I can hear, I should think that dear Mr. Wilberforce had given himself up almost from the commencement of his illness; he was not at all sanguine about himself. I cannot tell you how grieved I am. We had seen but little of him this winter on account of his being at the Academia. He used to come to us sometimes of a morning. Last year we saw him often, and he frequently went out with us. I feel that I have lost a friend whom I loved. No one who knew him could help loving him. Learned and clever though he was, I never felt afraid of him, because I could trust in his goodness. Mr. Dean brought us the sorrowful tidings. I have been thinking much of the Bishop of Oxford; it will be such a sad blow to him. I had a talk yesterday with the Italian doctor who had been to Albano to see Mr. Wilberforce. His illness was a low fever, not of an infectious character. He has not been well for some time, and Rome did not agree with him, but he was so fond of being in Rome.

"*February* 5.—Mr. Palmer has just been here. He talked a good deal about Mr. Wilberforce. Dr. Manning, who was with him at Albano all the time, does not seem to have had the slightest idea that there was any danger till within the last few days.

"*Sunday, February* 8, 1857.—Since I wrote we have heard more particulars. Mr. de Vere was at Albano and, like the rest of Mr. Wilberforce's friends, was quite devoted to him. Two days after Mr. Wilberforce's death Mr. de Vere returned to Rome. He came at once to see us, looking so sorrowful, so worn, and really ill himself with the anxiety and watching. I think he talked of nothing hardly but the dear friend whom he had lost.

"On Friday afternoon, as we were walking down the Via Sistina, we met Dr. Manning and another priest. Manning only spoke a few words. He said his friend had left a message for us, and he would come and see us the next day between twelve and one. He looked so ill, such deep sorrow was in his countenance. His eyes filled with tears, and I could hardly keep my own back. I felt for him so very, very much. He and Wilberforce have been so much to each other for thirty years that the blank his loss will make must be terrible. He called yesterday, as he said he would, and told us all about Wilberforce's illness and death, and the story was very touching. Mr. Wilberforce seems to have been most mercifully spared all suffering, except that which extreme weakness causes. His patience and his entire submission were perfect. He never expressed any wish to recover, but left all to the will of God. Dr. Manning seemed as if he could not say enough about his beautiful resignation. God permitted His servant to depart in peace. I should think that there could never have been a calmer and a happier death-bed. His mind was at times wandering, and once he fancied he was returning to England, that he was on the sea, going from Cività Vecchia to Marseilles. Manning told us so many beautiful little things about him, and said it all so simply. He said Wilberforce had a great regard for us, and used to speak of us. The last time we had seen him was when he and Manning called on us together, the day after Christmas Day.

"Mr. de Vere is anxious about Dr. Manning's health. Dr. Manning was looking for a lodging with the sun full upon it. This it was difficult to meet with. I was glad to be able to help him, and to tell him of the apartment above ours, which was to be let. He has taken it, and I hope he will get stronger. He will have two little balconies, and will look upon the gardens of the Barberini Palace. He will have a charming view, from being so high up. His nephew will be with him. His time is fully occupied, for he has very much to do, so do not be thinking that *we* shall see much of him, for I dare say we shall not have above one or two visits from him. He leaves Rome directly after Easter. You see I could not know of an apartment which would suit him, and not mention it, simply because it was in our house.

"*Monday, February 9.*—I have had a visit this morning from Celia. We went yesterday to hear Manning preach, and she wanted to talk about what he said. I have been longing to hear him preach for fifteen years, ever since you lent me his first volume of sermons, and told me how beautiful they were. What help and comfort I have found in his writings during these fifteen years! But how little I could have believed, had any one told me, that when my wish was gratified and I did hear him preach, it would be in a church at Rome, and that in his sermon he would be setting forth the comfort and the necessity of devotion to the Blessed Virgin! I could have wept bitterly all the time, so grieved and pained was I with what he said. His language was beautiful, his manner perfect, so simple, intensely earnest, and touching. His arguments were weak, and his conclusions were not forcible. They did not commend themselves to my mind as being true. Very many English were there. I should like to know what they thought. He quite came up to what I expected in grace and earnestness.... When he spoke of human love his lip quivered, and there was such an intensity of feeling in what he said. He looks very ill. What a thoroughly Christian spirit his must be! If you had heard him talk as we did of Wilberforce's death, you would have felt that whatever errors there may be in his faith, his heart must be as right with God as the heart of a poor human creature can be. There is such perfect charity in all that he says.

"*February* 17.—The Carnival is going forward in all its folly, and people are rejoicing in the splendour of the weather. We have given but little time to the Corso. On Saturday afternoon we went to the Villa Albani, where the girls sketched, and most delightful it was. The violets were smelling so sweetly. The view of the Campagna is lovely from the garden of the villa. I remember well writing to you about it last year and telling you how, whilst I stood gazing on the loveliness of the scene which entered into my very heart, I felt most sad....

"We had a busy day on Sunday. We set off for the Sistine chapel before seven, in order to see the Pope consecrate a Bishop (for Clifton), Dr. Clifford, Lord Clifford's son. It was a beautiful, solemn, and impressive service, for the Pope does everything so completely from his heart. Dr. Clifford evidently felt a great deal—as much as Robert did when we saw him consecrated. We were quite near enough to see comfortably, indeed Minima got the best place in the chapel. I should have been very sorry to have missed being present at this service. Col. Y—— went with us. We got home just in time to have breakfast, and to get to our own church. After the afternoon service we went to hear Manning preach again. There were parts of his sermon that were beautiful, but nothing to my mind that came up to his written sermons. It was a continuation of the one on the previous Sunday upon the duty of devotion to the Blessed Virgin. Again I heard nothing that in the least convinced me. We have not seen him to speak to since I last wrote. Oh, yes, I think that we saw him the day our letters went to the post. I must tell you about it. Mgr. Talbot came to see him before eleven, and not finding him in, came down to us. Mgr. Talbot stayed a long while, and was exceedingly entertaining. I sent up to inquire for him whether Manning had come in. When afterwards Manning did come in, he came down and stayed a little while. He talked about sorrow so very beautifully.

I quite longed to be alone with him, and to tell him a great deal about myself, for what he said made me feel that he thoroughly understands grief in all its intensity, and in all its phases. I can quite enter into what people have told me who have seen him in times of sorrow, that it was wonderful how he ministered to them, and showed them how sorrow should be turned to its best account. I believe it would do me good in many ways to talk to him, if he would talk without making any allusion to Roman Catholic doctrines. It seems to me that it is a gift which few of our clergymen possess, that of knowing how to talk to one on spiritual matters, so as to encourage one to bring out the innermost feelings and yearnings of the heart. Manning can do this. If he were but still in our Church, what a blessing and a comfort it would be to have him under the same roof! His Sunday sermons seem to have struck people so differently that it quite astonishes me. Yesterday evening at the Doria, Lord T—— told me that *his* impression was that Manning was making the most of a subject into which he did not fully enter, and that he was upholding a doctrine which he could not with his whole heart believe. Lord T—— thought that his arguments were weak, and that the sermon was illogical. I told him that I did not understand logic, but I was quite sure that Manning believed the doctrines that he endeavoured to teach; for he was no trifler with his conscience.

Afterwards I had a conversation with Mr. C——. Evidently *he* had been struck with a great deal that Manning said, and thought the reasoning deep. I should like Manning to put aside all questions of doctrine, and to preach a spiritual, practical sermon like his old ones, and not to preach *at* Protestants, but to address himself simply to Christians. There are many things in the world and about the world that puzzle me—thoughts about the end and value of sorrow and happiness. There are times when I cannot see these things in the light that the Gospel places them before us, and this disturbs me. I think that Manning could help me if he would preach on these subjects.

"Two evenings ago Dr. Manning came to see us, and talked so delightfully, so like his old sermons. He told us on what occasions and under what circumstances he had written some of those sermons. Then he spoke of the world, and of the danger of mixing too much in it. Life seemed so different while he was speaking of its duties and of its snares, and of what it *might* be to us. You know that I have longed for many years to see him. He quite comes up to all the ideas that I had formed of him. He is so very saint-like, and so thoroughly above the world."

It seemed impossible for my mother to shake off the prejudices and misunderstandings of the generation to which she belonged with regard to the doctrine about which Manning had been preaching. *Now* I believe that the very same doctrine is to be heard in Ritualist churches. Even at the end of 1857, when I returned to England, I heard a discourse at the chapel in Margaret Street on the honour due to the *Mater Creatoris,* which set forth as strongly as Dr. Manning had done her claims to our veneration. So strongly indeed were these claims urged, that I expected the Litany of Loretto to follow. It did not. There was then no practical result. I am told, however, that the Angelical Salutation and the *Stabat Mater* are, at the present day, to be heard in some Anglican churches. We may hope much from the use of such devotions.

My mother's objection to having recourse to the Blessed Virgin by no means arose from that spirit of pride, which was so severely condemned by Mr. Palmer's friend, the *Archimandrite*.[1] It arose from an idea, of which she could never rid herself, that to invoke saints and angels was to invest them with the Divine attribute of omnipresence. She could not understand that those who see God see all things, which it becomes them to see, in God.

I thought that to honour Mary rightly, to honour her as the "Mother of Jesus," we could not possibly honour her too highly. If honour were due to her, it must be a very great honour indeed.

[1] P. 344.

"He that is mighty hath done to her great things." The utmost reverence that we could offer would be incommensurate with the dignity to which her Creator had raised her.

> How can we rightly love thy Son,
> Dear Mother, if we love not thee?

Could it be pleasing to our Blessed Lord that we should be indifferent and cold towards her whom He has loved and exalted above every created being? Ought not rather our prayer to be earnest that our love and devotion to that Holy Mother might increase every day, that so we might become more and more like to our Divine Model, her Son.

A friend had given me a rosary of the Immaculate Conception. In saying this Rosary we offer praise to each of the Three Persons of the Blessed Trinity for benefits conferred on Mary. For some time I made daily use of this Rosary, the words for which I found in the *Vade Mecum*. It taught me a great deal about Almighty God, and about the praise to which He is entitled from us, for all that He has done for His Blessed Mother, and through her for us.

A Catholic friend wrote to my mother on this occasion:

"So you did not like Dr. Manning's sermon! Well, I hardly know whether that is a bad sign of you or not. I should be very sorry to think that there was not a great deal in you that sympathized with all he said, and all that could be said in honour of the Mother of our Redeemer, but even where this is the case I know that those who from their inherited position, external to the Fold, have ever been compelled, as it were, to look at the wrong side of the tapestry, can sometimes only see confusion where otherwise they would see harmony and truth. I know well that there are those who, not from heartlessness or lack of Christian instincts, but from prepossessions, and an imperfect appreciation of other parts of the Catholic system, stand practically alienated from the Blessed Virgin. They honour her in words, and sometimes in fancy, but between her and them there exists none of those living and practical relations through which the Communion of Saints becomes a reality. Everything depends on the way in which this misconception arises, for assuredly it is a great misconception which makes us mistake her, who is a bond of union between us and Christ, for a bar of separation. Wherever the misconception is wholly involuntary, however, and the jealousy against Mary's exalted place in the dispensation of grace proceeds from real love and loyalty for her Son and zeal for His glory, the film may at any time drop from the eye. Indeed, as long as the misconception exists it is actually a good, not a bad sign, that a feeling corresponding to that misconception exists also. That very feeling of strong repugnance, so far as it proceeds from love of our Divine Lord, is a pledge that the feeling will change into one of the exactly opposite sort whenever God gives us grace to see that the honour we give to Mary is in some respects like that which loyal subjects give to the representative of their sovereign, and is exactly the reverse of that which rebels give to the rival of that sovereign. What is really to be feared on such subjects is not the feeling you describe, but, on the contrary, indifference, apathy, and the habit of regarding as of no importance, and therefore as worthy of no laborious and painful investigation, differences of religious belief which really are of the deepest moment, differences which prove the existence of grievous and dangerous error on one side or the other.

"That you should feel disturbed, alarmed, and in part displeased at a sermon which proves that the most learned and spiritually-minded Catholics think with the poor on these matters, and are neither able nor willing to contract for a separate peace for themselves—this may be natural, nay it may be hopeful even, provided you do not, as self-willed people do, mistake strong *impressions* for certain *convictions*, and neglect the inquiry which God demands of all who believe that God has given a revelation to man. All such must believe also that to know aright which is the true version of that revelation and which the spurious one, must be our first duty, cost what it may. You cannot forget that Manning, and your departed friend Wilberforce, and some 200 beside of the English clergy, were brought up to see the thing as you see it; that they gave up all to testify to a higher truth; that they were learned in the Scriptures; that they ever affirmed that their new convictions had taken from them no single one of their old convictions except what was merely negative, and that they ever gave and give God thanks for the change..."

I was glad that my mother's wish that she could hear Dr. Manning preach a sermon in which there was nothing controversial, and which should remind her of his old sermons, was gratified one day at the Franciscan Church of St. Isidore. A great deal of this sermon was about the evil influences of the world. Speaking of those words of our Lord's, "How hardly shall they that have riches enter into the Kingdom of God," Manning said that the mere *possession* of riches (independently of *trusting* in them) had a tendency to form, and in many cases did form, a character of mind contrary to the spirit of the Gospel—artificial habits, artificial wants and pleasures, love of ease, love of pleasure, self-indulgence, indifference to the wants of others, love of the world, and attachment to the things of the world—whereas poverty tends to produce separation from the world, conformity to our Blessed Lord, simplicity of mind, self-denial, a true estimate of the world, and a more earnest desire for Heaven. The text was, "Blessed are the poor in spirit." Manning gave us some tests by which we might know whether we had this poverty of spirit. Then he told us what we must do in order that we might acquire it, and this part of the sermon was extremely profitable and practical, although it was somewhat painful. I thought how difficult it was to wish to possess humility when we knew that we could not get it without first submitting to humiliations. That this was the only way in which we could attain to humility, Dr. Manning taught us very plainly. He put before us the example of St. Francis of Assisi. There was much that was inspiriting in the lives of saints like him. Those only had really ruled the world who had been above it, who feared it not, and who would not be patronized by it. If we would not be the slaves of the world we must be its masters. We must care nothing for its opinions and its judgments, and its rules of right and wrong. They were as directly antagonistic to our Lord's precepts as were worldly ideas of happiness to His Beatitudes.

Dr. Manning used often to talk to us about the dangers which intercourse with the world involved.. In this sermon he spoke very strongly on that subject. The sermon disquieted me. It made me uncomfortable, and this his sermons on the honour due to our Blessed Lady had not done. Did it not suggest a way of honouring her, that was more difficult than that of saying Rosaries and Litanies? For it encouraged us to aim at that lowliness and humility, that poverty of spirit, that hiddenness and unworldliness, that complete submission to the will of God which must be found in all those who would be near to Jesus Christ, and which shone forth with greatest splendour in her who is the Queen of all Saints.

My mother wrote:

"Dr. Manning preached his last sermon (he has only preached four) yesterday, and a very beautiful one it was, quite like one of his old sermons. He preached at St. Isidore, the Church of the Franciscans. The church has just been repaired. First he spoke about the Franciscan Order and its work, and then he spoke about humility and poverty and trials. I never heard anything more in accordance with the spirit of the Sermon on the Mount. He set up such a high standard of goodness, and such pure motives for action."

The subject was one that was peculiarly interesting to my mother. She had an immense admiration for those who she saw were unworldly in spite of outward prosperity. On this subject she wrote:

"Certainly the things of the world—rank, riches, talents, &c.—do give a great deal of happiness to some, and *real* happiness, and happiness of a high kind. I mean when they are given to people who know how to make a good use of these gifts of God. The happiness of the merely worldly-minded must be of a very inferior kind, but when people *are* aiming high and *are* religious, and these things are added to them, I consider that they are blessings, and that certainly their possessors would not be as happy, and perhaps even not as good, without them. The feeling comes sometimes very strongly upon me that trials and poverty are much greater temptations, and take the heart farther from Heaven than happiness, and I could illustrate this by many examples."

No doubt the poverty of spirit which Dr. Manning had been advocating may be practised and has been practised, in the midst of outward worldly prosperity. But this I thought should not lead us to overlook the fact that under such circumstances the practice of it was much more difficult. Probably those who had attained to it must have undergone an amount of interior suffering of which not many souls are capable. If, although they possessed riches and honours, they were detached from them, that detachment must be the fruit of prayer and penance and mortification, and from these sources came the serenity and joy which no mere earthly prosperity can guarantee.

In the same letter my mother cited a passage that a friend had written to her about the happiness which he enjoyed in his home life.

"I know how uncertain is all such happiness, but I bless and thank God for it while it is here. You, too, know what is its happiness, and alas! too well the precariousness of it. How swiftly the years whirl round! How differently things look after one has passed the meridian! Life seems so short that one wonders how young people can take the trouble of settling themselves, 'building themselves houses as if they should abide for ever.' Happiest are they who go through their little round of life, their duties, their joys and sorrows, thinking of nothing but what is immediately before them, looking neither before nor after, feeling and acting, but not reflecting or speculating, at least happy if they have known nothing of the world of thought. But they who have once entered that region would not willingly sink into that unreasoning state I have just eulogized. No, they must go on struggling with a sublime discontent—sublime because it is engendered of conceptions and aspirations which find no type in the actual—and schooling this discontent with a patient acquiescence in that which after all may seem evil only because it is so imperfectly understood, and hoping that somehow, 'good will be the final goal of all!'"

My mother remarked that this did not seem to

her sound doctrine. She thought that her friend took a wrong and uncomfortable view of life, and of what its aims and objects ought to be. The truth is that the explanation of all that perplexes us with regard to happiness and sorrow and the meaning of life, is to be found in the right understanding of the end for which we were made—an end so glorious that we may well acquiesce in all that conduces to the attainment of it. Meanwhile we may give full encouragement to the highest aspirations of which our hearts and minds are capable. We may be certain that such aspirations will one day find their realization in a contentment, which will abundantly compensate for the temptations to discontent with which we may be tried during this our time of probation.

. . . .

From my Mother.

"*March* 6.—On Saturday we drove a long distance on the Appian Way. The day was wonderfully exquisite, the lights and shades so glorious. There was a delicious smell of grass, and larks were singing. Such fine shadows were cast upon the long line of ruined aqueducts and nearer ruins, on the hills of the Campagna, and on the more distant mountains still covered with snow; Frascati, Rocca di Papa, &c., seemed so near owing to the clearness of the atmosphere; and then I turned and looked back on Rome and the dome of St. Peter's—it was really *too* lovely!

In spite of the gay sunshine and the singing of the larks I could have *cried*, and had I been alone I *should*. You know as well as I do how a very lovely scene moves every spring of sorrow in the heart. A yearning for perfect happiness, pure happiness, comes over one, and the intense longing for those who are gone, and who we trust inhabit a world far more beautiful than this we look upon.

"I am writing now in the grounds of the Villa Nigrone. Minima is sketching Santa Maria Maggiore. Olivia has chosen the mountains for the subject of her sketch. The air is perfect and a fountain is babbling near me. . . . On Sunday morning Mr. Manning came down to bring back some books which we had lent him, and I had a talk with him alone, of which I was very glad. We did not touch upon doctrine. What a difference it must make in a person's life being able to *realize*, as he seems to do, the love of Christ and the presence of God! He seems to have made so many things *his own*. He spoke from his heart. How strange it must be to be living in the world and not to be caring in the least for the things of the world. I think *he* is the only person I have met with, whom I can imagine among the Apostles. I can quite believe what I have heard was the case with those who knew him, that constant intercourse with such a spiritual mind did even more good than the reading of his sermons. There is nothing in

Manning that ever jars upon my feeling of what a thoroughly religious man ought to be. I don't think I can explain per pen what I mean.

. . . . . .

"We had a drive by moonlight yesterday. We summoned Mr. de Vere and Mr. G. C——, and set out at eight, and were not in till nearly eleven. We went first to the Fountain of Trevi, where we got out and drank of the water; then by the Forum of Trajan. The broken columns of that Forum looked so fine in the moonlight. We passed by the beautiful remains of the Roman Forum, under the Arch of Titus, to the Colosseum. There we walked about a little, and sat down on the stones, Mr. de Vere recalling the scenes that had been enacted there by heathens and Christians. The night was too beautiful to think of going in, so we drove on to the Church of St. John Lateran, and contemplated its grand *façade* under the influence of moonlight. In the dim distance we made out the hills of the Campagna. It was so silent there, and the Church of Santa Croce, near the walls of Rome, looked so lonely. Then we proceeded to the Quirinal, where you know there is a fountain and the grand statues of Castor and Pollux and the horses, and finally on to St. Peter's. This drive was so delicious, only I felt very low all the time. There was something in the scene, the associations, and the glorious beauty of the heavens, which to me was quite overpowering—yet I would not have missed it on any account.

"We had a very pleasant afternoon with Mr. Palmer and Mr. G. C——. We traced the line of the wall of Servius Tullius, and very interesting Mr. Palmer made it, telling us snatches of Roman history.

"I must tell you about the Palazzo Spada. There are not many fine pictures there. The chief interest is a very fine statue of Pompey the Great, by which Julius Cæsar was standing when Brutus and the others struck him. It seemed so strange to look at it and to think of that event, to realize it, and to remember that it happened' before the Birth of Christ. I thought of the enthusiasm you and I used to feel for Cæsar when we were reading that old Roman history, and how intensely interested we should have been could we have come to Rome in those days. I believe at that time the remains of Pagan Rome would have found greater charm in our eyes than Christian Rome.

"*Wednesday in Holy Week.*—We do not mean to attempt going to the Sistine to hear the *Miserere* this afternoon, for there will be such a crowd; we are going to S. Ignazio, where we shall hear the same music in comfort, without people talking around one. Of course the music will not be so fine. We hope to go to the Sistine on Good Friday morning. Mr. Grey says that the music is so very beautiful: the Passion is sung in the most touching way. When one has a book and can follow it, the service is most impressive and lovely. I do so look forward to it. On Easter Sunday we shall go to St. Peter's for High Mass, and shall hear the silver trumpets in the dome, but we mean to take things much more quietly *this* year than we did last year; in fact I could not now run about as I did then."

The preceding year we had not attended the morning services at the Sistine on the three last days of Holy Week. We did so now, and as strangers were not in the habit of frequenting them, there was the space and quiet which conduce to the better appreciation of a religious function. We did not attempt the crowded service of Tenebræ at the Sistine. We went instead to the Church of S. Ignazio, where it was sung in a very edifying way by the Jesuit novices.

My mother wrote, April 14, 1857:

"I wish so much that we could adopt these services in our churches. With the exception of one Litany of the Saints, there is not a word to which the most rigorous Protestant would object if he did not know the services were used at Rome. Many chapters from the Prophecies are read, or rather, most beautiful and judicious selections from them and from other parts of the Bible. What impressed me greatly was the singing of the Passion from the nineteenth chapter of St. John's Gospel. It is so very touching, so deeply solemn. One voice sings the narrative, another the words of our Saviour, and a third those of Pontius Pilate. The shouts of the multitude are sung by a quantity of voices. The effect is most wonderful. I never heard anything more moving, and I would not have missed it on any account. . . . We had to be up very early on Easter Sunday, for we went to St. Peter's. We were very well placed, and the Pope sang the Mass beautifully. He has a very fine voice and is *very* devout; he seems quite wrapt in prayer. After he had consecrated, there was a moment of perfect silence. Then the silver trumpets sounded, and they quite thrilled through me. I don't think that I was ever so overcome by *sound*, though solemn music always has a great effect upon me. It seemed such a strain as might accompany a blest spirit to Heaven, or greet her entrance there. Oh! how I wished that it could have been prolonged. Shall I ever hear it again? Somehow, it was far more beautiful than on Christmas Day."

To our sorrow, the time for our departure drew near. Each succeeding day did but reveal to us that we had not nearly seen all that there was to be seen in Rome. Its interests seemed ever to multiply, its attractions to increase. We found that Rome should be lived in to be *understood*, though we *loved* it from the moment we entered its gates. Very different, alas! is the Rome of to-day from the Rome of my youth. Those who have usurped the sovereignty have done their best to efface its Christian character, and to make it resemble the least interesting parts of Paris. Twenty years of Piedmontese occupation must have had its effect on the spiritual atmosphere of Rome, and have weakened that supernatural influence of which many of us, although we were then outside the Church, could not but be conscious. Some of the charm must be gone, but a great deal must ever remain. In the days of which I write, though we gave a good deal of our time to the things of this world, it was yet very difficult to be in Rome and to forget that there was another and a much better world. Everything spoke of the supernatural.

On some expeditions we made, our good angels must have accompanied us gladly. Mother had proposed to Mr. Palmer that he should take us to all the places connected with SS. Peter and Paul. This idea met with his approval. "We began with the Appian Way," my mother wrote. "We passed under the arch which St. Peter must have passed under when he entered Rome. Then we went to the Pretorian Camp, where St. Paul would have been taken, the walls of which extend round what is now the Jesuits' garden. In this garden the bay-trees were smelling so delightfully. Mr. Palmer did not like us to enjoy the delicious perfumes or the lovely views. We were to think only of the Apostles!

We ended that first day with going to a church in the Corso built on the site of an old Roman house, the one in which St. Paul dwelt—'his own hired house'—with the two soldiers who guarded him, and from which he wrote the Epistles to the Ephesians," &c.

Another day we visited the churches, &c., where it is known that the Apostle went, such as Sta. Prisca, which stands on the site of the house of Aquila and Priscilla; and S. Pudenziana, the house of Pudens and Claudia. St. Claudia was a British captive who was converted by St. Paul. She was the *first* British Christian, and through her, therefore, Christianity was first introduced into Britain. This probably gave rise to the tradition that St. Paul himself had visited England. . . The Mamertine Prison, of course, came into our pilgrimage, and the chapel called " Domine quo vadis," and the spot where the two Apostles separated on their way to martyrdom. St. Peter was thence taken to the gardens of Nero to be crucified. St. Paul was taken a mile or two further on the Ostian Way. He was beheaded on the spot where now stands the Church of S. Paolo alle tre Fontane.

I look back on our visits to these holy places with much delight. They gave me a more intimate acquaintance with the Apostles, and inspired me with an increased devotion to them. There was also the interest of being associated with the numberless servants of God, who in every age of the Church had come from all parts of the earth to offer their thanksgivings and supplications at these sacred shrines. Here had come our holy Saxon forefathers. Here had come the founders of great Religious Orders. Here had come, ere yet he was twenty years of age, and here had lived and died, the fervent Florentine who earned the title of Apostle of Rome, and with whose life and character Newman and Faber and others of his illustrious sons in England have made us so familiar.

"St. Philip Neri," his biographer tells us, "would frequently visit the seven greater churches or basilicas of Rome, feeding his love on the memorials of God's goodness they contain. It is a distance of ten or eleven miles, and it takes seven or eight hours to make this pilgrimage with befitting composure and with the necessary pause in each church. The way lies partly in the city and partly in the country; in part, amidst the throng and bustle of men; and in part, through the still and pensive loneliness of the Roman Campagna. It is an excursion of singular interest and pleasure, even when made solely with a view to the grand memorials of times past; but when made with the soul fixed on God, and in due dispositions, it is one of those consolations we can never forget. All along the way, in the basilicas we visit, in the sacred bodies there enshrined, a thousand records of love and self-sacrifice are presented to the mind, or rather, the one great record of the great love of Jesus Christ, repeated anew in the saints from year to year, from day to day, in their martyrdom of blood or of desire. Sometimes in the day, but most usually by night, when all was still around, Philip would leave his little room and take his way to St. Peter's, slowly and absorbed in prayer. Then through the Lungara and by S. Maria in Trastevere, and over the bridge called the Ponte Quattro Capi, he would walk the long distance which separates St. Paul's from St. Peter's. From St. Paul's he would continue his course to St. Sebastian's, and so along the Appian Way to St. John Lateran and Santa Croce. Thence he would turn his steps to San Lorenzo, and back to Sta. Maria Maggiore, the close of his pilgrimage. Those who met him as he walked along, so humble and poor, alone, and rapt in meditation, would hardly suspect the mystery of that pilgrimage, or the consuming love hidden within that heart.

"As he went on his way, the expanse of green by day, or the starry sky by night, would raise his soul towards God in adoration and praise. His prayers at the doors of each basilica, so near the relics of the martyrs, would bring back vividly to his mind the memory of their conflict and their triumph, and lead him on in thought to the great martyrdom of Calvary. St. Peter, St. Paul, St. John, St. Sebastian, St. Laurence, whose memory is stamped on five of these basilicas, were martyrs very different in the circumstances of their martyrdom, but all well fitted to enkindle and increase the flame of his love. Sta. Maria Maggiore, where is preserved the cradle of the Infant Jesus, and Santa Croce, where is venerated the holy Cross of our redemption, would bring before him the beginning and the end of the earthly life of our Divine Lord, together with the dearest name of Mary, who, as Mother of Jesus and as participating in the great act of our redemption, is so inseparably bound up with the mystery of Bethlehem, and with that of the Cross. Both would go straight to Philip's heart, and nourish that tender, ever-present thought of Jesus and of Mary which characterized all his life. Both are interwoven with the memories of martyrs, of the Popes who raised those churches, of the saints who rest in them in peace."[1]

O dear St. Philip! how in after-years have I again visited these holy sanctuaries and asked that I might imitate you in your faith and burning charity! How have I knelt in the little oratory which was once your room, and assisted at the Holy Sacrifice, offered there where you used to offer it! How have I prayed that I might not be unworthy of the glorious gift of faith which now is mine, and that through your intercession those whom I loved might also obtain that gift, that at the altars of your Oratory in London we may all be enamoured of the beauty, and be animated with the spirit, and breathe the atmosphere of your own beloved Rome!

[1] *Life of St. Philip Neri.* By Capecelatro. Translated by Father Pope, C.O.

CHAPTER XII.

Painful impressions that some Protestants receive from foreign churches. They do not understand the Catholic idea of worship. Advantages of familiarity with foreign lands in youth. The choice of a state of life. Necessity of coming to a decision about religion. Motives which conduced to the decision. The Sacrament of Penance.

Dr. Pusey's satisfaction in the Church of England. Dean Church's views. Mr. Keble's views. The *Christian Year*. Ash Wednesday. The Commination Service.

Father Faber's books and sermons. Difficulties and their solutions. Interview with Father Faber. Reception into the Church.

THE thought of Italy is so pleasant that I could willingly linger over it and record memories of Siena, Bologna, Padua, and Venice. But were I to do so, the purpose of this narrative would not be furthered. I have said enough to show the impression that foreign travel made upon me, and that it did not increase my appreciation of England and its religion. I was not scandalized, as I had been told I should be, by many things that are stumbling-blocks to the Protestant mind. The behaviour of the poor people who crowd the large churches and who seem quite at home in the house of God, treating it so naturally as their Father's house, saying their prayers with such simplicity and utter absence of human respect, bringing in their bundles and their babies, assisting at Mass with unaffected devotion, is misunderstood by the Protestant who is above all things else—*respectable*. To him such behaviour seems irreverent. He cannot understand unceremonious prayer. He is painfully alive to the fact that these peasants have partaken largely of garlic, and have not meddled with soap and water. He notices, moreover, that they do not scruple to spit when it suits their convenience. No doubt such habits are unpleasant. They are annoying to the cleanly and more refined worshippers, but they are not sins. In the Italian churches there are hardly any seats. People stand or kneel. How uncomfortable! How different to the enlightened worship of a reformed Church! Most of all is the worthy Protestant distressed, if he should chance to frequent these foreign churches during the month of May, at the worship which he says is paid to wax dolls. He sees crowds gathered round life-size figures which represent the Madonna and her Child, arrayed in gauze and silver, with artificial flowers. Such representations are far more attractive to these simple minds than is the most beautiful marble statue to us, and elicit from them far more fervent ejaculations than we perhaps have ever made. What a shock does the enlightened islander experience when he beholds such a degrading spectacle! And then how unintelligible to him appear the grand functions which he may witness! Perhaps even more unintelligible are the Low Masses at which he sees crowds of poor assisting with deep attention and devotion. Must it not be superstition, and not true religion, which collects such multitudes in the churches? The people cannot know what the priest is about. Is not Mass said in Latin? Is it not difficult to catch even the Latin words? Still the fact remains, the churches are crowded with poor. Popery is not the religion of a class, and it is specially to the poor that its Gospel is preached.

Every nation has its own peculiarities, but in every nation the Catholic religion finds itself equally at home. In France and in Belgium, in Germany and in Italy, the same faith is professed, the same worship is offered, the same sacraments are received. Such was the case in England also, ere she was torn away from Catholic unity. Poor English! They would make such good Catholics if only they had the chance.

Why is it that even pious Protestants have so much repugnance to Catholic worship? We know how distressing a simple choral service, such as is sung in their own Cathedrals, is to some persons. They do not regard public worship as a tribute offered to Almighty God, but rather as something that is to appeal to themselves. If it has not the effect of exciting their devotion, they consider that it has failed in its object. Many think that the Creator is content with a minimum of worship from His creatures. Such is not the language of the Psalms. Perhaps Protestants of this class do not attach more meaning to the Psalms than they do to our Blessed Lady's *Magnificat*. " Praise the Lord, O my soul, and let all that is within me praise His holy Name. . . O praise the Lord, ye angels of His, ye that excel in strength. . . Bless the Lord, *all ye works of His*, in all places of His dominion." I knew an elderly Protestant lady who happened to go to her own service one weekday in Lent, and heard instead of the *Te Deum* to which she was accustomed, the *Benedicite, omnia opera*. She was quite indignant. How could the green things upon the earth bless the Lord? or how could the wells and the dews and frosts? Vain to remind her that the canticle was in her own prayer-book. She did not care where it was, *it was nonsense!*

It is certainly an immense pleasure and advantage to have had the opportunity of travelling and of becoming familiar with foreign lands in the days of one's youth. To look back on the happiness thus enjoyed, is a solace amid the inevitable worries and anxieties of middle life. As life advances so many ties are formed from which it is difficult to break loose, and very seldom are we able to exchange the cares and responsibilities of home for the pleasant sensation of being a pilgrim and a stranger with no abiding city. The work of life has to be done, and as a rule it cannot well be done by those who are ever wandering from place to place, taking root nowhere.

For most persons a time comes, sooner or later, when the choice of a state of life is forced upon them. However satisfied they would be to go on without making any irrevocable change, they find that it is no longer possible to do so.

I can imagine no greater happiness than receiving and following a vocation to religious life. Blessed are they on whom Almighty God deigns to bestow so choice a gift, choosing them for Himself, that they may love Him with an undivided love, and allow no human affection to come between Him and them. But those who regard the religious life as the highest and holiest life to which any human being can be called, have at the same time a nobler conception of the dignity of Christian marriage than have those who regard the married as the most desirable of all states of human life. God's will is the one thing that all must look to. It is His will that the greater number of His children should serve Him by living in the world, and carrying on that continual warfare against the over-solicitude for the things of the world—its cares, its business, and its pleasures—which such a life involves. With regard to the choice of a state of life Catholics have a great advantage (would that they more frequently availed themselves of it!) in the opportunities which are given them of going into retreat. What a satisfaction to have made the choice, seriously and deliberately, and with the aid of the rules laid down by St. Ignatius! Devout Anglicans do their best according to their lights, by prayer and reflection, but how often must they not long for more definite guidance!

I was glad that when I had to settle down, after those pleasant years of foreign travel, my lot was not cast in the country. I was to live in England, but in or near London. A more or less prosaic existence seemed to be opening out before me. If my life were to be rescued from commonplaceness it was evident that this could only be by my not acquiescing in the easy-going indifference to the supernatural world that prevailed around me. There were the great responsibilities of life to be dealt with. Sooner or later, some definite decision with regard to religion must be made. My doubts would not be silenced, however much I might try to be content with Anglicanism and to persuade myself that it might suffice for me as it sufficed for my betters. London provided every form of Anglicanism from which to choose. The best preachers were to be heard there; Masters' shop offered continually new and tempting little devotional works. But from none of these could I get the help I needed. Was there now any insurmountable obstacle to my seeking that help elsewhere? Must I not make one great effort to remove any such obstacle?

However much we may feel attached to the Church, and however few may be our difficulties with regard to her doctrines, however well we may have made ourselves acquainted with her ritual and devotions, there is a shrinking from taking the final plunge, a dread of actually making the change, which I can only account for as being inspired by the devil, who works on the imagination, when he cannot convince the reason, and who represents difficulties as being almost insurmountable.

Happy are those who do not keep God waiting, who do the right thing at the right time, who, directly they see the truth, do not hesitate to embrace it, who recognize Divine inspirations and promptly and generously act on them! From how many temptations against faith, from how much bitter regret are not such valiant souls saved!

Very leisurely did I proceed, alas! Mine was not an impulsive disposition. Now that I was free to choose my own place of worship, I usually went to Mass instead of to " Dearly Beloved." Abroad I had attended many grand functions, but I had not had opportunities of assisting at Low Mass. I wanted to get quite familiarized with Low Mass and with Catholic devotions and practices, in order that I might be sure that it was not the novelty of them to me, or their attractive surroundings which made them seem profitable. With regard to external attractions indeed, many people would prefer those which the Church of England had to offer. The Psalms and Anthems as they were sung in our old Cathedrals, the devotional music, and simple but impressive ritual of the choral "celebrations" that had now become more common; what could be more in accordance with a refined taste than were these? And from some of the sermons there was much to be learnt. Mr. Evans, who occasionally preached in St. Andrew's, Wells Street, was striking and original. Dr. Neale introduced us to the mystical interpretation of Holy Scripture. Mr. Carter, of Clewer, set before us rich examples of practical holiness from the life of the Blessed Virgin Mary. No less practical were the "courses" which Mr. Yard preached at All Saints', Margaret Street.

There was a feeling of comfort and of snugness in the Low Church temples, and in their pews, which was not without its attractions. It was, indeed, a lower form of attractiveness than that which was offered by the architectural beauty of All Saints', Margaret Street. We could turn in to a week-day Matins at St. Mark's, North Audley Street, and join in the Psalms and Prayers, and listen to the Lessons, and enjoy that satisfied feeling which we used to have as Anglicans when we went to a week-day service, a feeling that we were rather better than were other people, and that we had done a good work which they had not done. One does not have that satisfaction as a Catholic.

I could not be contented, however, with the services which the Anglican Churches, High or Low or Moderate, provided. I wanted something more than they had it in their power to give.

I found that the Low Masses which I was in the habit of attending were becoming more and more of a necessity to my spiritual well-being. It did not seem to me sincere to be going on in this way. I hated insincerity. I could not bear that others should assume that I believed in Protestantism when I did not believe in it. I knew that I was only waiting for a convenient season to have done with Protestantism for ever. Many converts have known how long that "convenient season" was in coming, how slow they were in discovering that it probably never would come, and how at last grace was given to them to see that it was not their own convenience, or the convenience of their relatives which ought to be considered, not their own inclinations and likings, or those of others, but simply and solely the will of God in their regard. Who has not taken refuge in the hope that a severe illness would supply an opportunity for reconciliation with the Church, the motives for which could not be misunderstood, even by the most malicious? Illness came to me. It took the form of great prostration. It was then that

I realized how impossible it was to nerve myself for so important an act at a time when I was weak both in body and in mind. I must get well first; such a step required health and strength.

A friend of mine, when telling me what was the final motive-power that brought him into the Church, said "that it was a general craving for the forgiveness of his sins." If our Lord had instituted the Sacrament of Penance—and it was impossible for us not to see that He *had* instituted it in the power which He gave to His Apostles to forgive sins—were we safe in not availing ourselves of it? "The forgiveness of sins" is an Article of the Creed: if the explanation which is given of this Article by the Roman Church is not the true Catholic doctrine, what is the true doctrine? What did the words mean? Could the most learned Protestant point to any century in the Church, when the Sacrament of Penance was for the first time introduced? Could he deny that St. James said, "Confess your sins (not only to God, but) to one another"? Could we be sure that God would forgive our sins if we should refuse to make use of the means which He had appointed whereby we might obtain forgiveness? That was a question which could not but present itself to one who was making a preparation for death.

In consequence of their having rejected the

Sacrament of Penance, many Protestants have come to think but lightly of the reality of the guilt and punishment of sin. It is often difficult to convince them that they themselves have any need of forgiveness, or any obligation to do penance for past sins. They assert confidently, that all that is necessary to secure Heaven for them, was done long ago by our Lord, and that to examine into their sins and to make acts of sorrow for these sins would encourage a morbid tendency and be an insult to the plentifulness of His Redemption.

I had been taught a different doctrine. In my childhood I had been taught that self-examination was a duty, that sorrow for sin must be a reality, and thus as I grew older I was led to long for reconciliation with God in the way which He has Himself chosen. I saw that it was for me a duty to seek that sacrament of mercy which can only be found with certainty in the Roman Catholic Church.

When men like Archbishop Tait talk of confession and say that it is not in accordance with the spirit of "our Church"—though it may be allowed to certain weak minds, who cannot otherwise quiet themselves, and who probably are just those who need it least—the question whether confession is not commanded as implied in the Gospels, never seems to disturb their consciences. They take it for granted that confession is quite unnecessary and superfluous, even if it is not positively harmful. They assume that it would be unworthy of Almighty God to attach such conditions to His pardon. " Who can forgive sins but God alone ? " Why should they believe that He has given such power unto men ? Why should they believe that the power entrusted by Christ to His Apostles was to be continued to the successors of those Apostles throughout all time ? "The sins that you forgive shall be forgiven." Often and often, notwithstanding, have they read St. John's account of that Easter evening in the upper chamber at Jerusalem ; how their Risen Lord, in His glorified Body, passing through the closed doors, suddenly stood before the Apostles, and gave that great gift—so fitting a gift for the day of His Resurrection—the Sacrament of pardon and peace which was to remain in His Church for ever. For through this sacrament did He ordain that the soul which had been dead in trespasses and sins might rise to a new life; that the soul which had been bound and helpless in the winding-sheet of evil habits should be bidden to come forth like Lazarus from his tomb and hear the voice of Jesus to His followers —Loose him and let him go.

Jesus had said, "Peace be to you." He had shown to His disciples His hands and His side, and the disciples were glad when they saw the Lord. The peace and the joy were not for them alone, but for all who should believe through their word. "He said, therefore, to them again, Peace be to you. As the Father hath sent Me, I also send you. When He had said this, He breathed on them, and He said to them, Receive ye the Holy Ghost. Whose sins you shall forgive, they are forgiven them, and whose sins you shall retain, they are retained."

If we regard confession simply as a pious practice, a practice that is advisable perhaps in some cases, but which, as a rule, should not be recommended to people in the mass, we are in harmony with the Church of England. She makes no practical provision for confession; her clergy are not so trained in a system of Moral Theology as either to qualify them or to justify them in dealing with immortal souls; her Bishops discourage their so dealing, and the Bishops herein do well. Are not their persistent denials that any change can possibly be effected in the elements of bread and wine by the words of consecration, and the attitude they have always held towards those of their clergy who have claimed authority to forgive sins, sufficient indications that in their own opinion they themselves had never received such powers, and that they most certainly had no intention or idea of conveying such powers to those whom they ordained? Are these Protestant Bishops not right in this notion of their office? Even if we have not examined the history of Barlow and of Parker, can we be blamed for agreeing with them? But

... death is rapidly approaching, and after death the judgment, and we must have our sins forgiven before we die. We have seen that Jesus Christ, when the sick came to Him to be healed, taught them to care rather that their sins should be forgiven. We have seen Christ instituting the Sacrament of Penance for the remission of sin. How shall we tell Him that we reject a sacrament which He has Himself appointed, that we prefer a more comfortable doctrine invented by Reformers in the sixteenth century and still held by their descendants in the present day?

It is difficult to set down in detail all the motives that induced me at last to take the final step. I know that one motive was "the general craving for the forgiveness of my sins" (and especially in the view of preparing for death), of which my friend had spoken. There was the wish, moreover, to possess myself of the means of grace which in their abundance are to be found alone within the Church—undoubted Sacraments, Indulgences, devotion to Mary and the saints, and above all, daily Mass and the continual presence of our Lord in His sacramental tabernacle. In trying to do without these privileges I was sensible of a want of loyalty and gratitude to God. This became at last too painful to be endured.

Dr. Pusey seems to have found all that he wanted for the necessities of his soul, in the

Established Church of England. He thought that those who could not satisfy themselves as he was satisfied must be deficient in humility and in self-discipline. He impressed on them most strenuously that they ought rather to reckon themselves unworthy of the helps which the English Church did provide than to carp at the incompleteness of those helps. It is evident that no doubt of her capability of satisfying all his own spiritual wants ever entered into his mind. Others, like Dean Church, if not so enthusiastic in their allegiance, came to the conclusion that the English Church was after all as well worth living in and fighting for as is any other Church. They did not blind themselves to her defects, but they looked abroad and saw defects elsewhere and everywhere. There might be much to be preferred in foreign systems, but they need not shut their eyes to the goodness of their own Church, and that a goodness which was so manifestly on the increase. And that most excellent of men who was the originator of the movement, he who first sounded the note of alarm and called on his brethren to arm themselves to defend the principles of Catholicism—the good and gentle Keble; he too, more clear-sighted as he was than Pusey, less sanguine, and sorely tried as was his confidence in his Church, he too thought he saw in the goodness of the lives, and in the peaceful deaths of Anglicans so great an evidence that the Spirit of God was at work in the Church of

England, that he need not fear to remain within her pale.

> No voice from Heaven has clearly said,
> "Let us depart." Then fear to roam.

But Keble did not deceive himself with regard to the contradictory principles which were struggling for mastery within the bosom of the Church of England.

In his Preface to *Eucharistical Adoration* (Second Edition), he says: "Unless I am greatly mistaken, the real point at issue in most of the controversies which have troubled us in the Reformed English Church might be expressed as follows: 'Is the Church, mingled as we see it of good and bad, a supernatural body, separated off from the world to live a supernatural life, begun, continued, and ended in miracles—miracles as real as any of those which befell the Israelites in the wilderness—as real but infinitely more gracious and awful; or is it only a body providentially raised up to hold the best and purest philosophy—helped, as all good things are, from above, but in itself no more than the heroical and Divine phase of this present life?' It is plain at first glance which side of this alternative brings with it the more intense obligation to holiness, and represents sin as more exceedingly sinful."

.   .   .   .

"It is a sad habit of thought for a theologian to train himself up in—that of instinctively adopting, out of various expositions, that which is most earthly and least supernatural."

Mr. Lock[1] quotes the above as showing "how the sense grew upon Keble that the one question at issue in the conflict of Churchmen was the reality of the supernatural."

The reality of the supernatural! That is impressed on the minds of the poorest and most illiterate Catholic peasant by the sacrificial act of worship in which he is daily invited to join. Is not that act the substance of which the miracle worked for the Israelites in the wilderness was but the shadow? It is impossible to unite in offering to Almighty God the Holy Sacrifice of the Mass without being made conscious of the reality of the supernatural. Was it not a sense of the supernatural that so powerfully impressed me when I first entered a Roman Catholic church in my childhood? However men like Keble may deplore the absence of this sense, they will strive in vain to make it live in the minds of those who are severed from that one supernatural society of men on earth, the members of which form the One Body with the One Spirit, and the One Faith.

The view of the Church which is most prevalent in England is, as Keble says, that "it is only a body providentially raised up to hold the best and purest philosophy—helped, as all good things are, from above, but in itself no more than

---

[1] *Biography of John Keble.* Second Edition, p. 234.

the heroical and divine phase of this present life."

Such a body is not the Church which our Lord established and left behind Him on the earth, and which He promised should be ever guided by the Spirit of Truth.

I have said how when I was in Rome I enjoyed spending a long time in St. Peter's—sometimes in the subterranean church before the altar of St. Petronilla, where the great Apostle was buried —or kneeling at the confession in the church itself, where the golden lamps are ever burning. We kneel there, and our thoughts go back to the Sea of Galilee and to the fishermen mending the nets which symbolized the nets that were to gather countless souls so long as the world shall last—to our Lord teaching the multitudes from the ship which was Simon's, as He will teach men to the end of time; or to that earlier day when Andrew found his brother Simon, and brought him to Christ, and Jesus looking on him said, "Thou shalt be called Cephas—a stone"— on to the time when the full meaning of that name was unfolded after the confession of faith in the Divinity of Jesus had been made by Simon. We think of those poor fishermen gathered round Him Who spoke as never man spoke, and as we gaze up into the vast dome above us, can we fail to comprehend the significance of the words which there we read: *Tu es Petrus, et super hanc*

Petram ædificabo Ecclesiam Meam. Et tibi dabo claves regni cælorum?

Shall we tell our Lord that we have explained away these words of His, that we attach no meaning to them, that we have settled to our own satisfaction the way in which His Church ought to be governed and His teaching perpetuated, and that we reject absolutely and entirely the infallible authority which He has provided for us? Our own interpretations of Scripture, our own views of what doctrines were held in the early Church—are sufficient for us.

Thus did the question present itself to my mind as a question that would have to be answered one day, when no evasions or excuses would avail. I could not be amongst those who can put it aside as a matter that does not concern them. Because there were so many men and women who lived good lives, and who died peaceful deaths amongst Evangelicals, and Anglicans, and Latitudinarians, and the various schools into which these are subdivided, it did not follow that the Church of Rome was not the one true Church of Christ. I did all that I could to settle down in the National Church, but in vain. The "signs of life" in it so confidently appealed to by Pusey, and admitted at last by Keble, as satisfactory evidence in its favour, failed to inspire me with confidence. Yet I can sympathize most truly with those to whom the Anglican Church is very dear, who have made for themselves a home in it from which they cannot bear the idea of parting. Some I have known who felt that it would be a real grief to them to give up reading the *Christian Year* as a religious exercise every Sunday. To me the *Christian Year* never was what it has been to countless souls in the Church of England—the one book that they prized next to their Bible and their Book of Common Prayer. In my youthful days I preferred the *Lyra Innocentium*, in which there is a poem for every Sunday and holy day. It was written in a more cheerful strain, and contained more of Catholic dogma than did its predecessor.

There were two poems in the *Christian Year* that I liked very much and learnt by heart. These poems were more especially characterized by that spirit of sadness which pervades the whole work. One was that for the Eleventh Sunday after Trinity—beginning,

>Is this a time to plant and build.

It described the critical state of the Church and deprecated the idea of acquiescing in a soft and comfortable life. We were "to steel our melting hearts."

>To watch with firm unshrinking eye,
>Thy darling visions as they die,
>Till all bright hopes, and hues of day,
>Have faded into twilight gray.

The time would come when we should

>Bless the pangs that made us see
>This was no world of rest.

The other poem spoke of a rest that we might have here—the rest that there is in perfect resignation. It began:

> O Lord my God, do Thou Thy holy will—
>   I will lie still—
> I will not stir, lest I forsake Thine arm,
>   And break the charm,
> Which lulls me, clinging to my Father's breast,
>   In perfect rest.

It went on to speak of the Crown, the special reward—

> . . . the radiant coronet,
> All gemm'd with pure and living light,
> Too dazzling for a sinner's sight,
> Prepar'd for virgin souls, and them
> Who seek the martyr's diadem,

and of how there were many meek, self-forgetting souls, hidden from the eyes of men, who without undergoing a death of blood or fire, would find their sufferings so patiently borne, rewarded in Heaven by the martyr's palm.

Nor were those whose lot here was happier and more prosperous to despair of reaching the highest seats in Heaven.

> And there are souls that seem to dwell
> Above this earth—so rich a spell
> Floats round their steps, where'er they move,
> From hopes fulfill'd and mutual love.
> Such, if on high their thoughts are set,
> Nor in the stream the source forget,
> If prompt to quit the bliss they know,
> Following the Lamb where'er He go,

> By purest pleasures unbeguil'd
> To idolize or wife or child;
> Such wedded souls our God shall own
> For faultless virgins round His throne.

I was a little annoyed when a Protestant friend who had not long to live, and who knew that his days were numbered, criticized these lines. He said that he thought it was hard that the happy, comfortable, married people were to have as high a rank in Heaven as those should have who renounced these worldly joys! Mr. Keble perhaps had in his mind the pious occupants of many a bright and cosy parsonage.

Yet there is one verse in the penitential season of Lent which suggests that the purest affections and pleasures of earth may have to be renounced if we would attain to the true liberty of the children of God.

> Sweet is the smile of home; the mutual look
> Where hearts are of each other sure;
> Sweet all the joys that crowd the household nook,
> The haunt of all affections pure;
> Yet *in the world even these abide*, and we
> Above the world our calling boast:
> *Once gain the mountain-top, and thou art free:*
> Till then, who rest, presume; who turn to look, are lost.[1]

Not inappropriate lines for the first Sunday I spent as a Catholic—the First Sunday in Lent—when in the exhilaration and delight of new-found liberty, that mountain-top seemed already scaled, and that city of refuge reached, of which

[1] The *Christian Year*. First Sunday in Lent.

it was said, "Haste thee, escape thither; for I cannot do anything till thou be come thither."[1]

But I am anticipating.

At last I followed my convictions. I could no longer endure the responsibility of remaining outside the Church which I now recognized to be the One Church of Christ. The fear came over me that my faith might go. I saw that faith was a gift, a great gift, and that the Divine hand which bestowed it might withdraw this gift if it were not cherished. I fixed on Shrove Tuesday as the day on which I would take some step. But when that day came, there came also relations to spend the afternoon. I had been in the habit of going to the ten o'clock Mass in Farm Street Church. What should I do on Ash Wednesday? I had a vague idea that it would not be seemly for me to receive the ashes, and so I turned in for the last time to an Anglican church.

> And now Ash Wednesday came, the day
>   When few to church repair,
> For on that day you know is read
>   The Commination prayer.
>
> And our late vicar, a kind man,
>   He oft has said to me,
> He wished that service was well out
>   Of our good Liturgy.

The Commination Service used in England on the first day of Lent does savour of the Old Law. It would seem to be more in accordance

[1] Genesis xix. 22.

with the Gospel spirit that we should spend our time rather in praying for sinners than in cursing them. We were, however, invited to curse them until that much to be wished for time should arrive when the discipline of penance may be restored. I left the church feeling no heart to join in these denunciations, and wended my way towards the Brompton Oratory.

It happened that I had a Catholic friend who was living close to the Oratory. Through his books and sermons I seemed to know Father Faber, and I felt impelled to seek for an interview with him, rather than with one who would be a complete stranger to me. I consulted my friend. She promised to arrange for my seeing him. In much trepidation I went the next day to learn whether the interview could take place. Having gone so far, it was a disappointment to find that Father Faber was engaged for the whole of that day. He would perhaps be able to see me on the morrow. This was the message conveyed to me by another Father.

Strangely enough, I, who had waited so long, became suddenly afraid that I might die in the night, or that if I waited any longer my courage would fail me. I considered whether I should not beg this Father to receive me at once. He was not, however, himself a convert, and I thought he would not understand me so well as one who was. He might insist on my spending some time in receiving instruction. This I wished to avoid. The necessity of taking the step had come before me as a pressing and urgent necessity. I believed implicitly every doctrine that the Church taught. Why should I any longer postpone the avowal of my belief? Further delay, even for a week, appeared to me to be fraught with danger.

The same evening I received a letter telling me that at two o'clock on the following day Father Faber would see me. Then I felt not a little frightened. Throughout the night that ensued, imagination was very busy in conjuring up difficulties. It was a dreadful and an entirely sleepless night. An undefined terror possessed me, and did but increase every hour. However, as I had made the appointment, I was resolved that I would keep it.

Mindful of my experience on the previous Tuesday, and fearing lest some unforeseen occurrence might again detain me at home, I went early to the house of a friend and spent an hour with her before I started for the Oratory. My friend was also on the point of being received into the Church. We passed the time in discussing difficulties, and in fortifying each other for the step which we had both resolved to take.

I never go into the house of the Oratorian Fathers in London without thinking of that day. The house remains unchanged. The temporary church, which was then in use, has been swept away, and has given place to the present magnificent building.

I had not to wait long before Father Faber appeared. I could not feel that he was a stranger. His writings had earned from me, as from many, a great debt of gratitude. Two of his books—*All for Jesus* and *Growth in Holiness*—had taught me a great deal about the spiritual life. They had made me wish to know more about the Saints, and about that science of the Saints which is so little understood outside the Roman Church. Familiarity with the lives and writings of the Saints is indeed a great characteristic of Father Faber. *Growth* was intimately associated in my mind with Rome. The book had been lent to me there. In anticipation of the time when I should have to return it, I had made copious extracts, especially from the chapters on "Prayer" and "Abiding sorrow for sin." These extracts had been my constant companions ever since. During the time that I had been living in London I had taken every opportunity of hearing Father Faber preach. His manner was singularly quiet, as far removed as possible from that of a popular preacher. There was a charm in his voice; mastery of language and originality of ideas were amongst his most remarkable gifts. Perhaps, as a compensation for not understanding music (though I am far from being insensible to its influence), I intensely delight in eloquence and beauty of language. As a rule an orator must be heard. His words fall comparatively flat when they are read, apart from the fire and energy of the speaker. There are some orators however—such as Lacordaire and Faber—whose words when reduced to writing do not lose their power of enkindling enthusiasm, and of rousing even in the most timid souls a desire to reach heights of perfection which had hitherto appeared to them to be unattainable.

There was to me a peculiar attraction in Father Faber's sermons. There were sentences in them which I have never forgotten: rays of light came from them that have suddenly illuminated hours of darkness, whilst they have given additional brightness in moments of spiritual joy, and have encouraged perseverance in vigorous resistance when temptations presented themselves with almost overwhelming force. But still I am inclined to think that great as was the charm of his writings, and of his sermons, Father Faber was even more attractive as a talker.

Before I left my friend she begged me not to be hurried into the Church without first getting a solution of any difficulties I might have.

When people who are endowed with common sense have the grace to see that if God has given a revelation, the Roman Catholic Church is the one Church which even claims to be the sole depositary of that revelation, they recognize that the [only safe and sensible course for them to pursue is that of becoming humble and docile learners. It is not for them to question the teachings of an Infallible Teacher. Difficulties they may have, but they need not fear to recognize them, and it is best to face them. Sometimes a few words from a theologian will solve their perplexities; the very statement of them indeed may go far towards the solution of them. How often has not the convert experienced that when he has stated his difficulty, and has said all that he has to say about it, the difficulty itself has vanished. In formulating it, he has answered it.

Hell was a difficulty to me—a difficulty to the imagination perhaps more than to the reason; for the reason cannot but admit that a will which remains always and irrevocably at variance with the will of its Creator must ever remain dissatisfied, and must entail eternal misery on itself. But in truth, is Hell as great a difficulty as Heaven is? Heaven means an eternity of happiness; pure, unalloyed, perfect happiness; a happiness not dependent on our senses, though the senses also after the Resurrection Day will have their complete satisfaction; not dependent on creatures, though God will make use of creatures to increase the joy of the Blessed; but a happiness which has its source in the vision of Him from Whom all that is beautiful derives its beauty, all that is attractive draws its attractiveness, to Whom all that is loveable owes its love-

EE

ableness. God Himself is to be our eternal great reward! Perhaps we may with effort succeed, in exciting within ourselves for a minute the desire of Him, but the next minute, the sights and sounds of the world, its pleasures, its cares and anxieties, our own perversity, our impatience and uncharitableness take possession of us again; and that we, such as we know ourselves to be, should ever be capable of seeing God and so of becoming like to Him, is in truth a difficulty, a wonder that does but increase each day with our greater knowledge of ourselves, and the more the sense of our utter helplessness is brought home to us. Ah, in truth, Heaven is the wonder, not Hell! If here on earth where we are continually pursued, however little we may advert to it, by the kind solicitude of a Heavenly Father's love, we can never realize what it is to be "exiled from the Eternal Providence," no more can we conceive of the ineffable bliss, the transformation that is to be ours when God shall appear and "we shall be like Him, for we shall see Him as He is." All this was conveyed in those few words of Father Faber's: "To me the wonder is that any one should be saved."

There was a difficulty, too, in the aversion that I felt at being obliged for the future to give up entertaining those Latitudinarian opinions which no doubt are very attractive to the young. They appeal to that love of independence which is so inherent in our nature, they recommend themselves as freeing the mind from unworthy trammels, and as imparting breadth and largeness of view. Their shallowness and worthlessness are not perceived, and to the juvenile intellect they present themselves in favourable contrast with sectarian narrowness. Since I became a Catholic I have learnt that the mind is no more fettered by the truths of revelation than it is fettered by the laws of mathematics. It is no hardship to be certain that two and two make four, and can never make five; nor is it a greater hardship to be certain that there are Three Persons in One God, and that one of these Divine Persons assumed our human nature, and came on earth to be our Teacher as well as our Redeemer. To profess to acknowledge Christ as our Teacher, and at the same time to reserve to ourselves the right to interpret His words according to our own ideas, is one thing; to recognize that as our Teacher He left behind Him on the earth the Divine authority of an ever living voice to proclaim and guard and explain His doctrine to all succeeding generations, is another. If He did this, then we have no right to choose those doctrines which we like and to reject the rest; it cannot be a matter of indifference whether we submit to this Divine authority or not. I saw this in a dim sort of confused way so long as I was outside the Church. I feared that if I became a Catholic I should have to be continually condemning others, and should become intolerant and narrow-minded. It seemed hard that the many good Anglicans with whom I was acquainted should not be allowed to believe with Dean Church that the English Church is as well worth living in and fighting for as any other. It suited them. They were leading useful lives. They were sincerely attached to their own form of religion. Apparently they had never had the call to inquire into the claims of the Roman Catholic Church to their allegiance. Should I be required to blame them? Should I have to do my best to open their eyes? Would not this make social life very tiresome?

I was relieved to find that I need not blame them. I was not their judge. I might hope that they were in good faith, and in the state of invincible ignorance. As to opening their eyes, unless they invited me to do so, I need not undertake it so far as talking to them was concerned. I should be bound, however, by showing kindness and by setting a good example to attract them to the faith; and above all by prayer, continual earnest prayer, I should endeavour to obtain for them the grace to receive and embrace it. That the increased sense of responsibility in social intercourse would be tiresome, was not to be denied. It was a thing that must be faced. The out-and-out Protestants would not indeed occasion much difficulty, for they would avoid having any intercourse with a convert beyond that which was demanded by the barest civility. With

Anglicans and with Latitudinarians, however, it is hardly possible to be sympathetic without giving a wrong impression—the impression that you think they may be quite content with their own views of religion and that they may ignore with impunity the teaching of that Church which you know to be our Lord's representative on earth. The more charitable and kindly they consider you to be, the more sure they feel that you must regard their position and opinions with indifference. They have never grasped the fact that "truth—and this," Father Faber said, "is one great distinction between Catholics and heretics—*truth is not ours, but God's.*"

If, however, we are ourselves penetrated with this conviction, we may hope in some way to convey it to others, without assuming an attitude of offensive superiority and increasing in them the spirit of contradiction.

I had read many Catholic books. I had become familiarized with Catholic worship and had but few difficulties to be solved. My wish was to be admitted at once into the Church, and to this the Father saw no objection. It was the first Friday in Lent, the feast of the Crown of Thorns. He said that there could not be a more appropriate day. I repeated the Creed, made my confession, and received conditional Baptism. The process was simple, straightforward, and business-like, very unlike the ways of Anglicanism. There was no vagueness and hesitation. The

Church knew exactly what she was about and what was to be done. She was my true mother and her arms were around me. There came a sense of security, a feeling of unutterable peace, a joy such as I had never before experienced. When I found myself again in the Brompton Road I asked what had happened. The shops and the cabs and the omnibuses were the same, but how changed was I!

.   .   .   .

It may seem presumptuous to assume that the record of my own thoughts and feelings in the search for truth will interest others. My excuse is in the certainty I feel, that to many it will but recount an experience which they have themselves undergone. I think they may welcome it, not because it records my experience, but inasmuch as relatively it records their own.

www.ingramcontent.com/pod-product-compliance
Lightning Source LLC
Chambersburg PA
CBHW051850300426
44117CB00006B/336